rockface books
7189 Paul Lake Road
Kamloops, B.C.
V2H 1N9
e mail: rockface@telus.net

Canadian Cataloguing in Publication Data
Cowley, Glen 1949-
The Seventh Man:The History of the Kamloops Blazers Franchise
Includes bibliographical references.
ISBN 0-9686331-1-0

1. Kamloops Blazers (Hockey team) --History. 2. Hockey--British Columbia --Kamloops --History. 3. Hockey --Canada, Western --History.
GV848.K35C69 2000 796.962'09711'72 C00-911063-1

Cover design: Larry Macko

Printed and bound in Canada by **Peerless Printers Ltd.**
Kamloops, British Columbia

The Seventh Man

In sport there are teams so associated with success their very names come to symbolize grasping for the Holy Grail. Teams that have something extra every time they go against the competition. That seem to pull the rabbit out of the hat at the last moment. That bring out the best in even mediocre players. That set the standard.

Every sport has them. Baseball has the Yankees, soccer Manchester United, basketball the Celtics, football the Edmonton Eskimos and Dallas Cowboys, lacrosse the New Westminster Salmonbellies and hockey, the greatest of them all, the Montreal Canadiens. That a junior hockey team and franchise, with its constant changing of players, should ever achieve that pinnacle is an even more remarkable story. Yet it is a story that exists and continues to be told.

A story whose faint beginnings in Humboldt erupted into life in Estevan and thundered upon the National stage in New Westminster before re-emerging along the shores of the Thompson River. The Kamloops Blazers and their franchise's storied history share the mystique. That something that gives them an edge; an expectation of success.

Every sport has a phrase or word analysts struggle to define. Team pride! The fans! Team cohesion! Each year the list goes on but the definition always eludes them. But in hockey we know him.

When the lights go out at the arena and the stands empty; silence sits briefly in the dark. A flutter stirs a championship banner. Faint echoing laughter follows the cutting blades of a ghostly shade. The Seventh Man dances forever young. The link in an unbroken line of players and bench bosses that stretch back over the years. The link that stands behind today's Blazers and expects them to carry on the tradition if they are prepared to put on the sweater.

The Seventh Man draws upon the fans, work ethic, teamwork and all those intangibles that go into the making of Champions. His price is dedication and hard work but his gift is the elation of being a part of the tradition and glory. To be forever young in the moment.

To become the Seventh Man.

Acknowledgements

The author would like to extend thanks to the many people who helped make this book possible.

To Jennifer Hoesgen of the Humboldt Museum and Gallery, former Indian Reg Beliveau of Surrey, former Indian and Bruin Jim Stewart of Regina, Doris Rubel and Kerry Rubel of Kamloops, the Estevan Bruins of the Saskatchewan Junior Hockey League, the New Westminster Museum & Archives, Richard Lapp and the Kamloops Blazers who all made major contributions to the compilation of photos. To Sharon Domotor of the Humboldt Journal and Norm Park of the Estevan Mercury who helped me negotiate my way through years of newspaper material. To the Kamloops Museum and Archives staff who afforded the patience and assistance that has come to be their hallmark.

To Ernie "Punch" McLean, Andy Clovechok, Dean Evason and Rick "The Bear" Wile who poured over the drafts to help correct and embellish the product.

To my wife Karen Hopkins for the painstaking task of editing so key to creating a presentable finished product; who put up with the travels and endless hockey talk that filled the last few years.

To Wilf Schmidt, publisher of Rockface Books, whose talents in photography and publishing made this book possible. Without his assistance neither of my books would have seen the light of day.

Dedication

This book is dedicated to all those who contributed to the creation of the Seventh Man. The players, parents, management, fans and media of Humboldt, Melfort, Estevan, Bismarck (North Dakota), New Westminster and Kamloops have all played a part, big or small, in the never ending story the Seventh Man has become.

Photo Credit Abbreviations

Credit/Courtesy	=	C.
Humboldt & District Museum & Gallery	=	HDMG
Kamloops Museum & Archives	=	KMA
New Westminster Museum & Archives	=	NWMA

INTRODUCTION

It had been a storybook year. The Blazers were ranked number one Nationally all season. They were secured of a birth in the Memorial Cup regardless of how they did because the annual battle for National honours was being played at Riverside Coliseum in Kamloops. Not satisfied with coming in the back door they went out and earned the right to be there by winning the Western Hockey League Championship.

To be a hockey fan and living in Kamloops in the late Spring of 1995 was Heaven. A fervent hockey town every season this one was electric. The Blazers had a chance to win it all in their own backyard; in front of their own fans.

Not since Paul Henderson's game winning goal for Canada in the 1972 Canada Cup had I felt the excitement that came with the last seconds of the deciding game. The Blazers were there amid the single breathing entity that was their fans. The clock ticked away. Fans rose to their feet screaming as one. White towels waved. The Seventh Man owned the ice and the moment. For the third time in four years the Kamloops Blazers were Memorial Cup Champions. Elation surged through us all and for that moment the team, fans, Seventh Man and Kamloops itself were as one.

The roar of the fans continued in lulls and crescendos as the Champions took turns hoisting the Cup and skating around the rink. The look in their eyes said it all. The moment would be with them for the rest of their lives and rekindled whenever they chanced to meet with team mates or fans. The Seventh Man grew stronger and his roar echoes still in my ears.

Shaking my head in wonderment a special smile pulled at my lips as I saw Kamloops' own Aaron Keller hoist the Grail. He embodied the marriage of Kamloops and the franchise which had reached the pinnacle of success. A success story that had started 50 years earlier far from the mountains and valleys of British Columbia.

It is a story that rings like a puck off the crossbar across time. The Seventh Man saw it all. He saw the birth, struggles, successes and disappointments. He was a part of the personal stories of the people who gave it life. He knew the laughter, tears, tragedies and happiness. Though it is a hockey story in the truest sense it is also a story of life from the spring of youth to the aches of age.

It is even more so a Canadian story; a story Canadians can relate to like no one else. Though its meaning is greatest for those who shared the ice with the Seventh Man and the fans of Humboldt, Melfort, Estevan, New Westminster and Kamloops who cheered it on, it is more than that.

The Montreal Canadiens do not have to be your favourite team for you to admire them. Their tradition and success compels admiration and respect though you are pulling for your NHL heroes when they go up against Les Habitants. And so it is with the Blazers for those who love the game and the mystique that goes with it.

So find a quiet corner where your mind's eye can travel through time. Where sights, sounds and smells can come alive. Go for a skate with the Seventh Man.

The Seventh Man
The History of the Kamloops Blazers Franchise

by Glen Cowley

rockface books
Kamloops, British Columbia

PART ONE

1 (H)

THE INDIANS

Beginnings 1946/47

The War was finally over. It was a time of new hopes and dreams. A good time for beginnings.

Humboldt, Saskatchewan is not a large community, nor was it in 1946. Yet here, in the land of the "Sure Crop" the seeds of the franchise were sown in fertile soil. Never more true was the adage that from tiny acorns do mighty Oak trees grow.

Humboldt's hockey legacy can be traced back to as early as 1905 and by 1909 it sported a combined skating & curling rink. In 1912 it joined the Northern Saskatchewan Hockey League which included Saskatoon, North Battleford and Prince Albert. In the 20's the "Sunocos' " playing roster included one Leo Parker, who was to prove an integral part of the birth and formative years of "the franchise".

The Humboldt Arena which later went by the name the Wigwam and finally the Leo Parker Arena. Where it all began. (C. HDMG)

In the 30's the senior team took the name Red Indians. The result of new sweaters and stockings being donated by the McColl-Frontenac Oil Company whose symbol was a "Red Indian". Unfortunately the war put many things on hold and league hockey was one of them.

So it was, until October 10, 1946 when, with winter fast approaching, the Humboldt Journal proclaimed

"Humboldt to Enter Team in Junior Hockey League"

The franchise was born!

W.A. Slater, former manager of the junior Moose Jaw Canucks and new Rink Manager and Winter Sports Promoter for Humboldt, approached the Board of Trade with an idea. A special board meeting heard him explain there was a 24 hour deadline to file an application for a new franchise in the Saskatchewan Junior Hockey League. Slater was no stranger to junior hockey success as his 1945 Moose Jaw Canucks made it all the way to the Memorial Cup final before losing out four games to one to the Toronto Saint Michaels Majors.

The Board supported the idea as a first class winter attraction and opportunity for the district youth to again play organized hockey. Their intention was to "temporarily" sponsor the team which would join the Prince Albert Black Hawks, Moose Jaw Canucks, Saskatoon Legionnaires, Regina Pats and Father Murray's storied Notre Dame Hounds from Wilcox.

Scotty Melville, of the Regina Leader Post, commented that "Slater, former manager of the Moose Jaw Canucks, pulled off something of a surprise by tossing Humboldt's hat into the ring." With the exception of the unique Notre Dame Hounds, a private college team, Humboldt was the smallest community in the league; a claim maintained through its existence.

Leo Parker The first Godfather of the franchise

The October 17, 1946 Journal announced City Council had backed the proposal and the franchise was in. Bill Slater and Mr. B. Laskin, president of the Board of Trade, were to oversee sponsorship and the team was to play out of the community arena which had been built in 1932 and still sported natural ice.

Most of the players in the first year were from either Moose Jaw or Regina but inquiries about the team came from around the Province as well as locally. Defenseman Bob Parker, son of Leo, hoped to make the cut.

Lacking artificial ice the team was scheduled for a late season start on November 30. As a result they had to make up many of their games in December. The 28 game season had them facing an imbalanced schedule playing more games against Saskatoon and Prince Albert.

Slater was optimistic. Despite being a new team he forecast the squad as fighting it out for 3rd or 4th. Regina and Moose Jaw were picked to battle for first with Humboldt and Saskatoon fighting for third. Prince Albert and Notre Dame were marked as also-rans.

The November 7th Journal proclaimed the Board had decided upon a name for the new team. Certainly pleasing to former Indian player Leo Parker, the Vice President of the Board, the team took on the old senior team name. November 30 could not come early enough.

If first games are any indication of a team's future game one of the franchise was an ill omen. Playing at home, before a near capacity 1400 fans, the Indians were humbled 13-2 by Moose Jaw. It didn't start out badly and the Indians looked to have a star in Dick Warwick, who had come up from Regina. He scored the first goal for the franchise and they were holding on to a 1-0 lead at the end of one period. Warwick netted the team's second goal in the middle frame but the period ended with the locals down 3-2. Then the roof caved in in the third. The lack of practice time became apparent as the Canucks scored 10 unanswered goals.

Still the fans embraced them. The CPR put on coach cars to run behind its freight trains and shuttle league fans to away games. At 75 cents for a reserved seat, 50 cents for rush seats and only a quarter for students game prices were reasonable.

Despite the efforts of their top line of Dick Warwick, "Ickey" Daurie and Doug MacDonald the squad struggled, losing their first four games. Unfortunately the score of their initial win, over Prince Albert Black Hawks, escaped the news but when they won their second, 4-1 over Saskatoon, their record only improved to 2-7. Don Smith knotted two goals and one assist and Ickey Daurie potted two assists. Unluckily Ickey also received a broken jaw and took up residence on the injured list.

Following up their win with two losses changes began to be made. Jack "Foo" McFarlane (who was to reappear in the unfolding of the franchise story), Neil McClenaghan and Webb Simpson suited up and Bill Yeo, Bud Andrews and Melvin Payne were released.

By late January 1947 the team continued to struggle but the fans stuck with them. Lack of practice time was still hurting.

A small item in the paper commented that the Juvenile Indians were going to the Provincial final. In net was a young local lad, named Glenn Hall.

The intensity of the fans and the team were not in question as attested to by a 4-4 tie against Saskatoon at the arena. The Indians had lost 13-3 to the Legionnaires earlier. The Journal commented that in response to fights on the ice between players "most of the small crowd that braved the cold jumped on the ice but were quickly chased back by the Mounties who broke up the fights."

The fates bedeviled the team to the end. On February 20 Harold Gorsalitz was lost for the season due to a cracked skull. Then they got good news as the Notre Dame Hounds forfeited them four points because they decided to play out the intermediate league playoffs rather than finish the junior season.

In their season ending match they climbed out of the basement but not into a playoff position. Bob Parker's winner at 12:40 of the 3rd over Saskatoon allowed them to leapfrog over the now non participating Notre Dame Hounds. Their playoff fate had been sealed in an earlier conflict ridden game against Prince Albert.

Prospects versus Prince Albert looked good after the Indians had beaten them 7-3 at the arena. Rookie Murray Parker made his first appearance in that game and Doug MacDonald starred with two goals and three assists. They had to take Prince Albert again to stay alive but when Bill Slater pulled his team off the ice in response to what he believed was biased reffing the team was given a $100 fine and forfeited the game. Slater made his move after the ref called a questionable penalty on Dick Warwick after what Slater saw as numerous non calls against the Black Hawks.

The first season had not been good and the team lost $2000. Would it survive? The community rallied behind their new local heroes and the Board of Trade covered the deficit. The Indians were coming back next season.

Hugh Coflin spent two more seasons in the SJHL, both with Moose Jaw but also put in half a season in 50/51 with the Chicago Black Hawks. Don Smith spent two more years at junior, both with the Medicine Hat Tigers of the Alberta Junior Hockey League before enjoying a brief 11 game stint with the New York Rangers in 49/50.

Dick Warwick went on to the greatest fame, though not in the NHL. Along with brothers Bill and Grant he led the 1955 Penticton Vees to the World Championship. In 1954 the Russians had burst on to the World Hockey scene and the Toronto Lyndhursts had the dubious distinction of becoming the first Canadian team to lose to the Soviets. They fell 7-2 in the final World Championship game. The Warwick led Vees restored pride with a physical 5-0 victory to regain the World Championship Cup.

It was said that the March 6, 1955 championship game was heard by the largest radio audience in Canadian history, up to that time.

The 1946/47 Humboldt Indians (C. HDMG) **Also suiting up** Bud Andrews, Bob Quigley, Melvin Payne, Fred McNaught, Neil McClenaghan, Webb Simpson, Bill Yeo

Some years later all three Warwick brothers suited up in Kamloops on the Senior A Chiefs squad for one brief but colourful season. Other Indians from that first year that made their way to Kamloops' senior hockey included Jimmy Van Buskirk and "Moose" McNaughton.

The first chapter of the franchise closed with little to suggest that the team would achieve any degree of dominance or that it would even survive for any length of time. Yet a star was on the horizon. A star born and bred in Humboldt itself. If the first shadows of the Seventh Man dimly clung to the Warwickian mystique then Glenn Hall was about add a bit more substance.

2 (H)

Local Hero ________________ 1947/48

A dream common to many. Local boy makes good and saves the day. Friends and family cheering him on. For most it is just a passing dream with little chance of reality. But for some!

The Indians second season opened with more uncertainty than promise. Slater was gone; returned to Moose Jaw. Players expected to return didn't as the teams that contributed them called them back. The struggling squad was told the players had only been on loan. Gone were goalie Freddie Ives, Hugh Coflin, Dick Warwick and Jimmy Van Buskirk. Basic building blocks were removed as the franchise struggled to be competitive and financially sound.

In their first season the team had appealed to local businesses for support. Businessmen put in $100 each on a loan and received $50 back at the end of the campaign. The same was called for again in season number two in the hopes of reaching $2500. The consequences were clear. Get the funding the team stayed, don't and it was gone.

Four potential coaches were in the running for a job which promised a staggering $250 per month.

Once again the town came through and fan support increased as well. Ted Brockman came up with a team bus. New sweaters sporting alternating bands of red, white and black hung in the dressing room. The paper was calling it a do or die season.

Leo Parker was elected manager and Don McIntyre came in as the new coach. November 29, 1947 was D-Day. Notre Dame rejoined the league.

It did not start well. In game one they fell 6-1 to last season's playoff killer Prince Albert, now named the Mintos. Insult was added to injury as former Indians McClenaghan and McNaughton skated for the foes. They then fell 6-2 to the Saskatoon Quakers and 5-3 to Regina.

For their fourth game they were joined by Ray Bouchard and Al Camponi who took up positions on a line with veteran

Harold Gorsalitz. Magic! The line garnered 11 points in their first win of the season; 5-3 over Saskatoon. Bouchard himself got 3 goals and 1 assist.

Last year's Provincial Champs, the Moose Jaw Canucks, with Coflin and Van Buskirk in the lineup brought the tribe back down to earth with a 6-0 drubbing. Still, the improvement was there as they came back with a split in the next two games, enjoying in particular a 6-0 shutout by Bill Wilson over the Mintos.

Despite better play January 1948 closed with the team sporting a dismal 3-10 record.

Down 5-1 to number one Moose Jaw in their next game a number of fans left at the end of the period thinking that the game was all but over. They should have stayed. The Indians stormed back to earn a 5-5 tie. Then they took out Saskatoon 7-5 with Peco Chorney, the winner of the neatest name contest by a long shot, scoring three times. That was followed up with a 7-5 road victory over Notre Dame. Though they lost their next two road games the squad was showing definite signs of pride and life.

47/48 Indians **Standing - Left to Right** J. Christian, Leo Parker, Bud Andrews, Bob Parker, Don McIntyre (coach), Harold Gorsalitz, Murray Parker, Irwin Grosse, Gus Kruse, Ken Dust **Kneeling** - Frank Pickering, Harold Hall, Ken Kinnon, Glenn Hall, Ray Bouchard, Peco Chorney, Lloyd Penner (C.HDMG) **Also suiting up** ? Bowles (goal), ? Bayne, ? Chow, ? McKinnon, Bill Wilson (goal), Al Camponi, ? Lang, ? Smith

When they took Notre Dame 6-3, largely on the back of Erwin Grosse's five points, they moved to within one point of 5th place. By the time February was closing their 5-2 win over Prince Albert had them in 4th and the winners of six of the eight games played that month.

A dark cloud appeared on the horizon when the team's goalie quit. Word went out for a replacement with five games remaining. It was not a time to be picky and the squad called up a local lad. Sixteen year old Glenn Hall backstopped the final five games. Joining cousin Harold Hall he shared in the moment when the Indians, led by team scoring leader Bud Andrews' five points, secured 4th with a 9-3 win over 5th place Saskatoon.

Winners of eight of their last ten games they put their 21 point season (11-16-1) against powerhouse Moose Jaw in a best of three. It was no contest and even 1500 fans at the arena could not help their boys as they went down 7-3 in their one home game. The series ended quickly but the season was not a loss.

Starting the campaign at a disadvantage with players and finances they exceeded expectations.

The Board of Trade sponsored a banquet honouring the team and gave special attention to young Glenn Hall, held largely responsible for the squad making the playoffs. Though they were losing graduates Gorsalitz and Bob Parker; Bud Andrews, Erwin Grosse and Glenn Hall had fans hoping for a brighter future.

Up to that time Humboldt had but one star in the NHL, not in itself a bad accomplishment for the small community, by the name of Tony Leswick. "Mighty Mouse's" 12 seasons with New York Rangers, Detroit Red Wings and Chicago Black Hawks saw him sip three times from the Stanley Cup as a Red Wing. No one could have guessed the greatness that awaited the second star, Glenn Hall.

Glenn had learned all his hockey in Humboldt and taken in Indian games at the arena. His friends Bob and Murray Parker, both teammates, were instrumental in helping him develop the competitive edge he needed to succeed. For him the joy was simply playing the game not just winning. Leo Parker also proved a major player in Glenn's rising star.

In those days there was no organized hockey for kids between the ages of 13 and 18. For Glenn to play at a more advanced level he had to get permission to play with older players. It was Leo Parker who gave him the support he needed and the rest became history. It was a comfortable 16 year old who suited up as an Indian when the opportunity came. An opportunity which was not lost.

He and the Indians were coming back for 1948/49 with more promise than the team had known to date.

3 (H)

Best Yet ______________ 1948/49

48/49 saw the league turned upside down and a class distinction started that lasted for years to come. New rivalries began and Humboldt's opportunities to grab top notch players were made harder yet.

The Saskatchewan Junior Hockey League broke up. The Regina Pats and Moose Jaw Canucks joined the Medicine Hat Tigers, Lethbridge Native Sons, Calgary Buffaloes and the Crows Nest Pass Coalers (Bellevue, Alberta) in the new Western Canada Junior Hockey League. As well as being the top junior teams they also had in common one particular thing; artificial ice. The new league was tabbed the "Artificial Ice League".

The remaining teams in Saskatchewan came up with a creative solution. The new Northern Saskatchewan Junior Hockey League was comprised of an East and West Division that included two Senior B teams. The squads played an imbalanced but interlocking schedule with the league champion entitled to go up against the top Saskatchewan team in the WCHL for the right to challenge for a Memorial Cup birth. Prince Albert, Humboldt and Saskatoon Junior Quakers were joined by the Flin Flon Bombers, North Battleford Beavers (Senior) and Prince Albert Monarchs (Seniors). Flin Flon's involvement , given its geographic isolation, was destined to cause dilemmas for years.

Erwin Grosse (last year's league rookie of the year), Murray and Bob Parker joined Glenn Hall at the Detroit Red Wing tryout camp in Saskatoon. Glenn was not initially invited but the scout who tabbed Bob Parker gave him extra forms and told him to bring along some others. The scout had never seen Glenn play. What tricks the Fates can play.

When the Indian training camp rolled around Glenn was joined by cousin Harold, Alvin Duke and Jim Kocourek as local hopefuls. Last year's leading scorer, Bud Andrews, was off to Moose Jaw for Hugh Coflin. The former Indian never did return though

The 32 game season started out with a tie against Saskatoon, a pleasant departure from the last two seasons' opening game losses. Although a poor start saw them sitting last in the division their record at the end of December 1948 proved marginally better than last year. Yet by the end of January they were in a three way battle for first with Saskatoon and Prince Albert, sporting a plus .500 record for the first time. The Grosse/Chorney/Herb Stoll line was stealing the show.

The battle ended with Prince Albert taking first but the Indians had their best finish yet at second. They had home ice advantage going into the best of three against Saskatoon.

In game one, at the arena, Erwin Grosse netted five points in a 6-4 victory. 200 fans joined them on the trek to Saskatoon where they almost pulled it off before losing 3-2. The third and deciding game was in front of the home faithful. It was no contest. Grosse and Twardosky shone in clinching a 9-3 victory that sent them to a division final for the first time. It also marked the start of the franchise's playoff dominance over Saskatoon.

48/49 Indians **Standing Left to Right** Ken Kinnon, Herb Stoll, Murray Parker, Don McIntyre (coach), Irwin Grosse, Harold Hall, Peco Chorney, **Kneeling**- Dave Wall, Lloyd Penner, Glenn Hall, Allan Buchholz, Ray Bouchard, Adam Twardosky (C. HDMG) **Also suiting up** Alvin Duke, Les Parker, Jim Kocourk, Jim Beckman, ? Martin, Bob Pickering

Glenn Hall came down with the German Measles and missed game one of the final. Allan Buchholz backstopped the team in the opening 6-4 loss in Prince Albert while Glenn came back for game two and made it a bit closer in a 5-4 loss. With a loss at the arena in game three the Indians were facing elimination in four straight, in front of their fans.

Sucking it up they took a 4-0 lead into the second period and a 5-1 spread into the third. Prince Albert, led by Guyle Fielder, stormed back to make it close but the Indians held on for a 5-4 victory. That was all that the tribe could muster as the Mintos nailed the coffin shut with a 10-4 triumph in Prince Albert, despite 300 Humboldt fans in attendance.

The team's play evoked optimism for the next season but in junior hockey success can be a two edged sword. Their number one star Glenn Hall, along with top scorer Erwin Grosse, caught the eye of Detroit, and they wanted them on their number one junior team, the Windsor Spitfires. Although Leo Parker eventually got some compensation and Detroit took on sponsorship of the Indians, it was still a devastating blow.

The story of Glenn Hall's success is a book in itself. Four times an NHL second all star, seven times on the first all star team, Calder Cup in 1956 (Rookie of the Year), three times winner of Vezina Trophy (best goalie), Conn Smythe Trophy (most valuable player in playoffs) 1968, one Stanley Cup and seven Stanley Cup final appearances. Nicknamed "Mr. Goalie" while playing for the Chicago Blackhawks, his 18 year career saw success in Detroit, Chicago and St. Louis before he hung up his skates in 1971. His accomplishments earned him entry into the Hockey Hall of Fame in 1975. The only franchise player to ever earn that supreme honour.

The season ending deficit improved to $1828.58, helped out by the playoff gates. The Board of Trade picked up the tab again but the constant deficits hurt, especially with the added expenses incurred traveling to Flin Flon. With Notre Dame gone Humboldt was the smallest community in the league and sustaining a team was no easy challenge.

How would they manage if the team started doing poorly and attendance declined?

4 (H)

Detroit's Farm 1949/50

Promising players Grosse and Hall were gone as six players in total were signed by the Detroit Red Wings. The promise of last season netted Leo Parker a working agreement along with some financial and player assistance in return for the players and the submission of an 18 player list to the Wings. It remained to be seen how the changes would pan out on the ice.

The Senior B teams did not return and Saskatoon, which had been Detroit's affiliate, changed its name to the Wesleys.

New coach Mike Horbul led his team in an imbalanced schedule which had them play Prince Albert Mintos more than any other team. A good way to build a healthy rivalry.

49/50 Indians **Top Left to Right** Leo Parker, Herb Stoll, Don Lardner, Murray Parker, Ray Selmas, Buck Morgan, Ben Wylie, Doug Frie, Hal Dunlop, Gordon Grest, Mike Horbul (coach) **Front** Charlie Sabo, Gordon Erhardt, Jim Kocourek, Al Buchholz, Adam Twardosky, Dave Wall, Harold Hall. (C. HDMG) **Also suiting up** Ed Barrack, ? Shawkey, ? Hammel, ? Gerling, Jack Adolph

By mid November 200 seasons tickets had been sold at $12 each. The Booster Club was putting on raffles and bringing in the movie "The Barber of Seville" for a one night fund raiser. Money remained an issue despite the Detroit agreement and it was yet to be seen how the fans would take the loss of Grosse and Hall.

Game one at the arena started well with the Indians breaking out into a 3-0 lead over the Mintos. Local player Jim Kocourek starred but his efforts were not enough as Prince Albert, who were destined to win the regular season, came back for a 7-5 win.

The Indians were not doormats either. They proved to be the only team able to win any games in Prince Albert. Splitting the season series with the Mintos and dominating over Saskatoon their greatest problems came against Flin Flon, especially on the road.

The end of the campaign saw the Mintos hold on to first with 32 points followed by Flin Flon at 29, Humboldt at 26 and the lowly Wesleys at 9. The Indians had garnered a plus .500 season and boasted Adam Twardosky as their top scorer. He managed to land 4th overall with 38 points.

Although Flin Flon had finished ahead of them and had home ice advantage there was no reason to believe that they were outclassed in the playoffs.

Games one and two went at the Whitney Forum in Flin Flon. Despite losses of 5-3 and 6-3 the Indians were in it. Better results were anticipated in game three of the best of five.
A disappointed crowd saw their heroes go down 7-3 to be eliminated in three straight; despite the heroics of Twardosky. Upset with the officiating they littered the ice and rained down cat calls.

It had been a good season with a disappointing end.

The worst was yet to come.

5 (H)

Nosedive 1950/51

It didn't look that bad to begin with.

Once again the Board of Trade came through to bail out the team; this time to the tune of $3000. Despite poor attendance through January and February, largely due to severe weather, the season had been good. An active booster club had secured a further $1400 for team coffers.

Even more optimism came from a commitment to install artificial ice. By May 33% of the necessary funding was secure and the plant was to be operational by November 1. It didn't happen and the cost of artificial ice came back to haunt the community. The plant never did become fully functional that season and the debt incurred added to the already formidable financial problems.

Detroit silently dropped its sponsorship. It arose farther west in Edmonton with the Oil Kings. A team destined to figure prominently in the history of the franchise.

On the ice locals Harold Hall and Jim Kocourek were back along with newcomer Steve Chorney, brother of former Indian Peco. Clark Burlingham took over as the new coach.

There were some long nights in a season to forget; particularly against front running Flin Flon. At seasons end they sported their worst record since 46/47 and were dead last. Still, as with any season, there were some highlights.

On January 1, 1951 Harold Hall, earned three goals in a 7-5 victory over Saskatoon. In February they played their first ever game against the Detroit sponsored Edmonton Oil Kings and managed a 4-4 tie.

Local product Jim Kocourek found himself on the trading block to Prince Albert for Frank Kuzma. Kocourek got the satisfaction of putting it to his old team with three goals in the Indians' second last game of the season; an 11-6 loss. Kuzma's worth was to, eventually, be proven.

Last place Humboldt had to face the powerhouse Bombers while second place Prince Albert squared off against

Saskatoon. The odds against the Indians were immense. Over 30 points behind the Bombers in the standings they had to try to unseat Flin Flon at Whitney Forum.

Game one showed that they had guts and class. It took double overtime before Flin Flon put them away 7-5. They kept it close in game two with a 3-1 loss. There had to be some optimism with the next game being on home ice.

It proved otherwise as Flin Flon finally exerted itself to win convincingly 6-0. A season of disappointment ended. The Bombers joy was short-lived as they then fell to second place Prince Albert on the road to the Memorial Cup.

A deficit of $3600, failure to ice a competitive team, bad weather, and the failure to get the artificial ice plant operational stung. It was a dark time for the league's smallest community. They needed something to pull the franchise out of the slippery slope that could spell its death knell.

What happened is the stuff of hockey legends. The flame of the Humboldt Indians was due to flare up like never before and begin the rise of the Seventh Man.

The 50/51 Indians (Unfortunately no photo available) **Players suiting up for the 50/51 season included** - Clark Burlingham (coach), Dave Wall, Adam Twardosky, Gordon "Chip" Erhardt, Jim Kocourek, Harold Hall, Steve Chorney, Glen Laughren (goal), John Pentz, Keith Megson, Cece Zimmer, Oscar Hanson, Chuck Gordon, Ken Jestin, Ed Malinowski, Chester Dobni, Bill Worth (goal), Hal Dunlop, Buster Green, ? Snyder, Nick Hampson, ? Schai, Al Kater, Jimmy Milne (goal), Spike MacDougall, Frank Kuzma, Dave Wilson

6 (H)

The Legend Begins__________1951/52

To date the Humboldt Indians had flirted with success and the Seventh Man watched quietly from the sidelines. They had had their moments on the ice and two of their own, Glenn Hall and Dick Warwick, were destined to carry their heritage to great heights. Yet it was with the 51/52 season that circumstances brought together a team and, in particular, two remarkable individuals. It was then that the Seventh Man truly joined the squad.

Scotty Munro was one of those people who did not simply participate in history but made it happen. He was a giant in Western Canadian junior hockey whose influence fell upon players, people and entire communities wherever he went. Those who knew him speak of him with fondness and respect. Yet it was not just his arrival in Humboldt which sparked the legend. There came another whose influence grew with the years until he took his place equally alongside the fabled Scotsman.

Scotty Munro With him came the rise of the Seventh Man (C. Estevan Bruins SJHL)

Fate or fortune brought Ernie McLean into the sphere of Scotty and the legacy rebounded off the boards with an echo heard to this day. McLean first came to the franchise as a promising 18 year old rookie centre but the connection between him, Scotty and the team more than survived his playing days.

Scotty Munro had a hard life but was living proof that you can't keep a good man down.

Born Roderick Neil Munro November 17, 1917 at Shackleton, Saskatchewan, life's cruel blow came early. His father, who had come from Glasgow, Scotland, died in the year of his son's birth. Before he died though he moved his family to Swift Current where he opened up a hardware store. Scotty was reluctant to talk about his early years but he did talk about hockey.

At age 15 he went to Edmonton to play as a goaltender. While there, at age 19, he met and married Rose Bashnik. They remained together until the end, producing two children in the process; Dawn and Jim.

Moving to Moose Jaw to take up play with a senior team he obtained work at the B.A. Oil Refinery. The job ended his playing days and almost his life. One night at the refinery he was making his way through the plant not expecting anything unusual. Unknown to him someone had left the top off an underground vat holding screaming hot tar. Putting down one leg he found not solid earth but the yawning mouth of the vat. His leg was engulfed. For six weeks he wavered in semi-consciousness in the hospital and then faced the long road back to recovery.

At age 20 his playing days were over. He turned to coaching.

For five years he coached in Moose Jaw and while there tutored Howie Milford, a player destined to rejoin him later. From there he went to Gravelbourg, Saskatchewan for one year and followed that up with two years coaching the Lethbridge Native Sons. The tiny town of Bellevue in the Crows Nest Pass then became home for four years as he managed the bench for the junior team. Wherever he went success and popularity followed.

When he joined the Humboldt Indians as coach for the 51/52 season there was reason for excitement. He quickly set about building a team with character. The acquisition of each player could well be a story in itself but one case in particular stood out.

Ernie McLean was a true son of Saskatchewan soil. Growing up in Estevan with his three brothers in a strongly religious family he became a star athlete in his hometown. He remembered receiving his first pair of skates for Christmas at age 12 and how his father hired Archie Running to teach his sons how to skate. Only Ernie pursued hockey with any long term enthusiasm.

He graduated to playing in the LERKS (Legion, Elks, Rotary and Kinsmen Hockey League) as a member of the Legion squad. By age 14 he was playing for the midgets and juveniles as well as starring on a basketball squad.

At age 16 he laced up with the midgets as well as the Senior Estevan Miners who played in the Soo League, a railway league encompassing Estevan, Weyburn, Carnduff, Yellow Grass, Wilcox, Gainsborough and Moose Jaw. Midget teammates included the likes of Bob Jackson, Irwin Kruger, Carl Maley, Ken McKersie, Ron Sperring. Mike Briltz, Larry Berg and Don Dupius.

Estevan hired former Humboldt Indian, "Foo" McFarlane out of Regina, to coach. He gave Ernie his first serious start, lining him up with two Regina natives Belicak and Dempsey. Ernie, as the league's top scorer, proved good enough to catch the attention of scouts for the New York Rangers Ernie Brochett of Lethbridge and Al Ritchie of Regina.

At age 17 he was in Winnipeg for the Ranger evaluation camp. His father, Tom, had been reluctant to let him go but eventually relented and gave him $40 to cover his expenses. Showing the frugality that eventually helped him to manage a junior hockey team he lived on the $5 per day living allowance provided by the Rangers and returned home with the same $40.

He impressed New York enough that they wanted him to play junior for the Prince Albert Mintos and coach Johnny Wilson. Enter Scotty Munro.

In those days NHL teams held closed evaluation camps, not wanting the opposition to scout up and coming potential. Scotty, in the course of building his Humboldt Indians, came to town in the company of future Hall of Famer Terry Sawchuk. He wanted to see what the Rangers had. The two managed to convince the security guard that they were two Americans who had never seen a hockey game before and just wanted an opportunity to watch a practise. That line and $5 gained them entry to the Winnipeg Amphitheatre.

Scotty got word to Ernie that he wanted to meet him and fellow Estevan product Jack Giles at the McLarenn Hotel. Ernie listened to Scotty's pitch and told him that he would think about coming to Humboldt. His next interview was with Johnny Wilson of Prince Albert.

It just so happened that Johnny Wilson was a smoker. Ernie, coming from a strongly religious family, was against smoking and was put off by the habit. Humboldt won the coin toss but there still remained the issue of convincing his parents to let him go.

A month after Ernie returned home Scotty came down to meet his parents. Tom McLean did not want his son going away and was concerned about stories he had heard regarding the lifestyle of hockey players. Anticipating some resistance Scotty brought along two of his former players as positive role models. Unfortunately the two decided to go out on the town and get drunk. Word got back to Tom and that was it. Scotty was leaving empty handed, or so it seemed.

Ernie's mother assured Ernie the matter was not closed. Two months later Tom relented and Ernie headed for Humboldt. Tom drove the 350 miles from Estevan to Humboldt to take in his son's first game, little imagining where it would eventually take him.

On September 3, 1951 Scotty Munro announced that another "outstanding" player was set to arrive the following Thursday. 18 year old, 175 pound centre Ernie McLean was lauded as the top scorer in the Soo League, an Honours student, captain of his high school basketball team and a top notch pole vaulter.

The team of Munro and McLean was formed.

Others joined the squad. Notables such as Melfort's "Little" Reg Beliveau, Eddy "Gabby" Panagabko, Lionel Heinrich on defence and tough guy Al Pyatt laced up as well. To this mix

51/52 Indians - Saskatchewan Junior Hockey League Champions **Top Left to Right** Dave Wilson, Leo Parker, Lionel Heinrich, Gordon Grest, David Brauns **Middle** Laurie Bursaw, Al Pyatt, Gordon Andre, Scotty Munro, Art Asleson, Ernie McLean, Reg Beliveau **Front** Dave Wall, Frank Kuzma, Peter Voykin, Glen Laughren, Eddie Panagabko, Orest Hryciuk, Oscar Hanson, **In Front** - Gerald Sedgewick (C. Reg Beliveau) **Also suiting up** Bernard Royal, Bob Robson, Lorne Harley, Jimmy Quinn, Ralph Britz, ? Wosik, ? Johnson, Spike MacDougall

Scotty brought over former Crows Nest Pass standout Gordon Andre'.

Scotty soon made his presence felt. Complaining the league was a weak sister to the Western Canada Junior Hockey League he lobbied for an interlocking schedule. The result was a bumped up season that went from 36 games up to 50.

There had not been promise like this since Glenn Hall's second season.

The campaign started on the road in Prince Albert. The number one line featured returning Frank Kuzma, Eddie Panagabko and Dave Wilson followed by the second string centred by Ernie McLean flanked by Dave Wall and Oscar Hanson. The third unit had Reg Beliveau, Bernard Royal and Bob Robson. They lost 4-3 with the winning goal coming with only six seconds remaining.

They dropped their home opener 3-2 to the visiting Wesleys on a goal by future Indian Peter Voykin; again in the last minute. The favour was returned as they then went in to Saskatoon and took them 4-1 in a game which saw Gordon Andre' play the entire 60 minutes.

By early November the Indians had grabbed first place after beating Lethbridge Native Sons and Moose Jaw Canucks of the WCJHL in road games. Even though they dropped their next two road games against WCJHL teams they proved that they could skate with them.

Scotty heated up the entertainment value in games as he managed to get himself ejected from matches on numerous occasions for his rather boisterous questioning of officials.

By early December Dave Wall had taken over the league scoring lead. Ernie was doing his bit as he popped the overtime winner in a 6-5 victory over Flin Flon which put them in to a tie for second.. That same month they went up against Scotty's old team, the Crow's Nest Coalers, and suffered a 6-4 setback. December also saw the Boston Bruins sign a working agreement with the team bringing both money and new uniforms. The connection with Boston was to span many years.

By February 14, 1952 their victory parade, which included a 5-1 victory over Edmonton Oil Kings on the strength of Frank Kuzma's hat trick, had them in second and chasing Saskatoon. They were on a eight game home ice winning streak.

The battle for first went to the wire. In late February they vaulted in to first by virtue of a 7-1 victory over the Wesleys at the arena. Ernie's contribution, two goals. Saskatoon never caught them.

The Indians won the regular season for the first time in their history. With it came the Robin Hood Trophy.

Final Standings

Humboldt	23	25	2	172	189	48
Saskatoon	21	24	5	192	239	47
Prince Albert	20	26	4	198	245	44
Flin Flon	18	27	5	212	236	41

Prince Albert was their first round foe. This time the Indians were the favourites. Despite Minto protests that Munro was not properly registered Humboldt downed them four games to one and extended their own home ice undefeated string to 13.

Thirteen proved an unlucky number as Flin Flon came in and stole game one of the best of five; 6-5. An irate Munro managed to get himself ejected from the game. The Indians came back for a decisive 4-0 victory in game two and followed it up with a 4-3 win to give them a 2-1 series lead heading into the final two games, at Flin Flon.

After the Bombers came back to tie the series by virtue of a 4-2 win it all came down to game five at the Whitney Forum. In a tainted game the Indians went down 3-1 and bowed out of the campaign. The paper claimed, and Ernie McLean later verified, Laurie Bursaw had scored the tying goal but the Flin Flon goal judge refused to put on the light. With the Indians cheering, Bomber MacKay took the puck and raced down to the ice to score the 3-1 insurance goal that secured the game and the series. The Indians had taken the regular season series six games to three and were dominating in the final game which only served to make the loss harder to take. Some Bomber players, including goaltender Lalonde, later told Indian players that the goal had in fact gone in.

Stories about biased goal judging in Flin Flon were rampant and only added to the advantages the home side sought over its visitors. Another story, recounted by more than a few, was that visiting teams were housed in a local hotel in an unheated wing that had teeth chattering all night and shorts put out the night before to dry solidly frozen in the morning. Just a little extra for the home side. Despite the goings on Ernie proclaimed that he enjoyed playing and coaching there. It was an exciting setting.

Regina eventually won the West and went on to the Memorial Cup where they lost out to Guelph.

The returning Indians were greeted by 800 faithful fans when they arrived home. They had lost the playoffs but praise heaped down on them for climbing from the outhouse to Penthouse in one year. Promise filled the air as their success had been achieved with 50% of the team being rookies.

Four year vet David Wall won the Most Popular Player Award from the Humboldt Journal and Frank Kuzma took home the MVP trophy at the season ending banquet. David Wall, Frank Kuzma, Eddie Panagabko and Ernie McLean finished in order as the teams' top scorers with Ernie finishing 10th overall in the league.

An optimistic Scotty Munro re-signed for another two years in February claiming

" I've never seen a town and district like this for real hockey enthusiasm and rabid fans. It's the sort of enthusiasm which makes the team want to give their best all the time. (Journal)"

Board of Trade President Mr. Grest proclaimed "What we want is the Memorial Cup for Humboldt and we're going after it (Journal)."

Making matters even better; the team actually made money that season.

The best season yet and the future looked even brighter. They had won the regular season and hungered for more. The smallest community in the league had the greatest of expectations.

7 (H)

Flin Flon Flu 1952/53

Despite the losses of David Wall, Gordon Andre and Laurie Bursaw the Indians had McLean, Beliveau, Eddie Panagabko, Heinrich and Kuzma returning. Promise was shown by Paul Strasser and Estevan's Al Nicholson as well as goalie Ray Mikulan. Fourteen year old Peter Panagabko, brother of Eddie, was outstanding at camp and figured to get in some games.

Gone was interlocking play against the WCJHL though the road to the Memorial Cup still went through them.

Early in the season it became a three way battle for first between Flin Flon, Saskatoon and Humboldt with Prince Albert drawing up the rear. The battles with Flin Flon proved the most intense with little to chose in calling favourites for the playoffs, despite Flin Flon's securing of first 13 points ahead of Humboldt. The front running Bombers, with sharpshooter McKay in their lineup, tasted some big losses at the hands of the Indians. The tribe handed the Bombers crushing defeats of 8-3, 10-1, 8-3 and 10-5 in the course carving out a plus .500 season.

The number one line consisted of McLean, Beliveau and Kuzma backed up by number two unit Peter Voykin, Bruce Lea and Eddie Panagabko. Al Nicholson, Paul Strasser and either Keith Christopherson or Len Friestadt made up the last line. Kuzma battled all season long with the Bombers' McKay for the scoring title before losing out. Line mates Beliveau and McLean joined him in the top ten at seasons end along with Eddie Panagabko.

Final Standings

Flin Flon	30	16	2	210	199	62
Humboldt	24	23	1	202	178	49
Saskatoon	22	26	0	200	214	44
Prince Albert	18	29	1	209	230	37

The playoffs started well with 4-2 and 3-0 home ice wins but they stumbled a bit in Saskatoon tying game three 3-3 and losing 7-3. A 3-2 victory back on home ice put them within a tie of advancing to the league final for the second year in a row. Saskatoon proved that they were no pushover as they took game six at home to force a 7th game at the arena.

No contest. Team scoring leader Kuzma potted a hat trick and Heinrich got two as the tribe rolled over the Wesleys 7-2. For the fourth year in a row they went up against Flin Flon and the dreaded confines of Whitney Forum.

Having the first three games at home the Indians took advantage in game one to come out with a 4-2 victory on the strength of Eddie Pangabko's two goals. Game two was preceded by honours being bestowed upon Reg Beliveau and Al Pyatt, both of whom haled from Melfort. The 388 Melfort fans on hand to honour the native sons suffered with the Indian fans as the Bombers stole game two with a goal at 15:07 of overtime; final 2-1. Facing a must win situation the Indians' defence failed them in game three as they went down 6-4. The remainder of the series was in Flin Flon. They had to win three of the remaining four games.

52/53 Indians **Left to Right** Bruce Lea, Lionel Heinrich, Art Asleson, Al Pyatt, Al Nicholson, Jack Giles, Ernie McLean, Will Bigelow, John Ewasiuk, Eddie Pangabko, Paul Strasser, Frank Kuzma, Peter Voykin, Keith Christopherson, Reg Beliveau, Peter Pangabko, Ray Mikulan (C. Reg Beliveau) **Also suiting up** Mike Vrabek, Ken Roenspies, Orest Hryciuk, Len Friestadt, Chuck Newmeyer (goal), Sid Humphries, ? Schmidt, Dave Steward, Gerald Sedgewick, ? Henderson

Game four had the Indians up 3-1 in the third only to lose 5-3 in the final two minutes.

Game five saw the tribe down 2-0 before they stormed back to knot it at 2-2 on goals by Al Nicholson and Peter Voykin.

Overtime would have to settle it and the Indians were proving they had a chance, having out shot the Bombers on their own ice. On one of the Humboldt goals the Flin Flon goal judge was up to his old tricks and refused to put on the light when the Indians scored. This time the ref was in place and overruled him.

For the second time in the series the Bombers took an overtime game. Their 3-2 game winner at 8:18 of OT ended the more than respectable season. For the fourth straight year the Bombers had dropped the Indians. If the franchise was to get anywhere it had to get an antidote for the Flin Flon Flu. As for the Bombers their glory was short-lived as the Lethbridge Native Sons of the WCJHL put them out in four.

Peter Voykin topped the local polls as the team's most popular player while Lionel Heinrich secured himself a spot on the league all-star team.

Back in January Scotty Munro was selected as one of Saskatchewan's top ten sports personalities. With him had come increased credibility for Saskatchewan's weak sister junior league and more recognition for the small community.

Big losses loomed as Kuzma, Lea, Voykin and, most significantly, McLean graduated.

Ernie, picked by Baldy Cotton of the Boston Bruins as pro material, was offered a spot on the Hershey Bears roster. Ernie however, made a decision that he never regretted. He returned home to Estevan to join in the family's construction business. He knew the limits of his talent and that his success was based much more upon his work ethic. The pros could not offer him what the family business could and Ernie was intending to be a family man.

Young Ernie McLean as a Humboldt Indian - 52/53 Indian Program (C. Reg Beliveau)

The Journal lamented "Ernie was one of the driving forces on the team and somehow managed to instill a lot of spirit into the boys. He'll be missed next season."

The words proved prophetic and Ernie's spirit was destined to be tied more intensely to the team than anyone could have imagined. The link between him and Scotty was welded by the Seventh Man.

8 (H)

Wigwam ____________________ 1953/54

Since 1946 the arena had simply been known as the arena. The start of the 53/54 campaign saw the importance of the Indians recognized as the rink took on the new and fitting name of Wigwam. The title stayed with it for many years until it was renamed the Leo Parker Arena in honour of Humboldt's greatest hockey citizen.

On the ice Scotty busied himself replacing the strength of outgoing players. Not an easy task.

The squad struggled out of the gate and matters got worse in November. With the team camped in last place they lost star forward Reg Beliveau for a month. Instead of folding, they rebounded to take three of the next four games to squeeze into third.

In December Beliveau returned to join team scoring leader Paul Strasser and Johnny Ewasiuk on the squads first line. The Panagabko brothers, Eddie and Peter, were the second unit along with Al Nicholson. The third line had Lawrence Leach, Larry Berg and Bob Lausen. They had fallen back to last place but were only two points out of second in a competitive season.

Scotty's intensity had not declined nor had animosity in games against Prince Albert. In one game, a 3-1 win over the Mintos, Scotty and Minto coach "Legs" Fraser were both suspended and a fan laid an assault charge against Indian defenceman Lionel Heinrich. The Journal complained that Minto fans threw debris on the ice and spit on Indian players during contests in Prince Albert. There was no love lost.

By February it was apparent they were not going to catch either Prince Albert or Flin Flon who were battling it out for first. It was between them and Saskatoon for third place.
In January they brought up a couple of players from the Canora Bruins, Ray Lariviere and Les Clark. Clark was not destined for stardom but his son Wendell eventually was.

With the season winding down the Wesleys were still close and the Indians had three of their remaining games against the front running and hated Mintos.

In the first they tied Prince Albert 4-4 with the all rookie line of Neil MacDonald, Will Bigelow and Larry Berg starring. They took the next one 6-3 on the strength of Reg Beliveau's hat trick. The final one went to the Indians again, this time by a score of 7-5. The squad scored five goals in nine minutes to erase a three goal deficit. Heinrich netted three goals and 1 assist. Fated to go up against the Mintos in the first round their season ending success gave room for hope.

Paul Strasser finished the season as the team's top scorer with 45 points.

Final Standings

Prince Albert	28	18	2	220	206	58
Flin Flon	27	21	0	279	204	54
Humboldt	20	25	3	163	202	43
Saskatoon	18	29	1	172	222	37

53/54 Indians **Top Left to Right** Art Howard, Ray Hamlin, Art Asleson, Peter Pangabko, Reg Beliveau, Jack Martin **Middle** Leo Parker , Dave Steward, Larry Leach, Al Nicholson, Al Pyatt, John Ewasiuk, Lionel Heinrich, Gordon Grest Front Keith Christopherson, Paul Strasser, Baldy Cotton, Red Nelson, Scotty Munro, Larry Berg, Eddie Pangabko, Bill Thieman - **sitting in front** (C. Reg Beliveau) **Also suiting up** Neil MacDonald, Bob Lausen, Les Clark, Bud McRae, Ray Lariviere, Will Bigelow

The Mintos had secured first and home ice advantage but could not take the Indians lightly. The tribe had managed a strong showing and taken Prince Albert six times.

Using home ice to their advantage, the Mintos, led by future star NHLer Orland Kurtenbach, took a quick two game lead on the strength of 8-2 and 4-2 victories. Game three was a back breaker for Humboldt as Prince Albert came in to the Wigwam and took them 6-4. It looked like a sweep.

Heinrich came to the fore in game four. His two goals led the team to a face saving 6-2 win to extend the season. It only lasted one more game however as the Mintos locked up the series with a 6-3 win in game five.

The season had not been bad considering the player losses. The team remained competitive and more than a few players had big nights. Paul Strasser, Al Nicholson, Peter Pangabko, Lionel Heinrich and Reg Beliveau had all managed hat tricks. Beliveau was voted the league's most gentlemanly player. Captain Al Pyatt was voted to the first all star team while Heinrich and Art Asleson landed on the second.

One night in late January the team thrilled the fans with a resounding 7-3 victory over the Saskatoon Wesleys. Peter Panagabko got his second straight hat trick and Strasser got two markers.

A great night but it was played before the poorest crowd of the season. Without the total support of the fans and the community the franchise could not survive. Dark clouds were gathering on a distant horizon.

9 (H)

King of the Hill 1954/55

It was Scotty's fourth year at the helm. The team had had more success in the three previous years than it had ever known; despite the financial pressures bearing down upon the small community. In the 54/55 campaign it all came together in a David and Goliath matchup.

In a forerunner to the season, western junior hockey clubs met and decided British Columbia was considered open territory which meant teams could take players from B.C. without considering them as out of Province imports. In addition the western teams were now allowed to bolster their squads by three players for the Memorial Cup. Decisions with profound impact.

Scotty's wheeling and dealing set the stage. All star Howie Hornby came over from Saskatoon in a deal costing goalie Red Nelson, three juvenile players and cash. Then he obtained Don Chiupka and Connie Madigan from Port Arthur Bruins of the Thunder Bay Junior Hockey League. Chiupka and Hornby were both in their last year of junior. Connie Madigan only suited up for five games with the Indians but went on to become a legend in the western pro leagues before finally hanging up his skates in his forties.

Graduation took Pyatt, Heinrich, Asleson and Eddie Panagabko. Both Pyatt and Asleson eventually spent time in Kamloops with the Senior A Chiefs while Heinrich and Panagabko put in part of the 55/56 season with the NHL's Boston Bruins.

On the positive side Scotty had Reg Beliveau, Al Nicholson, Paul Strasser (team captain) and newly acquired Chiupka returning from the Boston Bruins training camp.

The best of all seasons began with a road game loss in Saskatoon but revenge came in their own home opener against the Wesleys. The battle with Flin Flon started well with a 6-3 victory but they were smacked 15-4 in the return match. Their next meeting, at the Wigwam, saw Muenster's David Stewart slip three goals past former Indian goalie Red Nelson in a 9-5 win.

By mid November there was little to suggest a good season was in the offing. The Indians, though only briefly, found themselves in last place, despite some impressive scoring. Peter Panagabko was first in the league followed Chiupka (2nd), Beliveau (5th) and Nicholson (7th).

Scotty continued his player moves picking up disgruntled John Yanchuk from "Legs" Fraser's Mintos. Fraser was annoyed with the talented Yanchuk and had suspended him. On November 25 the paper boasted that the boys were in a first place tie with Saskatoon. Soon afterwards they took the Wesley's 4-2 with Howie Hornby getting the winner against his old team and moving in to the top ten scorers. Johnny Ewasiuk, who figured in the trade, was still skating for the Wesleys.

The teams next met in December. The Indians grabbing a 5-2 win and sole possession of first. The next tilt saw "Deker" Beliveau score the hat trick in a 4-1 win. They were on a roll.

They even rocked the WCJHL Moose Jaw Canucks 10-4 in an exhibition game.

As Saskatoon faded Prince Albert came up to challenge. A 4-3 loss in Prince Albert saw the Mintos vault into first. It was short lived as the Indians took a Boxing Day rematch 10-2 at the Wigwam. By early January six of the nine top scorers in the league were from Humboldt.

Mid way through the month Scotty pulled another rabbit out of the hat. He spotted a "hidden" talent on the Mintos and reached in to grab him from under their noses. Ron Larson was skating for Prince Albert but was not on their protected list. Scotty noticed it and nabbed him. The Mintos lived to regret the oversight.

By January 20, 1955 they were pulling away. Eight points up on Flin Flon and Prince Albert they had five of the six top league scorers while Ray Ethier had the best goals against average. February 17, 1955 the Journal headlined, INDIANS WIN LEAGUE CHAMPIONSHIP.

Their 4-1 win over the Wesley's clinched the Robin Hood Trophy for the second time in four years. Six games remained but no one could catch them. Munro was ecstatic, calling it the best team he had coached since the 49/50 Crow's Nest squad that almost made it to the Memorial Cup. The team was being picked, by some, to win the west. Six players in the top ten scorers (Chiupka, Beliveau, Nicholson, Peter Panagabko, Strasser,

Hornby), the league's best goalie and defencemen and the best record. What a season.

Even with the regular season sown up the excitement was not over. Melfort's Reg Beliveau, the four year vet, was honoured on a special "Reg Beliveau Night". Melfort Mayor Bill Frost led a contingent of 200 Melfort fans on a night to remember. Boston Bruin GM Lynn Patrick presented Reg with money and the Humboldt Journal MVP trophy while gold cufflinks were awarded by Mayor Frost. The ceremony continued with Leo Parker presenting Don Chiupka with the league scoring championship award and the team making Patrick an honorary "Chief".

The game. Well, right on cue, the visiting Wesleys fell to the Indians 4-1.

Standings

Humboldt	48	28	19	1	235	176	57
Flin Flon	48	23	24	1	218	215	47
Prince Albert	48	22	25	1	187	223	45
Saskatoon	48	21	26	1	175	201	43

Wigwam fans saw their heroes squeeze out a 5-4 opening game victory over Saskatoon in the playoff opener, on the strength of Strasser's hat trick, and then blow them away 7-0 in game two. In Saskatoon the tables were turned as the Indians fell 9-6 but then rebounded to take game four 9-3 going away. The Hornby/Strasser/Nicholson line netted 12 points. They could sew up the series on home ice. That they did with a 4-2 victory. They were on to play nemesis Prince Albert for the League Championship.

For years Flin Flon or Prince Albert had been the nail in the Indians' coffin. If they were to make it to the next level they had to get the monkey off their back. It had been the Orland Kurtenbach led Mintos who the year before stopped them cold and Kurtenbach was still there.

The March 10, 1955 Journal flashed the news that former Indian Dick Warwick shared in the glory of Penticton V's World Championship victory over the Russians. The first appearance of the Seventh Man on the World stage.

On home ice Ethier netted his second playoff shutout as the Indians blanked the visiting Mintos 2-0 in game one.
Ex-Minto Ron Larson had the joy of scoring the winner on his

old mates. Game two went to the Indians 5-2 with the squad scoring three goals in the final period after the teams entered the frame tied at two. Beliveau's three goals in game three gave them a 5-3 win and a 3-0 series lead heading to Prince Albert. The Mintos were not going out easily and shocked the visitors 7-1 in game four. Game five was set for the Wigwam.

Former Indian Frank Kuzma, who had tasted the bitterness of playoff defeat, was on hand for the prospect of seeing his former mates take the league. His stomach and that of the capacity crowd dropped within the first few minutes. Before many were even settled in their seats the Mintos struck for a quick 1-0 lead. It increased to 2-0 early in the second. If they lost, game six went in Prince Albert and in a seventh game anything could happen, despite the dream season. But the Indians hadn't won the league for nothing.

Reg Beliveau slapped a 30 footer that found the twine to put the Indians on the board. Nine seconds later, before the Mintos could recover, Chiupka skated through the defence and tied the match. This was the team they had watched all season. The rink tilted.

At 18:37 Strasser let go a 25 footer that was in and out so fast that the goal judge was slow to hit the light. The Mintos mildly protested but the goal stood. It stood as the winner.

For the first time in the team's history they had won their league.

On March 17, 1955 the Journal programmed in bold headlines:

INDIANS DEFEAT PRINCE ALBERT MINTOS - ENTER WESTERN JUNIOR FINALS.

As the winner of the Saskatchewan Junior Hockey League they went on to face the famed Regina Pats. Their odds against the top junior league in the west were long at best. No SJHL championship team had even won a playoff game against the WCJHL in the four preceding years. The Pats, the oldest junior team in the west, had been to the Memorial Cup three times in their long history and had won it once. In their lineup, coached by former NHL star Murray Armstrong, were six future NHLer's. Bigger and heavier, they were a formidable foe.

Another former Indian was on hand for game one, at the Wigwam. Ernie McLean, was spotted behind the Indian bench, cheering on his alma mater. The Seventh Man turned up as well for the Indians stunned the heavily favoured Pats 5-3. Regina took a 1-0 lead into the dressing room after one but it was the Indians who came out ahead after two; 4-2. The teams traded goals in the third.

The Indians were doing well in game two before the fates turned on them. They scored on their own net and never recovered. Final score 3-1 and the series was tied. Years later Reg Beliveau recalled the moment and the game. He felt the team would have won the series if they had taken game two as they were controlling the play in the series.

54/55 Indians - Saskatchewan Junior Hockey League Champions (C.Reg Beliveau & HDMG) **Also suiting up** Dick Todd (goal), John Yanchuk, Connie Madigan

Game three went to Regina 3-1 and when they invaded the Wigwam and stole game four 2-0 the odds piled up against the tribe. Despite outshooting the Pats in every game and keeping it close they were on the verge of elimination. The deciding game went in Regina.

The road to the Memorial Cup ground to a halt with an 8-1 loss. It was the first game where the Pats outshot the Indians and where they could clearly say that they dominated the game. The series went to Regina 4-1 but the Indians could just as well have taken it.

Just how good their performance was can be measured by the fact Regina went all the way to the Memorial Cup before losing to the famed Toronto Marlboros in a tough series. Final team honours came with the selection of Chiupka and Nicholson to the SJHL first all star team while Beliveau, Ray Hamlin and Peter Pangabko landed on the second.

Estevan native Al Nicholson went on to lace up for a bundle of matches over two seasons with the Boston Bruins.

For Humboldt it was the crowning glory of their existence. In the four years since Scotty took over, the smallest community in the league had twice won the regular season and had put the powerful Regina Pats on their heels before succumbing.

The Journal's Roger Barry commented that Lynn Patrick was astonished at the hockey interest in Humboldt. Patrick claimed he had never seen a place like it. Only 3500 people but a real hockey hotbed. An ideal junior setup with a good arena, fine coach and civic support. The warm fuzzies continued in April as Scotty signed a two year contract and proclaimed; "If the people stand behind and support it there will always be a good team in Humboldt."

Unfortunately you cannot spend words nor do they replace fans in the seats. During the regular season, despite the team's success, there were more than few nights when the Wigwam was not sold out. Board of Trade figures in December 1954 showed a $9800 deficit which included payments still being made for the artificial ice plant. Humboldt was straining to keep its team. A solution had to be found.

The people of Saskatchewan have always been known for resourcefulness and, in particular, their ability to pull together in bad times. Both qualities came together in a unique attempt to save what was a unique team. Those Melfort fans who had come to cheer on their locals on the team would be cheering a little louder next season.

10 (H)

Melfort 1955/56

For years the Humboldt Indians had been not only a community team but a district team. Players from nearby communities such as Meunster and, though farther afield, Melfort, had been as locals and received special note. Financial pressures brought the relationship closer for the 55/56 season and Melfort became an active member of the unique franchise.

It did not look good at the start. In June 1955 Humboldt and Saskatoon both withdrew from the league, contending the costs of traveling to Flin Flon were too high. Despite the withdrawal club president Gordon Grest promised the fans there would be a junior team in Humboldt and it would be a Memorial Cup contender. Within two weeks the picture altered. The Board of Trade approved amalgamation with Melfort and thus avoided the prospect of selling the team. It had been losing a bit of money every year and amalgamation was the only option seen.

The team was provided an 11 man Board with five representatives from each community and Scotty Munro as the 11th man. The 24 game home schedule was split between the Wigwam and the Melfort Teepee; which still had natural ice. Humboldt retained ownership of the players and remained the team's base of operations.

The Teepee was much the same as the Wigwam in size and capacity. Each rink could seat 1200. The team needed them all, the 229 season's tickets from last year just weren't enough.

With the arrangement in hand the team rejoined the league but Saskatoon did not. For the first time since their inception there was no Saskatoon team to face. The league did, however, expand to take in the Melville Millionaires and Yorkton Terriers.

To assist the new squads existing teams agreed to give up a top flight player to each new team. Johnny Yanchuk went to Melville to rejoin rambunctious coach "Legs" Fraser. On the good side, with the demise of Saskatoon, the Indians picked up Richie Van Impe, Buddy Bodman and Joe Kulbida.

Munro, hedging his bets, claimed third place was a reasonable goal for the young and inexperienced squad. Dick Thieman made the team; according to the Journal he was the first local to make the squad since Scotty arrived.

The season soon revealed that Flin Flon and Prince Albert were the class of the league leaving Humboldt and Yorkton to fight for third and fourth. Melville was a distant last.

Games in Melfort drew well but did not necessarily sell out. Still Scotty felt optimistic enough in January to comment on improved crowds. He also pointed out that with the exception of Flin Flon the Indians were playing .500 hockey or better with everyone else.

Munro's value to the league was acknowledged at league meetings. He was reimbursed for his costs and praised for his assistance in getting the two new teams off the ground. His credibility was widespread and not unnoticed by other teams and leagues.

As the battle for playoff spots intensified concerns were raised about financial costs if they had to play Flin Flon in the first round. Contending with Yorkton they were two points behind with each team having three games to go. Two of the games were against each other.

In the first of the remaining three they journeyed to Yorkton and fell 4-2 to fall four points behind. They had to win their remaining two and Yorkton lose theirs. Yorkton obliged however, in an embarrassing game in Melville the Indians lost 6-3 to the cellar dwelling Millionaires. Though they dumped Yorkton 6-1 in their final game they had already lost a chance at third. Making matters even worse the crowd turnout at the Wigwam was sparse. They had to face Flin Flon.

Standings

Flin Flon	37	10	1	301	149	75
Prince Albert	33	12	3	255	161	69
Yorkton	20	26	2	185	201	42
Humboldt	19	28	1	199	192	39
Melville	8	40	0	126	363	16

Peter Pangabko was the top Indian scorer with 85 points followed by Richie Van Impe, Lawrence Leach and Larry Berg. Flin Flon's rookie sensation Ted Hampson won the race with 113.

Round one against the Bombers was an uphill battle. They lost their first ever playoff game in Melfort 7-4 but at least they took it to overtime. Bouncing back they upset the league leaders 7-6 in game two. In the crucial third game, at the Wigwam, a close 3-2 loss put them down 2-1. When they lost game four 3-1 they were in trouble. The remaining games were all in Flin Flon.

Despite the long odds they did not roll over. Up 2-1 at the end of the first they ended the second period tied at 3-3. Flin Flon was not going to walk away easily. In the end rookie sensation Ted Hampson won the day for the Bombers as they took the game 4-3 and the series 4-1. The Indians had not been embarrassed.

Pangabko and Lawrence Leach were quickly scooped up by the professional Victoria Cougars of the Western Hockey League. Leach made the team and scored in his first game as a Cougar. Pangabko didn't stick but he did make the SJHL all stars.

If consolation could be found in the professional achievements of former Indians there was ample reason to feel good. Glenn Hall was not only playing in the NHL he won the Calder Cup, as rookie of the year with Detroit. Heinrich was up with Boston; Nicholson and Eddie Pangabko were in Hershey; Dave Wall in Trois Riviere; Ray Mikulan in net for the Vancouver Canucks; Erwin Grosse in Shawinigan Falls; Murray Parker with Saskatoon Quakers; Gordon Andre' with Seattle; and Paul Strasser, Chiupka and Beliveau in Victoria.

The biggest concerns were not on the ice though. Teams have good and bad years and the Indians under Scotty Munro had shown they had character and would rebound. The problem was could they keep Scotty and could they survive in Humboldt. Rumours sprang up that Munro was leaving or was buying another team in Medicine Hat or Yorkton. His answer "If there is a junior team in Humboldt next season I'll be there!"

That there would be a team was not at all certain. The deficit reached $14000 and the Board of Trade once again accepted liability. How long could it go on.

The rumours about Munro would not go away. Heading back east for a conference word had it he had an offer from Medicine Hat giving him a year lease on the arena with all proceeds from concessions, program and radio broadcasting. He insisted he still wanted to stay in Humboldt with the Indians and hold on to his bowling alley. It was known that he had been contributing financially to the team to keep it afloat.

In the end Scotty was true to his word. He came back.

55/56 Indians (Unfortunately no photo awailable) **Players suiting up for the 55/56 season included** - Richie Van Impe, Buddy Bodman, Joe Kulbida, Peter Pangabko, Dave Steward, Dave Beskal, Bill Thieman, Ray Hamlin, Larry Berg, Bill Drew, Henry Blanchard, Dick Todd (goal), ? Hamilton, Keith Christopherson, Lawrence Leach, Neil MacDonald, Keith Lawrence, Pat Tallis, Bob Seymour, Bill Wouters, Henry Blanchette, Dick Thieman, Chuck Passmore, M. Christopherson, Barney Krake, Duane Fagerheim, Steve Kuzma, Keith Lawrence, Oran Flory

11 (H)

Indian Summer________________1956/57

There is that time of the year when the first hints of winter are thrown back by a remembrance of summer. A time when we can pretend winter is not around the corner. A time when the inevitable can seemingly be put off. So it came to pass with the Humboldt Indians.

Munro spoke optimistically about the new season. The team budget was $25000 and he needed to get $15,000 from the gate. Another 500 seasons tickets would turn the trick. The team was again shared with Melfort but fans were promised at least one game a week.

The league was restructured with Regina and Saskatoon rejoining and Yorkton folding. The Indians picked up Garth Hayes and Jerry Serviss from Yorkton and added Chuck Passmore. The only down side was that Richie Van Impe turned pro with Winnipeg.

Lawrence Leach was lost to the pros as expected. His star climbed high enough to give him three seasons with the Boston Bruins. Peter Panagabko was back from Boston's training camp as was goalie Dick Todd. Dick Meissner, a promising rookie from Kindersley, turned up on the roster. Jim Munro, Scotty's son, was destined to put in appearances.

The season started poorly with four straight losses out of the gate. By the time they recovered a bit in November they were sitting 5th in a 6th team league. Thank Heavens for Saskatoon. But worse, the crowds were sparse.

In early December the front running Flin Flon Bombers, led by Paddy Ginnel, came to town and had their bubble burst 2-1 by the Indians, unfortunately, before one of the smallest crowds of the year. Claims poor attendance were due to cold weather somehow just didn't explain it. They moved to within three of Melville and a playoff spot.

When they next went up against the Millionaires Chuck Passmore gave them three goals and a 4-3 win to move them to within one. Melville still had five games in hand. Their playoff battle continued and saw them gain a tie for fourth when they tied runaway league leading Flin Flon 5-5 to stop their 18 game win streak.

Attendance woes continued. The experiment with Melfort collapsed in January and the remaining three games scheduled for the Teepee were reset at the Wigwam. Munro was busy putting out fires. Rumours were the team was intending to play all its playoff games in Saskatoon and move next season.

"There hasn't been a thought of it. After all we've got a three year contract and we intend to stick by it."

By early February the Indians and Millionaires were tied for the last playoff spot and had a home & home series coming up. Losing star centre Chuck Passmore for the season was not what they needed to hear going into the home stretch. The series split didn't settle anything.

In the end it came down to beating Flin Flon if they were to make the playoffs. Long odds as the Bombers had previously gone 33 games without a loss. The one positive was the game was to go at the Wigwam.

If character is defined by doing things the hard way and fighting through adversity then the Indians had character. Uncertainty about their future took a back seat as fans, players and everyone associated with the team shared one last moment of glory and remembrance.

They went up 3-1 at the end of the first. Late in the third nursing a 3-2 lead Flin Flon pulled their goalie. Wild cheering erupted when Jim Powers on a pass from Garth Hayes sealed the 4-2 victory. Dick Todd faced 14 shots in the third but kept his team in. After a season long battle they were in the playoffs. Melville couldn't catch them.

Their reward. Flin Flon in the first round.

What chance they had came from knowing that they had twice defeated the Bombers and earned a tie. Back to back 7-1 losses at the Whitney Forum did not bring much hope but the 3-2 loss at the Wigwam in game three showed that they could keep it close. Game four was the last kick at the cat. No one knew for sure what the future held but it wasn't the next round. The Bombers left no doubt with an 11-5 victory.

The season was over and so, although it wasn't definite yet, were the Indians.

The rumblings started with the Journal. It claimed that without 100% backing from everyone the team was a losing cause financially.

"The slim crowd on hand at Tuesday's game is evidence that not enough people are interested in keeping high calibre hockey here."

Scotty was no longer denying a move as emphatically anymore. His hopes for high attendance at the playoff games were met by a half empty arena.

Word had it that Rosetown, North Battleford and Estevan were all in the running. Estevan, with a population of 8000 and a new community ice rink scheduled for the Fall, was seen as the top prospect.

56/57 Humboldt Indians - The last Indian Team **Front Left to Right** Barney Krake, Red Bosscha, Mgr./coach Scotty Munro, Peter Panagabko (captain), Balfour Laskin (publicity Mgr.) Dick Todd, Keith Robson **Middle** Jack Martin (trainer), Chuck Passmore, Jim Powers, Bob Seymour, Brian Edwards, Garth Hayes, Garth Hayes, Don Anderson **Back** Jim Stewart, Bill Drew, Bill Wouters, Jerry Serviss, Dick Meissner, Norm Usselman (C. Jim Stewart) **Also suiting up** Don Anderson, Bill Thieman, Ernie Dyda, Harold Poelzer, Ron McLean, Gordon Dodds, Don Drummond (goal) Warren Back, Brian Edwards, Jim Munro, Keith Ernewein

On April 4/57 came word the Board of Trade had sold the team, with all the players and the North Battleford juvenile club, to Scotty Munro. Many years later and many miles away it eventually became community owned again as a means of saving it. For now the sale proved the means to move it.

There was a brief surge of renewed interest in keeping the squad when the same Bomber team that dropped the Indians dropped everyone else. Flin Flon won its first and only Memorial Cup. The prospect was not lost on Munro and he quickly called a meeting with businessmen to come up with a plan to maintain the team in Humboldt.

At a town hall meeting Munro and his supporters came away empty handed. He told them the team was losing up to $4000 per season and it was up to the businesses and citizens to make up the difference. It was proposed that a committee be set up to help with funding and keeping the team but the proposal was not approved. It was the last straw.

On May 23/57 it was announced that Munro was leaving town. The team was a losing proposition without total community support. Rumour had it Boston had been after him to move the team and that he had a job offer from Melville. Up to the very end he claimed that he would not rule out leaving the team in Humboldt if suitable arrangements could be made.

On June 13, 1957 the Journal announced:

ITS FINALLY DEFINITE

"Scotty Munro - coach, hockey promoter, manager etc. in Humboldt for the past five seasons is on his way to Estevan with a five year contract and a five year option to operate his hockey club in Estevan. The Community Centre is to be built by October 1, 1957."

Humboldt still held the franchise rights and Scotty had to make an application for a new franchise but the unbroken line of players and team spirit left with him. Though Humboldt's Leo Parker, who had been there at the beginning, sought and received a month extension to come up with a team, it was over. All the efforts proved in vain. Perhaps the declining attendance had come from a knowledge amongst the fans their community was just too small to hang on to the team. But like their team they gave it a long and glorious run before they let go.

The Boston Bruins gave formal recognition to the Godfather of Humboldt hockey when they donated the Leo Parker

Trophy to be annually awarded to the SJHL's MVP.

Humboldt dropped out of the league, expressing intentions of rejoining next year. It didn't happen and the birthplace of the Kamloops Blazers did not rejoin the junior leagues until 1970 when the Broncos took to the ice. By chance the same season the Estevan Bruins called their last in Saskatchewan.

When the new Estevan Bruins formally opened their home season at the new Agricultural Auditorium, dignitaries from Humboldt, showing the community's class, turned up for the celebration. Judge A.B. Gerein and Mayor B.T. Laskin, the same Laskin who 12 years earlier as President of the Humboldt Board of Trade joined with Bill Slater to sponsor the new franchise, came to offer their best wishes. The Seventh Man was with them with a hand on each shoulder.

In 11 seasons the Indians had their share of glory and adversity. The championships of 52 and 55, four league finals, one Provincial final, their thrilling runs for the playoff and playoff battles, stars exemplified by Dick Warwick and Glenn Hall and the influence of hockey legends Ernie McLean and Scotty Munro. Under Munro they had never missed the playoffs. But most of all it was the team and the concept of playing as a team that formed the groundwork that made the Seventh Man. The many players and support people who did not necessarily go on to fame or fortune but who made the team what it was. It is they too who were and are the Seventh Man and who are forever linked to the phenomena that it became.

In 1998 the Leo Parker arena was torn down. Three years after the team that was born there won its fifth Memorial Cup in its eleventh appearance.

But you can't tear down history or the fact that it was at that arena, in Humboldt, in 1946 that the Seventh Man was born. He is still living, proof of the flame that has been passed on non stop from team to team and player to player and which now blazes along the Thompson River in Kamloops.

12

PART TWO
ESTEVAN

Birth of The Bruins__________1957/58

Estevan and Humboldt differed in more than population and promise during the boom years of the 50's. If farming and the railroad were the keys to Humboldt's economy, energy was the foundation for the community of 8000 sitting just north of the American border. Boom times in the oil patch led to optimism. Just the type of environment for a team on the rise; and rise it did.

Estevan was no stranger to the franchise. "Foo" McFarlane, who coached Ernie McLean, had played for the team as had Ernie himself, along with Al Nicholson and Jack Giles. Ernie never lost touch with the squad or his friend Scotty Munro. Occasionally he traveled up to watch his buddy Al Nicholson and was there for the upset playoff win over Regina. When his old team moved to Estevan, Ernie began a new association rivaling Glenn Hall's "Local Boy Makes Good" story.

He had left his junior playing days behind in 1953 to return to Estevan and the family business. On August 5, 1953, at age 20, he married Francis Sparks of Estevan and settled into family life. But he was never far from hockey.

He turned to coaching in the LERKS and guided the first Estevan midget team to get by regional rival Weyburn. That was not enough so he laced up skates with the Senior Estevan Miners. As for his ongoing connection with the Indians it never ended. Even now, almost 50 years after they skated together in Humboldt; Ernie, Reg Beliveau, Art Asleson, Keith Christopherson and Orest Hryciuk get together down on the Lower Mainland of B.C. to compare notes and debate the old days. Ernie's affair with hockey was destined to be life long.

From the beginning of the days in Estevan Ernie was there with Scotty. By the time his story with the team was finally told he occupied every position in the organization from player to owner. Yet, in the beginning, who would have guessed.

He busied himself helping Scotty make the necessary political and business connections to help the team and the building of the new Agricultural Auditorium. Scotty made some bold promises to the community and implied a top junior hockey franchise would go a long way in covering the cost of building a facility with artificial ice. He claimed that obtaining the Indians would not cost Estevan a cent; adding that "Only a good team can make a $250,000 arena pay".

Then, just to ensure that he had the attention of city fathers he stressed at every meeting he attended, that Estevan would certainly not have another opportunity to get a top flight junior team for a long time.

The hurdles fell one after another. Estevan was sold on the team. The Boston Bruins agreed to the location. The SJHL accepted Scotty's application for a new franchise and momentum gathered for the new arena. It was to be complete by August of 1957, just in time for training camp in September. It was not, however, always easy sailing.

The community got involved in efforts to fund and construct the new centre. "Rinko" events were held to assist with financing. Much of the construction work was done by volunteer labour including farmers who came into town from the surrounding area. It was truly a community effort. Despite all the effort there were problems that took some creative genius and exceptional "cooperation" to overcome.

The arena roof cost $40,000 alone and in order to pay for it Scotty borrowed the money from Weston Adams of the Boston Bruins. He was making $5000 a year scouting for the Bruins and intended to pay the loan off over a few years. When he got a call from the Bruins accountant, requesting the remaining $35000 sooner than expected he blew his lid and told him he would have the money the next day. Realizing afterwards what he said he contacted Ernie.

Ernie called his friend, and team mate on the Estevan Miners, Bill Shinske. Together they went to see the Exalted Ruler of the local Elks club, Wally Morin, and sought a loan. The Elks agreed on the basis the city would allow them to run slot machines for a year. From there the expanding little lobby group set up a meeting with Mayor Harry Nicholson and Chief of Police Harry Casswell at the Woodlands Golf Course. The deal was struck and Boston had its loan repaid the next day as promised.

The police had previously confiscated the machines from the Elks. They were returned but, just to keep it legal, the police continued their inspections. Fortunately for the Elks arrangements were always made in advance to let the club know of impending visits. Everybody was happy.

It was a windfall at a time when there was lots of money flowing from the oil patch and the little prairie town was busting at the seams.

There was still the question of naming the new team. The Mercury set up a contest and the names rolled in. The Estevan Gushers, Oilers, Cups, Boomers, Wildcats and Soo Liners all made the shortlist but it was a non local who picked the winner. Mr. C.H. Hook, a visitor from Toronto, suggested Bruins and in time it became a name familiar even to hockey fans in Toronto.

1957/58 Estevan Bruins - The first Bruin team **Top Left to Right** Ken Hodson, Abe Berday, Chuck Passmore, Fred Knippel, Jerry Serviss, Jack Rogers, Paul Grundeen, Ed Hudson **Middle** Ernie (Punch) McLean, Red Bosscha, Dick Meissner, Barney Krake, Jim Stewart, Ralph Walker, Don Anderson, Bill Thieman, Herb Martell **Front** Ernie Dyda, Jim Munro, Moe George, Fred Cluff, Scotty Munro, Alvin Collins, Danny Muloin (C.Ross Portrait Studios & Estevan Bruins SJHL) **Also suiting up** Dallas Smith, Herb McMillan, Don Drummond (goal), Duane Fagerheim

And so they came. Former Indians Jerry Serviss, Bill Drew (from Melfort), Dick Meissner, Red Bosscha, Jim Munro (Scotty's son), Don Anderson, Barney Krake, Ernie Dyda, Chuck Passmore, Dick Todd, Jim Powers, Garth Hayes, Bill Wouters, Don Drummond, Norm Usselman and Humboldt's own Bill

Thieman. Nine of the former Indians were still there for the team photo. Peter Panagabko was to join the squad but Boston decided against it. They moved him back east to Barrie and Estevan got Jack Rogers in compensation. It did not hurt them. Scotty was behind the bench with new assistant coach Ernie McLean. For 11 years the terrible twosome were the formidable force behind the team's success.

On October 17, 1957 history was made as the new Estevan Bruins, before 1321 fans, played their first game (an exhibition match) at the Auditorium. Every one was smiling after an 8-4 win over Winnipeg. Dick Meissner got the hat trick and promising rookie Dallas Smith, from Hamiota, put in a few shifts. The season home opener was even better.

After winning their first league game, on the road, 7-3 in Melville, they hosted the Regina Pats for the first league game at the Auditorium. Bad weather hurt attendance but all the VIPs were there including an entourage from Humboldt, that got special recognition.

Despite two goals from Meissner, the lads were down 3-2 with seconds remaining. Moe George, who was behind the bench, pulled goalie Fred Cluff. It worked as Ernie Dyda netted the tying goal. As if that was not enough the Bruins took an inspirational 4-3 over time win. The arena and the new Bruins were baptised in dramatic fashion.

The year got tougher. Goalie Drummond was lost for the season with an injury. The team struggled and by the end of January 1958 they were fifth and facing league leading Regina who were riding a 14 game winning streak. With Saskatoon already ahead of them in the last playoff spot they could not afford a loss.

At the end of the second period Regina was cruising to their fifteenth win as they enjoyed a 5-3 advantage. The Bruins were clinging to the fact that they had, at one point, been down 4-1. Barney Krake's first two goals, of the three he had that night, had closed them to 4-3. The third belonged to Estevan. Goalie Knobby Graf proved stingy and the Bruins? Well, they stormed back with five of their own to win 8-5.

Next up was second place Prince Albert. Bill Thieman, who had earlier been sent down, scored the winner in a 4-2 victory. The Bruins were alive and climbing.

On February 13, 1958 the Mercury raved that the Bruins had moved into a 4th place tie with Saskatoon after beating Flin

Flon before 2700 fans at the AA. They had earlier beaten Saskatoon 8-4. The Bruins were the masters of their own destiny. With three games remaining they had one against bottom feeding Melville and two against 3rd place Flin Flon.

The smiles from a 7-2 win over Melville turned to frowns when they lost 10-2 to Flin Flon. It came down to the final game. They had to play Flin Flon while Saskatoon had a much easier tilt against Melville. It looked bad when the Bruins found themselves down 5-0. Cue the comeback. A three goal rally in the third gave them a dramatic come from behind 6-5 victory while Melville held Saskatoon to a tie. The Bruins made the playoffs by one point. The season had begun with and ended with drama. Scotty could only comment "It was a great finish".

Standings

	G	W	L	T	GF	GA	TP
Regina	51	36	12	3	246	160	75
Prince Albert	51	33	16	2	237	160	68
Flin Flon	51	24	25	2	220	177	48
Estevan	51	22	29	0	199	206	44
Saskatoon	51	20	28	3	156	203	43
Melville	51	10	39	2	134	286	22

Their next task was a difficult one. Try to knock off league leading Regina who finished 31 points ahead and had home ice advantage.

After losing the first two games in Regina the Bruins had a chance for some redemption at home. They got it with Dick Meissner's winner in a 2-1 victory. But that was as far as they got against a Pats team destined to make it all the way to the Memorial Cup final.

The Bruins had proven that they still had the character of Scotty's Indians. They had clawed back to make the playoffs and given star studded Regina respectable opposition.

For next season star forward Dick Meissner was being joined by promising rookie defenceman Dallas Smith. A good start and some promise for the future.

The Bruins had arrived and before they left Saskatchewan they were to leave an impression across the country.

13

Respect 1958/59

If season number one fell short of expectations season number two offered more promise, though part way into the campaign it didn't look very good. Both on ice performance and back bench problems tainted the optimism.

A strong returning core, including leading scorer Dick Meissner, was joined by hopefuls Herbie Martel, Ron Erne and two individuals destined to play a role in the team's future. Harvey Roy and Ivan Prediger were both to flit in and out of the franchise's fortunes long after their junior playing days were over. The greatest promise was in Dallas Smith, who was expected to be a regular this time around.

Munro kept his cards close to his vest and called for Prince Albert to be the season favourite. He couldn't have been more wrong.

The first sign of good things to come was a resounding 16-2 exhibition win over Brandon at the Auditorium, after having defeated the Wheat Kings in Brandon earlier 5-4. Barney Krake was paraded out as the new team captain and 17 year old Dallas Smith looked like a veteran on the blueline.

They opened against Fred Shero coached Moose Jaw, a team which had been out of the league for fully four years and started well with a 6-4 win.

By mid November they were playing sub 500 hockey and trailing both Prince Albert and front running Flin Flon. Still the fans were turning out as witnessed by the 2400 that came out to catch a match with the league leading Bombers.

When Scotty received a years suspension in early December, for hitting an official, it looked to be a long season.

Right up to game time Scotty was threatening to put wife Rose behind the bench for the next game, against Melville Millionaires. Instead Ernie McLean came out as the bench boss and guided the team to an 8-2 victory and a foothold on second place. But it was not yet Ernie's time.

To get him through the suspension Scotty reached back to bring up Howie Milford who had played for him over parts of six seasons both in Moose Jaw and in Lethbridge. It paid off.

In mid December, in the biggest win of the season, the Bruins mauled last year's league leading Pats 9-1 at the Auditorium. Vaughn Hensrud starred in net and 2350 fans saw their boys hang on to second place. The Mercury crowed that seven Bruins had been selected to the all star squad in the persons of Meissner, Dyda, Stewart, Munro, Knipple, Anderson and Krake. The only fly in the ointment was Flin Flon, which was busy running away from the rest.

In early January they took another from the Pats, this time 5-0 in Estevan. It was the first shutout for the team since moving from Humboldt and the pleasure was enhanced for Hensrud who had been traded by Regina. Later the same month an even bigger game had 3000 home fans screaming their support as the Bruins stoned the Bombers 6-2 to move within nine points of first.

Early February brought them a chance to pull even closer when the Bombers came visiting again. Once more 3000 faithful turned up in the hopes the black and gold could move to within three of the front runners. Not this time though as the Bombers got the winner at 18:57 of the third to take it 5-4. The Bruins were not destined to catch the Northerners.

With the season winding down Flin Flon was cruising to the wire while Estevan and Regina were squaring off for second and home ice in the first two rounds. A 3-1 win over the Pats in February gave them a six point bulge and Regina had to settle for third place.

Standings

	G	W	L	T	GF	GA	TP
Flin Flon	48	35	12	1	269	144	71
Estevan	48	30	16	2	207	163	62
Regina	48	27	17	4	163	140	58
Saskatoon	48	20	26	2	224	243	42
Melville	48	20	26	2	182	175	42
Prince Albert	48	17	27	2	213	231	38
Weyburn	48	11	38	1	166	428	23

(Moose Jaw had moved to Weyburn to finish the season)

The Bruins managed a winning record against every other team in the league except Flin Flon. Against the Bombers they had gone one and seven and had been outscored 42 to 22.

Melville came calling in round one. Game one was no contest as Ernie Dyda's four goals led the Bruins to a 7-1 victory. The Millionaires stunned Estevan 3-2 in overtime in game two but a 4-1 win at the AA put the Bruins up two games to one in game four.

Now simple math suggests you can't be up 2 - 1 in games after playing four matches. Melville coach Paul Bozak protested that goalie Hensrud should have received a game misconduct in the third game, after he got his second major penalty. The Bruins were up 6-3 at the time. Officials gave him the protest and 4:41 of the third game had to be replayed. An annoyed Munro threatened to put forward Jim Beckman in net just to make a point. The protest didn't help Melville anyway and they were eliminated three games to one. The trick of putting a forward in net as a protest was not lost on Ernie.

Their next opponent was their nemesis from last season. The Regina Pats kept game one at the AA close and forced it in to overtime by coming back from two goals down. Still, it was Bruin Ernie Dyda who was the hero at 9:12 of OT and gave the Bruins the series lead going back to Regina. Taking game two 2-1 they were looking to lock up the best of five at home. Regina stayed alive with a 1-0 win but finally fell 6-2 in Regina to go golfing. Some revenge for last year's defeat. Now came the Bombers.

On paper and from the season stats it did not look good, but the playoffs were a new season. More so than any other team, the Bombers had been the biggest road block to the team, both in Humboldt and Estevan.

When the Bruins bombed the northerners 9-1 at the AA in game one it looked like they were on their way to taking the Province for the first time in team history. Jim Stewart contributed three goals and rookie Dallas Smith added two. When Vaughn Hensrud led them to a 5-3 game two victory before 3000 at the Auditorium there was every reason to be optimistic. They only had to win one of the remaining three games. The only bad part was all three were in Flin Flon.

The unfriendly confines of Whitney Forum had not changed and the Bombers evened the series with wins of 4-0 and 7-2. It came down to one game. Down one goal in the third, with time winding down, Dick Meissner potted the tying goal at 15:15. The game and the series were to be decided in overtime. Alas their best game in many years at Flin Flon was not enough as the Bombers took it 8-6. Their last goal went into an empty net. The loss stung. They had been so close and they had played so well.

Top league playoff scorer Dick Meissner was picked up by Flin Flon which almost made it to the Memorial Cup before falling to eventual Cup winner, the Winnipeg Braves. Meissner piled up 31 points in the playoffs to go with his team leading 89 points in the regular season.

The Bruins knew they were losing eight players next season including standout Jim Stewart but Meissner's accomplishments had not gone unnoticed and the hopes they pinned on his return were destined to be dashed. He was scooped up and played the major parts of four NHL seasons with the Boston Bruins and the New York Rangers before retiring from the pros after the 74/75 season in Portland.

Promise for the next campaign fell on Harvey Roy, Ivan Prediger and holdovers Dyda, Ralph Walker, Jack Boehm and Dallas Smith. Howie Milford was to be back behind the helm.

The great season had ended with disappointment in the results but not in the team's play. Ernie Dyda expressed his feelings, regarding the loss to Flin Flon, "They won this year but we'll be back next season and we'll take them".

One could only hope that he would be right.

58/59 Estevan Bruins **Top Left to Right** Ed Hudson, Dick Meissner, Dallas Smith, Fred Knippel, Don Anderson, Jim Stewart, Dr. R. Inglis **Middle** Ken Hodson, Moe George, Ivan Prediger, Ralph Walker, Jack Rogers, Jim Beckman, Barney Krake, Mike Dayne, Lloyd Wheatland **Front** Dick Berday, Harvey Roy, Jack Boehm, Scotty Munro, Vaughn Hensrud, Howie Milford (coach), Jerry Bulitz, Ernie Dyda, ? (C. Ross Studios & Estevan Bruins) **Also suiting up** Irwin Young, Jack Boehm, Harvey Thibeault, Ed Kutz

14

Ouch — 1959/60

On the one hand it was the biggest training camp yet, on the other, rumours Boston was going to take Meissner up would just not go away. A raft of hopefuls came down from the North Battleford Beaver Bruins. The biggest news was that the Bruins had picked up star netminder Eric Reid from the Memorial Cup Ottawa Hull Canadiens. According to Scotty, ranked #1 in Canada.

The rumour proved true with Meissner as he turned pro with the parent Boston Bruins.

It proved a long and disappointing campaign. By November Jim Munro was brought back in the hopes of shoring up the team but the dismal season continued.

Not taking to losing well the combative Howie Milford managed to get himself suspended along with "Legs" Fraser, who was back behind the bench in Prince Albert. Shortly thereafter Scotty returned from his forced holiday to take up the controls once again.

He emerged in a game against the Mintos. Defenceman Dallas Smith played a full 58 minutes and Ralph Walker contributed a hat trick in a 6-4 welcome home victory. But one victory does not a season make and the team continued its campaign long struggle.

The experiment with Eric Reid did not pan out as hoped but Prediger, Dallas Smith and Ernie Dyda impressed enough to make the all star team. It was developments in Alberta which finally brought some needed light to the dark days. The Medicine Hat Tigers folded and the Bruins picked up goalie Jack Norris and skaters Jim Kozie and Murray Nellis. Though it proved too little too late the acquisitions were to make a difference in the season to follow.

One season high point was a 4-3 exhibition victory over the touring Edmonton Oil Kings. At that time no one would have guessed the rivalry that would grow between these two perennially powerful teams.

A glimmer of hope emerged in early February when the

team began taking some big games, including two against league leading Regina. Jim Munro played a big part in the team's emergence. They desperately needed a win over 4th place Saskatoon Quakers in order to have a hope of making the playdowns.

This time they just couldn't pull it off and a 3-2 loss eliminated them. For the first time since Scotty took over the franchise in 1951 and the first time in thirteen years it missed the playoffs. Even going four for their last six games could do little but offer hope for next year.

59/60 Estevan Bruins **Top Left to Right** Doug Dayman, Dallas Smith, Brian Williams, Jack Boehm, Gerard "Skip" Arnsten, Dave Padzerski, Ivan Prediger **Middle** Ed Hudson, Jim Munro, Roger Vermette, Bill Dyck, Ralph Walker, Ed Kutz, Lloyd Wheatland **Front** Owen Rogers, Terry Burns, Scotty Munro, Eric Reed, Howie Milford, Ernie Dyda, George Boychuk (C. Ross Studios & Estevan Bruins) **Also suiting up** Barry Crozier, Jack Norris (goal), Jim Kozie, Jim Nellis

They had to settle for an embarrassing 6th place ahead of last place Moose Jaw Canucks. Regina topped the league followed by Flin Flon, Prince Albert, Saskatoon and Melville.

Ivan Prediger was voted Bruins' Rookie of the Year and was the most penalized player on the league's second most penalized team. Dallas Smith was voted the team's most popular player. Not only that, he was called up by the Boston Bruins for their playoff run where he managed a goal and an assist in a five game stint. It was enough and, unfortunately for Estevan, he became the next star called up before the team expected to lose him.

He patrolled the blueline for 16 seasons, all but one with the Boston Bruins. Flourishing in the era of Bobby Orr and Phil Esposito, he enjoyed two Stanley Cups, four all star appearances and, in 1968 won the NHL's plus/minus award.

Ernie Dyda's prediction of the year before was far from realized but it was to be the last time the franchise missed the playoffs for 19 seasons.

Estevan was beginning its rise to prominence.

15

The Big Bad Bruins________1960/61

Milford was back behind the bench for a promising season that had 11 regulars returning; albeit without all star Dallas Smith among them. The North Battleford Beaver Bruins were sending down Barney Krake's little brother "Skip". The biggest acquisition though was one of the top rated juveniles in Saskatchewan last season, a lad named Terry Simpson from Shellbrook.

Also trying out were Ray Boehm (brother of former Bruins Jack), Ron Boehm (cousin of Jack), Don Smith (brother of Dallas) along with two British Columbians George Boychuk and, from Kamloops, Glen Madsen. A young Joe Watson, destined for fame in Philly, skated at training camp but was not quite ready for prime time.

The team shared the Auditorium with the professional Portland Buckaroos who brought former Humboldt Indian, and Estevan native, Al Nicholson back to town. Joining him was former Bruin Barney Krake.

The promise was well founded as the team stormed out of the gate to take its first seven games and a solid hold on first place. By late November they had 12 wins out of their first 16 games and were also maintaining the league lead in penalties. John Rogers was leading the league in scoring.

The luster came off a bit in December and the team fell into a slump which saw Regina and Melville gain ground. To add goaltender insurance they picked up Kamloopsian Jim Letcher from Regina. The goal tending duo of Letcher and Norris was to frustrate the opposition.

On December 8, 1960 the Mercury reported Howie Milford had been suspended for all future games against Regina. Complaints were coming in that the Bruins were the roughest and toughest team in the league. The Big Bad Bruins had arrived. But they were now skating in second place behind Regina.

Always looking for an advantage Ernie and Scotty experimented with a "spotter to coach two way radio system" which they employed for the first time in a 5-2 win in Prince Albert. When Commissioner Boucher got wind of it he put an end to it. A good idea before its time.

At mid season the Bruins were struggling with a slump but Terry Burns managed to land on the first all star team followed by Ivan Prediger and John Rogers on the second. As for Milford, he managed to get himself a second suspension; this time for the remaining games against Saskatoon. The question was whether he would run out of teams before the season ended.

In January 1961 first place Regina came to Estevan riding a 12 game winning streak and looking to put some distance between them and the Bruins. They were turned back 4-1. By February the Bruins were creeping closer to the Pats, with much credit going to former Pats' goalie Jim Letcher. They were on an 11 for 14 streak with Letcher being a major contributor to their success. The best was yet to come.

1800 fans were on hand to see Letcher stone his old teammates 7-0. He had allowed only 15 goals in nine games and had posted two shutouts since being picked up. The team had won 13 of their last 16 games but it was not enough as the Pats still secured first. Estevan was not quite done yet. Letcher garnered his third shutout with an 11-0 waxing of Saskatoon and John Rogers got three goals and two assists to set a new SJHL record with 124 points. The only sour note was that Bill Dyck and Terry Burns were out for the playoffs with injuries.

Regina topped the league followed by Estevan, Melville, Moose Jaw, Saskatoon, Prince Albert and Flin Flon. The Bruins were scheduled to go against Melville, who had runner up league scorer Ed Lawson, in a best of seven.

The Millionaires stunned Estevan in the first two games. Bowing out 9-7 in game one at the AA they went down 2-0 in games after an 8-3 loss in Melville. It was not looking very promising returning to the Auditorium. The Bruins clawed back to take the next two matches by close scores of 6-4 and 4-2. Finally they had recovered their form, or so it seemed.

With 3000 fans in attendance looking to their boys to finally take over the series lead Estevan forged a 2-0 lead. It didn't last. The Millionaires battled to a 5-4 overtime win to put the Bruins on the ropes in Melville in game six. There were no more tomorrows.

It was a different team that arrived in Melville. Up 4-1 going into the third they put away the Millionaires 7-2 to force a deciding game at home. The intensity of the game proved too much for one fan from Grenfell, he died of a heart attack on the spot.

Seventh game; 3000 fans. The Bruins had lost two of three on home ice. Jack Norris in net. Read 1-0 Bruins end of first. Read 4-1 end of second. This time there was no question as the Bruins took the game 5-1 and a hard fought series 4-3.

Going in to Regina for game one of the league final the team fought back from a 3-1 deficit to tie the game and force overtime. When Bill Dyck got the winner behind the Pats goalie the celebration began. Enter the referee. The goal was disallowed on the claim that John Rogers was in the crease. The next goal made matters even worse as the Bruins protested, to no avail, that Beaudin's winner did not even enter the net. In the end they went down 6-5.

60/61 Estevan Bruins **Top Left to Right** Ed Hudson, Paul Grundeen, Dr. R. Inglis, Abe Berday, Don White, Lloyd Wheatland, Ernie (Punch) McLean, Ken Hodson **Middle** Mike Demmick, Bill Dyck, Terry Simpson, Murney Nellis, Brian Collison, Dave Padzerski, Owen Rogers, Ivan Prediger, Ron McNaught **Front** Jim Letcher, George Boychuk, Jim Kozie, Scotty Munro, John Rodger. Howie Milford, Terry Burns, Ron Willy, Jack Norris. (C. Ross Studios & Estevan Bruins)

The Pats kept the Bruins off balance by coming right back to take game two 4-1 at the AA.

In Regina for game three the complaints about officiating continued. Losing 6-4 Scotty argued two of the Pats goals should not have counted. The Bruins claimed one went in after the whistle had blown and a Pats player was in the crease for another. End result the Bruins were down three games to zero coming home.

There were 3100 fans filled the Auditorium. Their boys were outplaying the Pats but were being stymied by goalie Art Koberinski. Finally at 16:32 of the second John Rogers gave his side the 1-0 lead. It almost lasted until the end of the period before Regina tied it up at 19:33. The battle seesawed in the third until Bill Dyck was assigned a charging penalty. Forty-three seconds into the power play Beaudin did them in again. The game ended 2-1 Regina and a great season came to an end. A season that had seen a great comeback from the disappointment of the year before.

Scotty's closing remark! " Lady Luck just wasn't with us."

The Pats picked up John Rogers, Dave Padzerski and Jim Kozie for their Memorial Cup run which ended at the hands of the Edmonton Oil Kings.

In the NHL Glenn Hall became the first member of the franchise to get his name etched on the Stanley Cup as he backstopped the Chicago Black Hawks in their Cup victory.

Ernie McLean had been busy with the team all season but he had also been putting in some time as a player. An April 13, 1961 photo of the George's Soo Line Cafe' team pictured the team's leading scorer Ernie along with a friend and team mate destined to leave his mark on the franchise. His name, Bill Shinske.

16

Home Ice Heaven 1961/62

This year Scotty was not hedging his bets. He called for his boys to take the regular season title. His reason for optimism lay in the fact he had Letcher and Norris returning in net; easily the best tandem in the league, and a host of returning vets.

Milford was gone and Scotty was back behind the bench with Ernie as his assistant. Don Smith, brother of Dallas was destined to stick with the squad as were Skip Krake, Joe Watson and Ron Boehm. Kamloops had another contribution in the person of Don Newman and his connections in his home town were to later have an immense impact on the team.

Nearby hockey rival Weyburn joined the league as the Red Wings, making it an eight team conference.

Norris and Letcher burst upon the scene in record shaking fashion. Letcher started with a 5-0 shut out over Moose Jaw and then got his second straight goose egg; 4-0 over Weyburn. Not to be out done Norris got his first shutout in a 16-0 shellacking of Prince Albert. When the Bruins won their 8th straight game 6-0 over the Mintos Norris racked up his second shutout to tie Letcher. His partner came back with a 5-0 win over Saskatoon to go ahead in the race and set a goal against average of .50.

The team wasn't sitting back in the win column either. By mid November they were in first and sporting an undefeated streak at home.

Norris got the next two shutouts, 8-0 over Melville and 4-0 over Weyburn, to inch ahead of Letcher. By seasons end Norris managed a league leading seven shutouts in 43 games. As for Letcher, the Kamloops native moved on before the season ended, but not for want of talent. Ten shutouts between them was a stunning accomplishment at any time.

As the Bruins star rose things began to look bad for their old time rival Prince Albert. In mid November the Bruins were managing the host Mintos quite well with a 4-1 lead at the end of two. Unexpectedly smoke began to make its presence felt and the building was quickly evacuated. Fire damage made the arena unusable and the Mintos finished the season as the Dauphin (Manitoba)/Prince Albert Mintos. The unfinished game went in Dauphin and ended 6-1 Estevan.

By late January 1962 the Bruins were closing in on securing first place and maintaining a season long undefeated record at home. It looked increasingly possible they could finish the entire season undefeated on home ice.

61/62 Estevan Bruins - **Top Left to Right** John Martin, Abe Berday, Dr. Inglis, Lloyd Wheatland, Ernie (Punch)McLean, Paul Grundeen, Moe George, John McDonald **Middle** Don Smith, Ron Willy, Doug Dayman, Terry Simpson, Dave Padzerski, Brian Collison, Owen Rogers, Don Newman, Skip Krake, Joe Watson, Lyle Bradley **Front** George Boychuk, Butch Norris, Ed Hudson (mgr.), Jack Norris, Jim Kozie, Scotty Munro, Pat Donnelly, Ron Boehm (C. Ross Studios & Estevan Bruins) **Also suiting up** Jack Boehm, Art Chiupka, Tony Bukovich, Harvey Wish, Mike Demmick, Gary Nellis, Brian Matheson, Murray Nellis, Don White, Jim Letcher

Scotty was positive enough to claim the Bruins could get to the Memorial Cup. Ken Pettit of Weyburn retorted the Bruins would never go anywhere with Munro at the helm and suggested they get Milford back.

On February 22, 1962 the Estevan Mercury could boast their Bruins were the regular season champs. Scotty managed that feat in his first year in Humboldt and did it twice in four years there. It took him five years in Estevan but the future was brighter. Joe Watson and Jim Kozie took the lead in dumping

Scotty, Ernie and manager Ed Hudson in the shower in celebration.

Add to all this the fact they set a league record for going the entire season without losing a game at home.

Their reward for grabbing first and setting a new league record? Nothing! No home ice advantage. Officials decided on a round robin format amongst the top six teams with the best two teams squaring off in a best of seven final series for the Robin Hood Cup.

Regina, Moose Jaw and Estevan were neck and neck for the two finalists. The round ended with hated Regina holding on to first by two points and Moose Jaw tied with Estevan for the second spot. Estevan had taken three of a possible four points from the Canucks but the league gave the Canucks the second spot on the basis they scored more goals. Scotty, the fans and the Mercury were enraged. Munro suggested the league could at least have the two teams battle it out on the ice in a tie breaker. The answer was NO and that was it.

Despite a record breaking and stellar season which solidified them as one of the best rep teams for Saskatchewan, the Bruins were sent packing. Over the years the frustration with officiating, goal judges and league officials had been as much the team's adversary as the other squads. The teams and locations may have differed, from Flin Flon to Regina, but the result was the same. Success would have to come by playing through adversity and controlling their own destiny.

What solace they could grab came from Norris and Padzerski making the first all star team followed by Brian Collison, Jim Kozie and Ron Wiley on the second string.

Scotty had managed to win the regular season three times with his team and once took the SJHL championship only to be denied by Regina from taking the province. It was about time that the squad moved up the ladder. Next time even outside forces were not going to stop the Bruins.

17

Champions 1962/63

Despite the disappointment of last season's playoff, enthusiasm filled the air for the 62/63 campaign. The optimism wasn't shared by league sportswriters who picked the team for 4th, largely because of lack of depth on defence. Joe Watson was the only returning defenceman.

That didn't deter the Bruins and Estevan. A big opener was planned for October 12, 1962, with a parade, seven bands, sales promotions and a visit by Maurice "The Rocket" Richard. The Rocket didn't make it but the popularity of the team was summed up by Scotty.

"Everyone wants to play with the Estevan Bruins."

Verifying Munro's words, Jack Norris, who Boston wanted to turn pro, decided to return for another year. Skip Krake was named captain and joined Ron Boehm and Don Smith as part of the family heritage component of the squad. Kamloops' Don Newman was back along with Terry Simpson, who was to figure prominently in the Bruins fortunes. In an effort to address the defence problems on the team he was moved back to the blueline, along with Newman, an idea that bore fruit beyond expectations.

Edmonton came to town for an exhibition match and was held to a 4-4 tie. It was not to be the only time the squads went head to head. Shortly afterwards the Bruins picked up Don Hughes from the Oil Kings in a three way deal with Regina that sent Doug Dayman to the Pats.

The hoopla of the opening ceremonies over, the Bruins started with a win over Regina 2-1 and followed it up with a 3-2 victory in Moose Jaw. A nice way to start after those two teams had thwarted its hopes last season. By late November they were knocking on the door for first place and relishing accolades for an alumni.

Sports Illustrated ran an article on the best prospect in the American Hockey League; the Bruins own Dick Meissner. Starring with Hershey Bears he had scored five goals in five games.

By early January they were tied with Weyburn, three points behind front running Melville. Norris was proving the key ingredient to success but others, who had been expected to shine, were not fitting in to the mix. In particular, Pat Donnelly, though leading the team in scoring, was sold to arch rival Weyburn. On the other hand, John Manchester, who had been a "problem child" in Flin Flon returned to the Bruins and was now a major contributor to their success.

Donnelly still impressed the league enough that he landed on the all star squad coached by Scotty. Former team mates Skip Krake, Jack Norris and Joe Watson lined up with him for the all star match against Manitoba. Saskatchewan won the day 5-2.

Coming down to the wire it was clear the Bruins were destined to finish first or second. It was between them and Melville. The winner also picked up a $1000 bonus.

At the wire it came to a head to head game between them and the Millionaires. Skip Krake, Joe Watson and Jack Norris shone in their 2-1 win over Melville and clinching of the regular season championship for the second year in a row. The Mercury crowed they were the first team, in the history of the SJHL, to accomplish that feat.

Prince Albert, probably their greatest rival from their Humboldt days, was without an arena and conspicuously absent from league play. Estevan was followed in the standings by Melville, Weyburn, Regina, Moose Jaw, Flin Flon and Saskatoon. Thankfully there were no round robins and the Bruins got some benefit for taking first overall.

It was fitting the first round was against the Pats. The Mercury claimed the smaller Bruins would have to rely on John Manchester and Lyle Bradley to keep the Regina players honest. They did more than that in game one. Both managed two goals apiece as Estevan rolled over Regina at the AA 5-1. In game two Manchester potted another while Skip Krake got the winner in a 2-1 triumph. Then it was off to Regina and some surprises.

Game three in Regina ended in a tie but game four held a surprise no one would have expected. With 6:35 left to go in a close game a construction bolt came hurtling out of the crowd and struck Scotty in the face. It was no minor wound and Munro had to be taken to the hospital. Whether the fan was around or not he was not likely popular as the game was suspended and scheduled for completion after game six. Some years later the matter came to an unexpected but happy resolution.

Back at home for game five, John Manchester's hat trick led his Bruins to a 5-2 victory and put Regina on the verge of elimination. The Bruins only needed a tie to wrap it up.

Despite a hat trick by Skip Krake the Pats scratched out a 4-3 win in game six to avoid elimination. They now had to finish up the remaining time from game three. Skip wasn't through for the night as he scored the winner into an empty net at 19:35 to end Regina's season.

The final went against their strongest competition of the season, Melville. The Millionaires managed three wins from Estevan but suffered five loses in the regular season. They also had to struggle past a stubborn Weyburn squad that took them to seven games. A rested Bruins team was waiting.

Estevan charged out to a quick three games to none lead with the third being an 8-3 thrashing right in Melville's backyard. Embarrassed but not dead the Millionaires produced their own heart stopper by gaining a 2-1 overtime victory with only one second remaining in the contest. Estevan could wrap up the series on home ice.

It was all over for Melville in game five. The Bruins were the champions of the SJHL and the province. Years of frustration dating back to Humboldt faded away in the glory of the moment. The squad had passed another hurtle on their long distance journey to the Memorial Cup. After grabbing first place in the regular season for the second time as the Bruins, and fourth time as a franchise, they finally won not only their league but the province.

They now faced a team that had established a stellar reputation of its own. Thus began an intense franchise rivalry that goes to this day. They took on an Edmonton Oil King squad with future NHLer's Bert Marshall (of Kamloops), Pat Quinn and Glen Sather.

Game one went at the AA and looked bad when the first period ended 2-1 for Edmonton. It got better for the 3100 fans as Edmonton could get no more goals past Norris while his team mates got five by the Oil Kings. Pick up Gary Peters, from Regina, helped out with two markers.

Even more fans turned up for game two (3200) and were treated to a thrilling game that went into overtime. Skip Krake put the Bruins up 1-0 and they held on until 9:43 of the third when Glen Sather netted the tying goal that sent the game into OT. Closing in on the four minute mark of overtime Joe Watson skated the puck to the Edmonton blueline, passed it over to Regina pickup, Fran Huck, who in turn put it over to Ron Boehm. From there it ended up in the twine and the Bruins had an unexpected two games to none series lead going to Edmonton. The win was no fluke as the Bruins outshot the visitors 46 to 36.

The next three were to go in Alberta.

Despite deserving a win in game three, according to some observers, the Bruins found themselves heading into game five all tied up at two games apiece. Making matters worse captain Skip Krake was lost to the team. Bill Flett, who they picked up from Melville and who had some starring years ahead of him in the NHL, gave them a 2-0 lead to start the fifth match. But Edmonton stormed back to send their 5000 fans home happy with a 9-2 victory. Down 3 -2 in the series the Bruins were coming home for game six.

62/63 Estevan Bruins **Top Left to Right** Ken McDonald, Fred Weisse, Ray Mercier, Don Hughes, Stan Gilbertson, Don Newman, Bill Sveinson, Lloyd Wheatland, Marvin Symons **Middle** Ernie (Punch) McLean, Don Jackson, Butch Morris, Wayne Green, Jack Norris, John Manchester, Lyle Bradley, John McDonald **Front** Ron Boehm, Ed Hudson, Terry Simpson, Scotty Munro, Skip Krake, Dr. Inglis, Joe Watson, Don Smith (C. Ross Studios & Estevan Bruins) **Also suiting up** Don Inkster, Rob Ruel, Pat Donnelly, Ken Schissler

The 3500 cheering fans urged them on and the game was close. Unfortunately not close enough. The Bruins lost the game 2-0 and the series 4-2. Edmonton went on to win the Memorial

Cup. It had been a good and close series. Edmonton coach Brayshaw claimed Norris was the best goalie he had seen in the West.

Scotty was predicting an even better team next year and that they would take Edmonton. He was calling North Battleford Beaver Bruin Ross Lonsberry an up and coming star and he also had returnees Terry Simpson and Skip Krake to build around.

Lyle Bradley, Fred Weiss, John Manchester and, most damaging, Joe Watson and Jack Norris, graduated. Norris had a sip of coffee in the NHL but enjoyed his best four years of pro in the WHA with the Edmonton Oilers and Phoenix Road Runners. Bradley also skated for a few games in the NHL, with the California Golden Seals and the Cleveland Barons.

Joe Watson had twelve seasons in the NHL capturing two Stanley Cups with Philadelphia after being picked up in the expansion draft from the Boston Bruins in 1967. He twice made the all star team in 1974 and 1977 and began a brother act with Scotty and Estevan. Brother Jim Watson later played for Scotty in Calgary while brother Glen eventually became coach of the Estevan Bruins of the SJHL.

The Bruins and Scotty had finally jumped the next hurdle but they were not yet through battling with the Edmonton Oil Kings. As for Saskatchewan the Bruins were the king of the heap and not easily removed. The image of the Seventh Man was materializing.

18

Triple________________________1963/64

Munro was brimming over with confidence as the exhibition season began. He was calling for the team to be holding down first place by the end of the year.

Despite the high hopes the season was not meeting expectations and by November that led to trades. Future NHLer Stan Gilbertson was sent packing to Regina in return for former Bruin Doug Dayman and Stan Fuller. Another American, Dick Paradise, was released.

When they went up against Regina shortly afterwards it was Gilbertson who knotted the tying goal in a 2-2 kiss off at the Auditorium. He proved a thorn in the Bruins side all season.

By late November the squad, with Ernie behind the bench, pulled ahead of Moose Jaw and grabbed first. By late December, on cue, the Bruins were holding on to first with Saskatoon breathing down their necks. The Quakers, Bruins and Pats were to battle to the wire.

In mid December an intensely played match with Moose Jaw at the Auditorium led to an incident destined to repeat itself, with more serious consequences, almost fifteen years later. A big fight erupted in a 5-5 draw. Moose Jaw kept its players on the bench while the Bruins jumped over the boards and entered the fray. Munro did not escape unscathed as he ended up being pushed over the bench after a verbal exchange with a fan.

With the year end coming to a close Ron Boehm, Skip Krake, Don Smith, Terry Simpson and Wayne Doll were picked for the all star team facing off against the Czech national juniors.

The schedule that year had an unusual element. The powerful Edmonton Oil Kings, who normally played in the Central Alberta Intermediate League, played a number of interlocking games against teams in the SJHL. In head to head matches the Bruins salvaged a tie but also fell 6-1 against last year's Memorial Cup Winners.

Early January 1964 had the squad battling Saskatoon

for second and a big night for Ted Hodgson and the team coming up. Ted's First Nation ancestry was to be recognized before a tilt against Melville scheduled for the Auditorium. A Cree from Hobbema, Alberta he was to be honoured by the Cree, Assiniboia and Saulteaux by being made an Honorary Chief. Band members from both Canada and the USA turned up for the ceremony and dance that bestowed the title of Chief He Who Runs on Skates. The dance, led by Chief Big Eagle, eventually had Scotty and Ted's family up doing their steps to the beat of the drums.

Hodgson was asked why he had turned down opportunities to play in Edmonton or Moose Jaw. His response! "If you want to learn how to play hockey Scotty is the man to play for."

As for the game the Bruins went out and took Melville 4-1 to grab sole possession of second place behind Regina. Hodgson did his part by contributing a goal to the victory. They then went out and took the Millionaires again 3-0 to mark Wayne Doll's 4th shutout and bring them up to one of the most important games of the season against Regina.

A near capacity crowd at the Auditorium saw the Bruins end the Pats 13 game winning streak by stopping them 8-5. They inched to within a point of first. When the teams met again later in January in Regina it was the Bruins again who came out ahead 3-1. Despite increasing their mastery over Regina the Bruins were still having trouble getting and holding on to first place.

Weyburn Red Wings, who were well back in the standings, proved to be one of their toughest competitors. The fact the two communities were near neighbours and had a healthy sporting rivalry in all facets of sport only added fuel to the fire. Scotty and Ken Pettit of Weyburn turned up the heat a bit with a bet on the ensuing match.

This was one Scotty lost as his Bruins fell to the Wings. His penalty! He had to push Pettit across the ice in a wheelbarrow holding a sign claiming "We (The Red Wings) are the Greatest".

On March 6, 1964 the Mercury proclaimed the Bruins, record third straight regular season title. While they were busy beating Weyburn 3-1 at the AA the Pats were losing 4-3 to Moose Jaw. Scotty was quick to give much of the credit to his rookie goalie Wayne Doll who had been brought up from the Bruins farm system. Doll topped the league as the number one goalie.

In the final countdown Estevan was first followed in order by Regina, Saskatoon, Weyburn, Moose Jaw, Flin Flon and

Melville. Their first round rivals were the Canucks whom the Bruins had not defeated all season in Moose Jaw.

The Canucks fell 5-2 in game one at the AA and found home ice did not help as they went down 6-2. Back in Estevan Skip Krake netted a hat trick in a 6-3 victory putting the Canucks on the ropes. Right afterwards he was whisked away to Boston for a two game tryout. Not a good time to lose your top scorer.

Returning to Moose Jaw the Krakeless Bruins fell 8-5. Game five went in Estevan and rookie Ross Lonsberry's hat trick could have won it by itself as the Bruins dumped the Canucks decisively 9-2. Not surprisingly Regina came through to meet the Bruins in the league final.

63/64 Estevan Bruins **Top Left to Right** Ken McDonald, Lloyd Wheatland, Wayne Green, Ross Lonsberry, Terry Simpson, Jerry Walker, John McDonald, Bobby Adderly **Middle** Ted Hodgson, Doug Dayman, Stan Fuller, Don Newman, Don Hughes, Bob Heaney, John Chapman **Front** Ron Boehm, Ed Hudson, Weston Adams, Skip Krake, Wayne Doll, Scotty Munro, Dr. Inglis, Butch Morris (C.Ross Studios & Estevan Bruins) **Also suiting up** Peter Neukom, Stan Gilbertson, Dick Paradise

After splitting the first two games Estevan was shocked by the Pats coming in to the Auditorium to take game three 4-3 before 2400 fans. Making it worse was former Bruin Gilbertson knotting two goals, including the winner. The Bruins were down 2-1 in games.

They regrouped to take game four 4-1 at home and tie the series. They needed a win on Regina ice and Krake's hat trick did it as they silenced 5259 fans with a 4-1 triumph.

Game six was a gutsy performance by both sides. Starting the third up 5-3 the Bruins saw the Pats pull their goalie twice in the last two minutes and force overtime. In the first OT Gilbertson again haunted his ex mates as he gave Regina a 6-5 lead. Three minutes later Hodgson tied it. The game had to be settled in sudden death overtime. Four minutes in Ron Boehm got a shot on goalie Sternig who stopped it but left a rebound. Wayne Green jumped on it and buried the winner. The Bruins were league and Provincial champs for the second straight year.

Once again the road block to the Memorial Cup was Edmonton. The Oil Kings had easily eliminated the B.C. Champs, the Kamloops Rockets, to advance. Playing on the Rockets was a young man destined to figure prominently in the future of both Edmonton and Estevan. No one yet knew what talent lay hidden in Jimmy Harrison.

They were in tough from the start in Edmonton. Wayne Doll made 57 saves in game one but the Bruins still came up short 5-2. Game two was no better as they went down 5-1. At least they were headed home for the next two games. Facing off against each other in the series were Kamloopsians Don Newman of Estevan and Bert Marshall of Edmonton.

Bruin fans had something to cheer about in game three as their heroes pulled out a 5-3 win before 2800 faithful. Fran Huck, picked up from Regina, led the charge with two goals and was a clear fan favourite. Another pickup, former Bruin Gilbertson, also contributed with his line netting three power play goals.

Saskatchewan's best were still no match for the prime time Oil Kings as they fell in the next two games 5-1 and 5-0. The Glen Sather captained Edmonton squad captured their fifth Abbott Cup on their way to another Memorial Cup appearance. The impressive squad picked up Bruin Ron Boehm but did not get to hold the Cup this time around.

Although the end was less than hoped for the Bruins had arrived as a junior power house. Personnel losses were to be deep and it would be a test of both team and organization to see how they fared. Gone were Terry Simpson, Don Hughes, Butch Morris, Skip Krake and Ron Boehm. Krake would get ice time in the NHL with Boston, Los Angeles and Buffalo over all or parts of seven seasons. Simpson eventually got to sip from the Memorial Cup as coach of the Prince Albert Raiders in 1985 before enjoying coaching in the NHL with a number of teams. Former Bruin Stan Gilbertson had eight solid NHL seasons with the California Golden Seals, St. Louis Blues and Washington Capitals before retiring in 1977. Boehm skated in 16 matches for California.

Despite the losses there was the makings of the strongest team yet to come out of Estevan.

The league was looking at some additions the following season and Scotty was beginning to entertain thoughts of the professional level. It was time for Ernie to come to the forefront.

19

Bend But Don't Break________1964/65

After three years as King of the Hill it was time to pay the price of success. The loss of stars ensured the squad would be hard pressed to threaten for first for a fourth time. It was time to rebuild. Time for new stars to emerge. Time for Ernie McLean to take over behind the bench.

Scotty was still involved but had his hands full. He was assisting the league in dealing with the troubled Moose Jaw franchise, overseeing the farm team in North Battleford and getting his hands dirty with his new team, the professional Jacksonville Rockets, who played in a southern pro league.

When the Rockets came to Estevan for their training camp there was something very familiar about them. Former Bruins Dick Todd, Fred Weiss, Don Newman, Jack Boehm, Butch Morris, Jim Kozie, Ron Wiley, Ernie Dyda, George Boychuk and Don Anderson were all in Jacksonville colours.

As for the Bruins they had 108 players turn up for camp, including nine returnees. Promising prospects included 14 year old defenseman Dale Hoganson, Barry Gibbs, Morris Stefaniw and Jim Harrison who were joined by Estevan's own Ken Anderson. John Chapman took over the reins as team captain. Star veterans Ted Hodgson and Ross Lonsberry were back along with Stan Fuller, Wayne Green, Bob Heaney, Jerry Walker and Wayne Doll.

The league expanded to take in the Brandon Wheat Kings and Saskatoon changed its name to the Blades. The team owner, Jim Piggot, was also the owner of the L.A. Blades of the professional Western Hockey League and obviously fond of the name.

Scotty picked his Bruins to finish a respectable third. The season proved a test of Estevan's farm system as many of the rookies had come up by that route. Nine of them suited up at the start of the season.

The team's teething problems were obvious as they carved out a fourth place finish and faced the prospect of taking on number one Regina. Still, they gave an indication of their future power in some overwhelming victories. Wayne Green netted three goals in a 13-3 drubbing of Saskatoon. Goalie Peter Neukom fought to stay awake in a 14-1 thrashing of Brandon where the Bruins outshot the Wheaties 51-16.

The playoff series opened in Regina and the Pats, as expected, took game one. The Bruins bounced back on home ice before 2200 fans to even the series with a 6-3 victory. They then put Regina on their heels with another win in game three to go up 2-1. A capacity crowd was on hand at the Auditorium hoping their boys could take a strangle hold on the series. It proved a hard fought contest but the Pats took the day 4-3. Upset fans littered the ice and fan favourite Ted Hodgson was lost to a game suspension. The balance shifted in Regina's favour.

The Pats didn't look back and took the next two games to end the Bruins' reign. For Estevan the rookies, in particular Barry Gibbs, Morris Stefaniw and Dale Hoganson offered great promise. Harrison remained the diamond in the rough. The best was yet to come.

64/65 Estevan Bruins **Top Left to Right** Dr. Inglis, Moe George, Bill Shinske, Marlin Thompson, Barry Gibbs, Bill Sveinson, Lloyd Wheatland, Abe Berday, Ed Hudson **Middle** Gary Mills, Jim Harrison, Terry Kerr, Bob Johnston, Stan Fuller, Ron Barkwell,Ken Anderson, John Chapman, Jerry Walker **Front** - Peter Neukom, Wayne Green, Ted Hodgson, Scotty Munro, Bob Heaney, Ernie (Punch) McLean, Morris Stefaniw, Ross Lonsberry, Wayne Doll (C.Ross Studios & Estevan Bruins) **Also suiting up** Jim Griffiths, Gary Mills, Aime Boey

20

Dynasty 1965/66

Minus standout, goalie Wayne Doll, the Bruins began the 65/66 season with a question mark. How good were they between the pipes?

A 16-0 blowout of Flin Flon at the Auditorium in November looked impressive enough and by mid December the team was neck and neck with arch rival Weyburn and Brandon for first. Still, goaltending was enough of a concern that Scotty made a trade sending Ron Barkwell to Moose Jaw for goalie Ken Brown. It paid off.

Together Peter Neukom and Brown compiled the best goals against average in the league while Ross Lonsberry skated away with the league scoring title. Jim Harrison and Morris Stefaniw lit up the score sheet while Dale Hoganson and Barry Gibbs shone on defence. Bob Heany finished with a league record for most points in a season by a defenceman.

The battle with Weyburn for first raged on. On February 3, 1966 the Mercury boasted that the Bruins had tied Weyburn for first when they beat Flin Flon 6-4 and Weyburn lost 9-2 in Brandon. The next day they took over sole possession of first with a 9-2 win over the Bombers. They followed that up with shutout wins of 6-0 over Regina and 12-0 over Flin Flon to pad their lead. Weyburn never caught up to them again.

On March 2, 1966 the Mercury proclaimed their Bruins as SJHL regular season champs. They left no doubt as they went into Weyburn to take a 6-4 win and then gave the Red Wings their worst trouncing of the season, 12-3 at the Auditorium. For the fourth time in five years they were regular season champs. Ernie's first as coach after one as a player in Humboldt. .

In round one the fourth place Canucks dropped the first three games 5-4, 5-2 and 3-1 before salvaging an impressive 9-4 win at home to stave off defeat. Any doubt as to the dominant team ended in game five in Estevan. Ross Lonsberry scored three goals in 25 seconds to set a league record for fastest three goals and rookie Grant Erickson garnered five points as the Bruins stopped the Canucks 11-3. They now awaited the winner of the Weyburn - Brandon series.

It was fitting the league final should be between rivals Weyburn and Estevan. The two neighbouring communities had a long history of sports competition. In hockey it had most often been Weyburn taking the accolades until a minor league team coached by Ernie McLean grabbed some respect back. Now it was major junior A.

The battle was a homer series. The Bruins took game one 5-2 but lost game two 4-1. They took game three 3-2 but lost game four 3-1. In game five they went up 3-2 in the series with a 3-1 win but the Red Wings would not lie down and took game six 4-3 in front of their home town fans. It took game seven to settle it.

65/66 Estevan Bruins **Top Left to Right** Bill Shinske, Dr. Inglis, Gary Mills, Wayne Green, John Chapman, Lloyd Wheatland, Abe Berday, John McDonald **Middle** Jim Harrison, Bob Heaney, Barry Gibbs, Stan Fuller, Terry Kerr, Dale Hoganson, Ed Kresnoski, Grant Erickson, Jerry Walker **Front** Ken Brown, Morris Stefaniw, Paul Melle, Ernie (Punch) McLean, Ross Lonsberry, Scotty Munro, Ed Hudson, Ted Hodgson, Peter Neukom (C. Ross Studios & Estevan Bruins) **Also suiting up** Ron Barkwell, Butch Morris

Some 3300 fans piled into the auditorium, Weyburn fans included. Jim Harrison put Estevan up 1-0 before many of the spectators had made it to their seats. The Bruins then killed off four minutes of overlapping penalty time to Chapman and Fuller in the first four minutes. A power play goal put them up 2-0 and a Ross Lonsberry slapshot improved that to 3-0. Terry Kerr's 4-0 goal secured the win and a 26 save shutout for goalie Peter

Neukom. Weyburn goalie Don Caley made 27 saves in the loss.

For the third time in four years the Estevan Bruins were league and Saskatchewan champs. This time the road to Edmonton went through the Fort William Canadians. Although he originally baulked at picking up other players from the SJHL Ernie eventually relented and accepted John Fisher (Moose Jaw), Corky Agar (Saskatoon) and future NHLer Bill Lesuk (Weyburn).

When Peter Neukom was diagnosed with a broken jaw Weyburn goalie Don Caley came on board. He played all seven games against the Canadians.

The Bruins returned from Fort William down three games to two. After tying the series at 3-3 game seven erupted into a brawl that saw the game suspended with the Bruins up 3-1. When play resumed the next day the Canadians were without three big guns due to suspensions and injury. Following a scoreless second the teams entered the third with Estevan up 3-2. It looked good when the home boys went up 4-2 but Ft. William fought back to tie and force OT.

Ten minutes of regulation overtime settled nothing and 3200 fans bit their nails as the two teams faced off in sudden death. At 7:33 it was finally settled. Terry Kerr became the hero in the Bruins 5-4 victory. Ted Hodgson, Morris Stefaniw, Ross Lonsberry and Greg Sheppard (called up from North Battleford) provided the Bruins other goals.

The powerhouse Edmonton Oil Kings were waiting for the third time.

After winning game one of the western final 5-2 at the Auditorium the Bruins fell 3-1 at home and faced the next three games in Edmonton. It looked bad when the Oil Kings took game three 6-4 but this time the Bruins did not falter on Edmonton ice. They came back to win game four 5-3. The Kings took the series lead with a 2-0 win and returned to Estevan up 3-2. The Mercury claimed the Bruins could easily have won games one or three on Edmonton ice.

At the Auditorium for game six the first period ended scoreless. In the second Ross Lonsberry got a powerplay marker to give the Bruins a 1-0 lead and pickup Bill Lesuk put the boys up 2-0. Edmonton surged back to tie the game by 5:43. At 10:34 Jim Harrison's power play goal put Estevan up 3-2 but, in just over one minute, the Kings tied it again.

At 15:30, with Jim Harrison in the penalty box, Edmonton took their first lead. They did not let up and at 2:02 of the third they managed the insurance goal in a 5-3 series clinching victory. The Bruins were out four games to two and Edmonton was on its way to its last Memorial Cup championship.

The fans erupted in applause for their Bruins. Edmonton was equally impressed and picked up Neukom, Lonsberry, Hodgson and Harrison for their championship run.

It saw them go up against the Bobby Orr led Oshawa Generals. In the 7-2 game one victory all three Estevan forwards figured in the scoring. Bruins stole the show in game six as Harrison got the Oil Kings first goal and Hodgson the second in a 2-1 win. The win clinched the series and the Memorial Cup.

Though they had not tasted the thrill of the Memorial Cup itself, loyal Bruins fans could share in the glory of their contribution to the Edmonton Cup win. The franchise had its first faint touch of junior hockey's greatest prize.

Though Ross Lonsberry and Ted Hodgson would not return Estevan had bright prospects moving up and key stars returning. Lonsberry's name shone for twelve years in the NHL and was etched twice on the Stanley Cup with Philadelphia. Hodgson managed a handful of games as a Boston Bruin and three years in the World Hockey Association with L.A. and Cleveland. Ken Brown moved on to Moose Jaw and was graced with an NHL match as a Chicago Black Hawk and one season with the WHA Edmonton Oilers.

Barry Gibbs went number one in the fourth year of the NHL entry draft to Boston.

The future remained bright.

21

The Clear Lake Massacre_____1966/67

There are seasons when events off the ice take on more meaning than the game itself.

When representatives of the (SJHL) met at Clear Lake Resort, in Riding Mountain National Park, dissatisfaction was brewing. Both Ernie and Scotty were in attendance and were sparks in a rebellion leading to the creation of the Western Canada Hockey League (WCHL), the forerunner of today's Western Hockey League (WHL).

The SJHL had been expanding under the Canadian Amateur Hockey Association (CAHA) without regard for the viability of its new franchises. The CAHA took the initiation fee but did not have to deal the effects of its decisions. Those rested with league teams. The SJHL was set to add a further two teams and opposition was expressed by some of the existing league governors.

Scotty claimed he was unable to pay his annual dues for the coming season and was therefore denied a vote in the proceedings. Other governors followed suite and the meeting deteriorated. Scotty left and was joined by others. They subsequently held another meeting in the same building and constructed the footings for their new league.

The end result was Estevan joined with Regina, Moose Jaw, Saskatoon and Weyburn of the SJHL in the new league which included the Edmonton Oil Kings and Calgary Buffaloes. The new circuit decided to operate outside of the national CAHA and was immediately branded an "outlaw" league not entitled to battle for the Memorial Cup. The CAHA, with the support of the NHL, was a powerful force but the new kids on the block were determined to go it on their own if they had to. The success of their venture, so strongly visible today, was no sure thing at the time and the first few years were marked by ongoing battles with the CAHA.

Titling themselves the Canadian Major Junior Hockey

League the rebels opened shop.

For the first time Estevan and Edmonton went head to head in the same league. A total of 1300 fans were on hand at the Auditorium to see their Bruins, captained by Morris Stefaniw, open against the Oil Kings. They fell 5-4 to begin their season long first place battle with Edmonton. It was not until mid March of 1967 that they finally took their rivals. Two thousand were on hand in Estevan to see Gregg Sheppard score two goals in the 5-1 victory.

By mid November they were trailing third place Regina by one point. Scotty remained optimistic. Despite losing seven players and being the youngest Bruin team yet he pointed to the squad, in December, being within one point of last season's performance. The stage was set for a memorable occasion.

When the Bruins lost 4-1 to Regina they were bumped back to 4th place. A return match was set for the Auditorium. 1300 fans were hoping for revenge but it did not look likely. Their boys were down 5-3, with 30 seconds remaining, against a team riding an eight game winning streak. High powered Regina scorer Rick Sentes rubbed salt in the wound when he taunted the fans by pointing to the scoreboard as he was led to the penalty box. The squad needed a repeat of last year's record three goals in 25 seconds set by Ross Lonsberry. But Lonsberry was now toiling in the pros. Cue Jimmy Harrison.

Most fans had already left the arena when Jimmy drew Estevan to within one goal at 19:31. The Bruins pulled their goalie for the extra man and Harrison was there again at 19:44 to nail down the tying goal. He was not done. At 19:55 he took a high shot that goalie Tabor misjudged and gave the home side a dramatic 6-5 victory. He had set a new junior hockey league record of three goals in 24 seconds.

Praise poured down. He received the key to the city, a trophy was donated in his honour by E. Fagerheim, the mayor of Kamloops sent a telegram congratulating him and a special Harrison night was arranged. He received the trophy before the home town fans and his proud parents. The WHL record still stands.

The very next game Gregg Sheppard netted three goals as the Bruins put it to Regina again, this time 8-4. Estevan was now in second three points up on the Pats. They were setting their sights on front running Edmonton.

On January 22 they added to the league record book.

Beating Calgary 18-2 at the Auditorium they set a record for most goals by a team in one game. It lasted for 23 years. They also set the record for most goals in one period at 11 that was tied 25 years later by the Blazers.

Harrison came up with three goals in a late season 8-4 win over Weyburn that pulled them to within five of first but that was as close as they got. A 4-1 loss to the Oil Kings killed any hopes they had of catching them. They ended seven behind and for the fifth year of the last six were the top team in Saskatchewan. It looked like another Edmonton Estevan matchup was a good possibility.

66/67 Estevan Bruins **Top Left to Right** Russell Brooks, John McDonald, Leroy Watt, Tony Mitchell, Gary Mills, Greg Sheppard, Brian Dickie, Wayne Gibbs, Bill Shinske **Middle** Lloyd Wheatland, Herb Howdle, Dan Schock, Barry Gibbs, Greg Polis, Brent Taylor, Roy Atcheynum, Dale Hoganson, Grant Erickson **Front** Gordon Kopp, Dr. Inglis, Terry Kerr, Ernie (Punch) McLean, Morris Stefaniw, Scotty Munro, Jim Harrison, Ed Hudson, Peter Neukom (C.Ross Studios & Estevan Bruins) **Also suiting up** Ed Kresanoski, Wayne Hogansom, Ken Fuller, Leroy Watt

Edmonton seemed to have an easy ride to the next round as they squared off against 4th ranked Moose Jaw, who sat 16 points behind them. The Bruins had to get by 5th place Saskatoon.

The Blades stunned Estevan 5-4 in game one at the Auditorium but the Bruins rebounded in game two on Grant Erickson's 3-2 winner with less than a minute left in regulation play. Down 3-0 in game three they came back for a 3-3 tie having to play without Harrison who had injured his back. Blade fans had reason to be optimistic and 4300 turned up for game four. They went home disappointed as the Bruins took it 4-3 despite being down two men for the last 25 seconds of the game. When the Blades came back for a 4-1 win in game six Estevan was clinging to a 3-2-1 series lead heading home. A win or a tie and they had the series.

The Blades pulled ahead 2-1 after the first and were holding on to a 3-1 lead after two. Ernie replaced goalie Kopp with Neukom. The Blades scored no more goals that night. Estevan pulled to within one when Saskatoon's Don Parenteau got a high sticking penalty at 17:44. The opportunity presented itself. Ernie put out five forwards. Harrison, Stefaniw, Sheppard, Erickson, Schock and Barry Gibbs on defence. The move paid off. Gibbs blocked a shot and then let go a slapshot. The rebound came to Dan Schock who put it in for the game tying and series clinching victory. The fans went wild and littered the ice, delaying the game by five minutes.

The next round featured Regina who had finished only two points behind. It started well with a 5-1 home ice victory but there were to be no more victories that season. Regina took the series four games to one with one tied. There would be no Edmonton Estevan rematch.

The mighty Oil Kings also fell in the semi finals. The Moose Jaw Canucks became the upset darlings of the new league as they bumped off Edmonton three games to two with four tied, then went on to take out Regina four games to one. The CAHA's outlawing of the league prevented them from taking their challenge further.

It was a great season for the rebuilding Bruins. Barry Gibbs and Morris Stefaniw were selected to the first string all stars while Harrison was picked for the second. Stefaniw was voted the league's most gentlemanly player and Barry Gibbs was named the league's best defenceman. Rookie Gregg Sheppard finished 4th in playoff scoring.

Only three players were expected to be lost for the coming season; Peter Neukom, Grant Erickson and Terry Kerr. The baby Bruins ended the season with 11 rookies in black and gold. It could only get better and it did.

22

The National Stage__________1967/68

The summer Sun of 1967 shone on Scotty Munro like a beacon heralding his past achievements and future promise. A beacon destined to stay alight throughout the 67/68 season and guide him and his team to their greatest heights. Its ending was unexpected.

With the first hints of the coming Fall the Estevan Mercury joined the community in praising Scotty as a citizen and a hockey personality.

Mayor John Barabash claimed "Scotty Munro has more influence on the future of Estevan than any other businessman in the city."

"Certainly he likes to win hockey games, after all what sportsman doesn't. Scotty's teams fight hard on the ice, even he himself gets involved occasionally, but when the game is over there is no animosity."

A special tribute pullout on Scotty hearkened back to his successes with Lethbridge, Gravelbourg and the Crows Nest Pass teams. Good-natured humour was poked at him; a photo of him in boxing attire from the 1950 Lethbridge Herald after he had been suspended for one game; his nickname as the "Fabulous Fat Man"; his informal title of Count Roderick Munro, 10th Baron of Roaringham, after an alleged Scottish inheritance.

In the end it all said that Scotty had charmed his way into the hearts of the people of Estevan as he had where ever he had gone. Just as he had in Humboldt.

All he needed now was the ultimate prize. The Memorial Cup.

At least his Bruins were going to have the opportunity to play for it.

After facing the prospect of a Court battle the CAHA came to terms with the CMJHL on a pre condition it change its name. So was born the Western Canada Junior Hockey League. The league mushroomed from seven teams to eleven. Flin Flon, led by Bobby Clarke and Reggie Leach exploded on to the scene and battled the Bruins season-long for the rights to first place and home ice advantage. The Bombers had played in the Manitoba league last year where Clarke had led the league in scoring.

The Winnipeg Jets, Brandon Wheat Kings and Swift Current Broncos also came on board along with the renamed Calgary Centennials, a team with a big part in the Bruins' future.

They expected the loss of Grant Erickson who went on to four years in the World Hockey Association with Cleveland and Phoenix as well as a handful of NHL matches with Boston and Minnesota. They did not expect to lose stars Stefaniw or Gibbs. Stefaniw put in 13 games in the colours of the Atlanta Flames while Gibbs went on to a 12 year NHL career with Boston, Minnesota, St. Louis and L.A.; playing on the all star squad in 1973.

The team, still stocked with the Hoganson brothers, Dale and Wayne, captain Danny Schock, newcomer Ernie Moser (from Saskatoon), stars Harrison, Polis, and Sheppard, stormed out of the gate to vie with Flin Flon and Edmonton for first.

By November 1 the paper was crowing about their seven game season opening winning streak after they beat Flin Flon 4-3. During the streak they took the Oil Kings 2-1 in their first meeting of the season. A big improvement over last year. The streak went to 22 games before they were finally stopped by the Saskatoon Blades 4-3 in mid December, setting a league record that stood until 1981.

Everybody was contributing. Ernie Moser netted four goals in an 11-2 waxing of arch rival Edmonton at the Auditorium before 1400 delighted fans. Sheppard, Danny Schock, Brent Taylor, Herb Howdle, Murray Mitchell, Greg Polis, Ken Silver and Jimmy Harrison all contributed big nights while Gordon Kopp collected five shutouts. Harrison came into his own playing as the stereotyped "Power Forward".

He didn't stop at scoring goals, he also took a hand in stopping them. In a battle against the Broncos in Swift Current (coached by former Bruin Harvey Roy) Harrison was put in net by Ernie after the goalie they borrowed from Swift Current let in five shaky goals. Having already scored three goals himself he only allowed one past him as his Bruins skated to a 9-6 victory.

Ernie kept the pot boiling and managed to get himself fines and suspensions during the heady season. Scotty got to go behind the bench for a bit as a result.

Despite a mid season slump, greatly contributed to by a virus which struck the team during a road trip, they still found themselves within three points of front running Flin Flon by late February. The Bombers' remarkable 47-8-5 season record proved too much in the end though and the Bruins had to settle for second, seven points back. Edmonton landed in third ten points behind them.

The season also saw them record a league record 21 game home winning streak that lasted until 1984.

For Scotty a forgettable incident of the past was brought back during a road game in Edmonton. He was approached by a man with a guilty conscience. The fan identified himself as the one who had hit him in the head with a bolt four years before during a Pats/Bruins game. They shook hands and when Scotty looked down there was a Pats/Bruins ticket in his hand.

It was obvious the Bruins had a contender but Scotty felt some tinkering was still needed. Bob Olin joined the squad along with Rick Pool from Swift Current (for Gary Swanson) and Jerry Dionne from Oshawa (who had played against Harrison in the Memorial Cup).

They entered the first round as clear favourites over 6th place Winnipeg Jets and took them out in four straight. Last season's champs, the Moose Jaw Canucks, were next after they eliminated Brandon in a tough eight game series.

It was obvious Moose Jaw was in tough when they were roasted 11-0 in game one at the Auditorium. Harrison and Dale Hoganson each garnered five points in the rout. An astounding 2715 fans were on hand for the next match, again taken, this time 4-2, by the Bruins. The series went to Estevan four games to none with one tied. Harrison was dominating and praise was being heaped upon him as the best junior in Canada.

Next came Flin Flon led by the league's top two scorers Clarke and Leach. Estevan didn't have a scorer in the top ten. The Bombers had topped the league in all departments and had taken out perennial favourites Edmonton. They also had the home ice advantage.

The Bruins, on the strength of Schock's tying goal at 19:54, pulled out a tie in game one at the Whitney Forum. Schock took Harrison's face off pass and fired a low close shot past Worthy. Harrison won four important faceoffs in a row against Bobby Clarke to make the difference.

If that stunned Flin Flon game two was a shocker. Kopp got the shutout while Schock posted two goals to go along with one each by Harrison and Atcheynum in a 4-0 upset.

It was no wonder that there were 2390 fans in the stands for game three. The teams entered the third period tied at two. The Bruins went ahead only to see the Bombers tie it up. Ken Silver put the home side up 4-3 at 18:04 from Harrison and Wayne Hoganson. Brother Dale got the insurance marker at 18:32. Kopp did his part by stopping a clear breakaway in the dying seconds.

When they took game four they headed back to Flin Flon knowing they were a game away from winning the league championship. A telegram with 1400 names followed them to the Whitney Forum.

67/68 Estevan Bruins **Top Left to Right** Lloyd Wheatland, Ron Lyons, Rick Lowe, Jerry Dionne, Greg Polis, Bill Shinske, John McDonald **Middle** Dr. Inglis, Herb Howdle, Dale Hoganson, Jim Harrison, Ken Brown, Brent Taylor, Ernie Moser, Garry Braun **Front** Wayne Hoganson, Ken Silver, Bob Piche, Ernie (Punch) McLean, Danny Schock, Ed Hudson, Roy Atcheynum, Tony Mitchell, Greg Sheppard **Stick Boys** Allen Biette, Brian McLean, Larry Dean (C.Ross Studios & Estevan Bruins) **Also suiting up** Gordon Kopp (goal), Gary Swanson, Murray McNeil, Bob Olein, Ed Dyck (goal), Rich Pool

Up 3-1 at the end of the second, on goals by Dale Hoganson, Atcheynum and Brent Taylor, the Bruins played disciplined hockey. Harrison refused to retaliate when Bomber tough guy Klewchuk hit him over the head with his stick. The pain was worth it as Klewchuk took a five minute major. The Bruins skated off with a 3-2 victory and the league championship. A victory especially pleasing after all the years of franchise frustration against Flin Flon. In doing so they established a still standing league record of 14 straight playoff games undefeated.

Harrison was awarded the Murray Balfour Trophy as the league MVP and praised for his all round abilities in skating, scoring, penalty killing, toughness and playmaking. He also took the playoff scoring title with 35 points on 13 goals and 22 assists. Boston scouts Gary Young and Rudy Migay agreed he was the best junior in Canada.

As for Ernie, he claimed "He amazes me with his stamina and his all round ability. The team looks to 'Harry' as our leader & his aggressive nature should make him a great pro."

The journey to the Memorial Cup was not over. The Bruins now had to play the Westport Hurricanes. They were joined by former goalie Ken Brown, who had been playing for the Moose Jaw Canucks. Harrison came to the fore in game one scoring two shorthanded goals, one when his team was two men short, for a 6-1 victory. Westport managed to steal one game and stop the Bruins undefeated streak at 16 but entered game five at the Auditorium down three games to one and facing elimination.

On hostile ice and facing the golf season the Hurricanes, largely on the strength of Trewin's goaltending, carried a lead into the third. The Bruins refused to let the game get away and forced overtime. Regulation overtime decided nothing and so the teams entered sudden death. Fittingly, at 4:15 of OT, on the night he was awarded the MVP trophy and scored four points, Jimmy Harrison netted the game and series winner.

Memorial Cup fever hit Estevan. The mayor proudly proclaimed the community's name was temporarily changed to Bruinville, Saskatchewan.

The long and winding Memorial Cup road now led through Penticton of the BCJHL, a team that put out the Kamloops Rockets on their way. The first two games were scheduled for Vernon and the next three in Estevan. The Broncos made a game of it in the first two matches, losing 3-0 and 5-4, but once they got to Estevan it was no contest. They fell 6-1 in game three and faced elimination in game four. The first goal belonged to Penticton but then the roof caved in. The Bruins crushed them 12-1 to take the Abbott Cup as Western Junior Champions.

Jim Graham, director of the Saskatchewan Amateur Hockey Association, awarded the Cup to the Champs noting that never before had such a small city won it.

For the first time in franchise history the team had won

the Abbott Cup as Western Junior Champs and were going to the Memorial Cup. Their foes were the Niagara Falls Flyers, another former Boston farm team. A definite tilt in the Flyers' favour was that all series games, with the exception of game two, were to be played at the Niagara Falls Memorial Arena.

The Bruins picked up reinforcements in the persons of Swift Current's Joe Zanussi and Oil Kings Kerry Ketter, Ron Walters and Ron Garwasiuk to go along with goalie Ken Brown. For Jimmy Harrison it was a chance to claim a second Memorial Cup though he wound up playing the series impeded by a broken hand that greatly reduced his effectiveness.

Game one went to the Flyers 7-4 before 3000 cheering fans. Game two, played at the Montreal Forum, was the Danny Schock show as he scored a goal and got two helpers in a 4-2 Bruins victory to even the series. Back in Niagara Falls the Flyers rebounded for another 7-4 victory. Goalie Ken Brown held his team in game four and the squads entered overtime tied at 3-3. The bubble burst at 12:56 of the second overtime when OHA junior scoring champ Tom Webster stripped Danny Schock of the puck, and deked out Brown for the winner.

Munro complained about the officiating and the number of penalties his boys had to kill off. The fatigued Bruins had relied heavily upon their goalie who faced 63 shots compared to the 31 the Bruins sent at the Flyers' goalie.

The tank was empty for game five played before 3813 excited fans. They fell 6-0 to end their greatest season ever.

They remained the Western Champs and holders of the Abbott Cup. Ernie was particularly fond of the Cup and when it went missing the Estevan police eventually found it in his care. He explained he had forgotten he had hidden it in his basement.

The Bruins achievement remained a high point. Referee in Chief Ted Yarnton claimed "Estevan is to hockey what Green Bay is to football"

As for Ernie, he was already looking towards next season. Commenting on the loss he saw it as a combination of the poor quality of competition in the last two series and the nine day layoff. He was predicting a stronger team next season. A tall order even if they could deal with the loss of some top players.

Great changes were in store for the team. Some of them expected.

Fan favourite Jimmy Harrison was lost to the pros and began a career that lasted 12 seasons in the NHL and World Hockey Association with Boston, Toronto, Edmonton, Cleveland and Chicago before his ailing back did him in. He set a Guinness Book of Records professional mark on Jan. 30, 1973 in Edmonton when he got ten points (three goals and seven assists) as an Oiler; a record matched three years later by Darryl Sittler of the Maple Leafs. His love affair with Estevan didn't end as he returned years later to put in time behind the bench as the SJHL Bruins coach.

Danny Schock went on to a few games as both a Boston Bruin, sharing in the 1970 Stanley Cup victory, and Philadelphia Flyer. Tom Mitchell and Ken Silver graduated.

Some of them were not expected.

As early as November 1967 Bob Kohaley, an Estevan native who was also legal counsel for the WCHL, was warning the community would have to come up with $20000 over the next three years to keep junior hockey in town. Primary problems were cited as Estevan's size, its distance from other centres, absence of air service and lack of educational facilities. Its biggest asset, he noted, was Scotty Munro. He further touted the benefits of the Bruins to Estevan citing how the town was widely known because of them; and this was before they made it on to the national stage at the Memorial Cup.

The surprise that came in August was not the loss of the team but rather Scotty himself. The August 7/68 Mercury lamented the godfather of western junior hockey was moving on as manager and Vice President of the Calgary Centennials. Scotty had 50% of the Bruins and had made an offer to the 36 businessman who owned the other 50% but they turned him down. Shades of Humboldt all over only this time the team did not go with Scotty.

There had been some rumours in July that Scotty's return was not certain and he might be trying to move the team. But when asked his comment echoed his last year in Humboldt. "As long as the people of Estevan continue to support the club it will stay here."

After 17 years with the team, which he led to six regular season championships, four league championships and one Abbott Cup, the master was moving on. Left behind was his star pupil and home boy made good Ernie McLean. Their friendship remained.

Uncertainty clouded the team's future. Not only was Scotty going but he was taking half the players with him, including Kamloops star Randy Rota.

In the end the team solidified with Ernie still at the helm

as coach and now joined by his buddy Bill Shinske as GM. Shinske had been associated with the club since the 64/65 season. The two were to leave a mark even Scotty would have envied. Though they would never again reach the same heights in Estevan incredible success lay ahead for the team that was now Ernie's.

The teacher had left and now the student had free rein.

23

New Era ______________ 1968/69

When training camp opened Ernie could look out on reliable returnees in Greg Polis, Greg Sheppard, Ernie Moser, Dale Hoganson, Herb Howdle, Brent Taylor, Jerry Dionne, goalie Gordon Kopp and a rookie prospect from Melfort named Lorne Henning. The question for those on the outside was "How will Ernie do without Scotty?"

The CAHA once again outlawed the WCHL denying any opportunity to get to the Memorial Cup. Regina and Weyburn, not wanting to deal with the sanctions, left the league. Ernie took the opportunity later in the season to accuse Regina of being an overrated team playing in an overage juvenile league. Regina did eventually go on to represent the west but fell in four straight to the Montreal Junior Canadians.

The answer to questions about Ernie came soon enough and Scotty's return to Estevan as bench boss with his Centennials formed part of it. Munro, who did not normally coach, went behind the bench for that first match against his old team. About 1500 fans turned up at the Auditorium for what was billed as the "Beat Scotty Munro Night".

And beat them they did. Moser got the winning goal at 12:24 of the third to prevent overtime and the Bruins skated away with a 4-2 victory. Scotty got into the game as he had in the past. Upset at a call he fired a couple sticks and his hat on to the ice to earn a bench minor.

The Bruins started well but McLean and Shinske had some tinkering to do. Jimmy Watson, brother of Joe Watson, was traded to Calgary because he wanted to play for Scotty. Along with him went Murray McNeil in a deal which brought ill fated Brian "Spinner" Spencer.

When Spencer finally joined the team he showed his potential in a 10-0 whitewash of in Saskatoon. Playing on a line with Greg Polis and Bob Fowler he garnered two of the five goals they scored that night. Ed Dyck got the shutout. In the very next game they waxed Brandon 10-4 with Polis getting five points and Bob Piche four. They were a firm second, again in a battle with Flin Flon.

The Bomber's Paddy Ginnel's practises and the officiating in Flin Flon had Ernie steaming mad. Injuries, more than a loss at Whitney Forum, had McLean so incensed he sent his whole team over the boards to complain to the ref and got ejected for his gesture. It seemed his anger was justified after Bruin Yvon Bilodeau was boarded from behind by Bobby Clarke and fractured his neck. Bilodeau was gone for the season and Clarke got a minor penalty. The Bruins dropped both crucial contests 4-0 and 4-3.

68/69 Estevan Bruins **Top Left to Right** Lloyd Wheatland, John Converse, Ernie Moser, Jerry Dionne,Dr. Inglis, Yvon Bilodeau, Rick Loe , Lorne Hennning, Ray Frehlick **Middle** Rick Shinske, Brian McLean, Brent Taylor, Willie Brossart, Bob Fowler, Greg Polis, Herb Howdle, Allan Biette, Larry Dean **Front** Bob Piche, Greg Sheppard, Gordie Kopp, Ernie McLean, Dale Hoganson, Bill Shinske, Roger Kozar, Roy Atcheynum, Ed Sidebottom (C.Ross Studios & Estevan Bruins) **Also suiting up** Brian "Spinner" Spencer, Cam Fryer, Wayne Inglis, Murray McNeil, Brian Dickie, Bill McFaddin, Ed Dyck, Gordon Button, Rick Lee

In December, after Estevan dumped the Winnipeg Jets 8-2, Jets coach Eddie Dorohoy levelled the same criticisms at Ernie. When they next met in Winnipeg the Jets theme was "Get the Bruins Night". They didn't and the Bruins won again; this time 6-3. December 15, 1968 saw them match their own league record 18 goals in one game when they demolished Brandon 18-1.

In January promising young goaltender Ed Dyck was "loaned" to Scotty's Centennials. He never returned but did go on to a brief NHL stint with the Vancouver Canucks.

A near capacity crowd saw their Bruins crush the Bombers 6-1 in the return engagement and extend their home ice winning streak to 17. What was even more pleasing was Spencer and Dionne both won their fights. If there had been doubts about how Ernie was going to do without Scotty around they were fast disappearing.

When they won their next home game 6-1 over Calgary they extended their overall unbeaten home ice record, including last season and the playoffs to an incredible 41 games.

It was not always rosy with the team and when friction between Polis and Spencer led to a fight during practice the incident resulted in Spencer packing his bags for Swift Current.

The tragic story of Brian Spencer eventually led to his mysterious death and a made for TV movie. From the heights of playing on National TV for the Toronto Maple Leafs to being murdered in Florida he symbolized how the greatest promise can turn to the saddest end.

There was no question the Bruins were ahead of the entire league save for their nemesis Flin Flon, who virtually clinched first by late February. On February 26/69 the Mercury paid Ernie one of the greatest compliments it could. "In McLean Estevan has found the complete successor to Munro."

He also resembled Scotty in some of his tactics. Tactics that both upset and entertained. In one game in Calgary he ordered his team to stand still and let Calgary score in order to protest a penalty. The league gave him a three game suspension but the leopard did not change his spots.

Their season ended with them in second place, 14 behind Flin Flon, but 12 ahead of nearest rival Edmonton. Moser, Sheppard and Polis ended up in the top 10 scorers. Polis finishing second with 125 points 12 behind Bobby Clarke.

The first round matchup against Brandon went according to script as they disposed of the Wheaties in five; despite being blown away 7-2 in Brandon in one game. Once again they faced Flin Flon and once again they did not have home ice advantage.

Dropped convincingly in game one 6-1 the Bruins fought back for a 3-3 tie in game two. A disallowed goal, that Ernie claimed was seen by everyone in the arena except the ref, would have won them the game and evened the series. He continued his tirade against Ginnel's tactics calling the club a travelling circus and complaining Ginnel had sent out a bit player like Mike Sauter to maim a million dollar star like Dale Hoganson.

This year it was Flin Flon's turn to take the series four games to none with one tied. They went on to beat out Edmonton but could not compete for the Memorial Cup because of the CAHA ban.

Polis, Herb Howdle and Dale Hoganson were named to the league all stars

Hoganson, awarded WCHL honours as the top defenceman, and Gregg Sheppard were not in the team's future. Drafted that summer both went on to NHL and WHA careers. Hoganson had 13 seasons split between the NHL and WHA with Los Angeles, Montreal, Quebec and Birmingham. Gregg Sheppard enjoyed ten years in the NHL with Boston and Pittsburgh and played in the 1976 NHL all star game. Willie Brossart also went in the draft and skated in and out of the NHL with three different teams over seven years. Ernie Moser and John Converse took the number of Bruins drafted to five.

It was another successful year and Ernie removed any doubts about his ability to step into Scotty Munro's shoes.

24

Rebuild 1969/70

Even the best organizations have their down years; when the promise of tomorrow gets them through the trials of today. They had been few and far between for the franchise and the key remained as to how they were handled by the team and the fans.

A major trade before the season began saw future NHL star Blaine Stoughton sent to Flin Flon for Gerry Petryk and Ken Baird. On the powerhouse Flin Flon team, still featuring Reggie Leach, Stoughton came back to haunt Estevan. Ernie Moser was lost to the pros but Polis and Henning were still in the fold and were joined by rookie Bernie Lukowich.

A rather unusual story surrounded the addition of defenceman Don Martineau to the team, according to the Mercury's Norm Park. Norm was there with Ernie and Bill when this unknown lad walked in to training camp, put money down on the table and asked directions to the dressing room, telling them he intended to make the team. Ernie and Bill just looked at each other. Neither knew who the guy was. Rough and tough but sincere Martineau made and stayed with the team.

Herb Howdle donned the C as team captain.

The CAHA still had the WCHL outlawed and word had it that teams from the OHA were looking to raid the western league. The league was still not out of the woods.

The club started well, winning their first three games. In doing so they took Scotty's Centennials 6-5 at the auditorium and then upset the visiting Bombers 3-2. Both teams that were destined to win their divisions. On Oct. 16 the Bruins set a record for the fastest opening goal of a game when Henning notched one only six seconds in against Calgary. It stood for 18 years. Then times got tough as they went on a seven game losing streak that had them in last place facing Flin Flon again. The Bombers fell 3-1 at the Auditorium as the Bruins snapped the slide. Still, at years end, they were mired in unfamiliar territory, last place.

With January and the start of a new decade came renewed hope. Wayne Harrison, Glen Irwin and Rick Metzler were added and by February 4th they were in third, just one point behind second place Winnipeg. An ominous sign though was only 969 fans in attendance when the club took an important 4-1 win over the Jets. Shades of Humboldt, Estevan could not afford poor crowds and keep the franchise. It was not the only time there were small turnouts for big games.

69/70 Estevan Bruins **Top Left to Right** John McDonald, Dave Matchett, Dave Bonter, Rick Metzler, Blaine Rydman, Jim Pudlowski, Yvon Bilodeau, Bernie Lukowich, John Converse, Dr. Inglis, Lloyd Wheatland **Middle** Larry Dean, Richard Shinske, Ed Sidebottom, Ken Ireland, Glen Irwin,Bob Fowler, Don Martineau, Warren Harrison, Les Jackson, Brian McLean, Kelly Pruden **Front** Grant Green, Herb Howdle, Ernie (Punch) McLean, Greg Polis, Ed Hudson, Brent Taylor, Bill Shinske, Lorne Henning, Ray Frehlick, Wayne Bell (C. Ross Studios & Estevan Bruins) **Also suiting up** Bob Piche, Ken Baird, Don Coombs, Rick Motaler, Mike Prodahl, Randy Smith, Doug Lachambre, ? Krehbiel

On March 18, 1970 the Mercury could claim the Bruins had secured second place after a dramatic rise from the cellar. The acquisition of Wayne Harrison and, fan favourite, Glen Irwin were seen as key reasons for the comeback. Irwin came west and was cleared to play by the WCHL. The Bruins were holding last place at the time so he landed with them. Seldom is last place a blessing but it was that season.

It was the first sub .500 season for the Bruins since the new league had formed and there would not be another for nine years. Greg Polis finished second in scoring, only seven points behind winner Reggie Leach, while Henning landed in 4th. Polis and Herb Howdle made the first string all stars.

Their opponent in the first round was third place Winnipeg, who finished five points behind. Only 938 fans were there for the opening game at the Auditorium. Brent Taylor scored all three Bruins' goals but the team had to settle for a tie. It was a bad omen and the club ended up on the short end of the series, bowing out in five.

Game five, at the auditorium, saw only 1027 fans staying with their Bruins to the end. In the stands was former Bruin Greg Sheppard who had been named MVP in the Central Pro League where he skated for the Oklahoma City Blazers. No one was happy with the 4-1 loss but there was a bright light in the season comeback and the promise of the Dave Bonter, Les Jackson, Lorne Henning line.

Brent Taylor, Bob Fowler and Wayne Bell were picked up in the NHL entry draft.

On the down side all star Polis, Brent Taylor, Herb Howdle and goalie Wayne Bell would not be returning. Greg "Pole Cat" Polis went on to ten seasons in the NHL with Pittsburgh, New York Rangers, St. Louis and Washington and played in three all star games (71,72,73). Ken Baird played only briefly with California in the NHL but skated for seven years in the WHA with the Winnipeg Jets and shared in their 1978 AVCO Cup victory.

Dallas Smith became the second franchise player, and first Estevan Bruin, to etch his name on the Stanley Cup as his Boston Bruins beat out Glenn Hall's St. Louis Blues.

"Be Proud to be a Bruin" was Ernie's comment during an interview focused upon the team concept and philosophy. The aim was not just to win but to make men out of boys and hockey players out of those with stumbling beginnings. It gave him as much pride to see ex Bruins making a living through hockey as it did winning championships.

He was destined to be proud a lot.

25

Goodbye Saskatchewan______1970/71

For 25 years they were a fixture in Saskatchewan hockey. From a budding franchise in Humboldt showing hints of future success to the powerhouse that emerged in Estevan to challenge for the Memorial Cup. When the expectant 70/71 season started no one knew it was to be the franchise's last on the Canadian Prairies.

The CAHA ended its sanctions against the league and rival Regina returned to the fold. Weyburn opted out and the Bruins took them on as a farm team to go with North Battleford and the Chilliwack Bruins of the BCJHL. During the course of their exhibition season they journeyed to BC and took on Calgary's (and Scotty's) farm team; the Kamloops Rockets. Medicine Hat came on board with the Tigers and Ernie unhappily lost defenceman Yvon Bilodeau He vowed to get him back and did, before the season even started.

Newcomers included youthful standout Barry Smith. The 16 year Prince Albert native was dubbed "Bubba" and looked to be a sure fire prospect when he made the team. His star shone ever so briefly and marked one of the saddest moments in Ernie McLean's hockey career.

Also coming on board was a goaltender named Doug Sauter who began his long association with Ernie and the team much as Ernie had done years before with Scotty. On the farm, in Chilliwack, a young prospect named Ron Greschner was to give Ernie and Bill reason for excitement. They were even to get future star Dennis Sobchuk, who played for Weyburn, to suit up for a few games.

The Bruins were quick off the mark and were getting nicknames, both complimentary and critical. In some circles they were the "Big Bruin Machine" while in others, particularly Regina, they regained their title of "The Big Bad Bruins." Ernie began referring to the Estevan flu some players, particularly from Saskatoon and Regina, used to get prior to coming to the Bruins' barn. They mysteriously got ill just before the trip. His philosophy was; if you can't play in Estevan you will never make it in the NHL.

Save for team scoring leader Lorne Henning, the squad threw balanced scoring at opposing teams all season while they battled down to the wire with Flin Flon for first in the East Division. Goalie Grant Green was doing his bit in piling up impressive shutouts and compiling the league's second best goals against average at 3:00, behind ex Bruin Ed Dyck in Calgary. One of his shutouts was a 6-0 win over the Edmonton Oil Kings who eventually won the league.

70/71 Estevan Bruins **Top Left to Right** Bud Johns, Dave Matchett, Bob Fowler, Yvon Bilodeau, Pete Kay, Ron Popadynetz, Dr. Inglis, John Gallant **Middle** Lawrence Gingras, Barry Smith, Dave Bonter, Bernie Lukowich,Don Martineau, Ken Ireland, Les Jackson, Ron Kennedy, Kelly Pruden **Front** Grant Green, Bill Shinske, Ed Sidebottom, Ernie (Punch) McLean, Glen Irwin, Ray Frehlick, Lorne Henning, Doug Sauter (C. Ross Studios & Estevan Bruins) **Also suiting up** Bob Stumpf, Mike Randolph, Rick Metzler, Dennis Sobchuk, Boyd Anderson, Bob Miller, Murray Fleck, Darryl Fleck, Larry Drader, Rick McDonald (goal), Brian Back, Ed Lavigne

Fan turnout in Estevan was still not good and was exceeded by turnouts at Bismarck, North Dakota, where the team played a number of its home games. Fan support dropped during the rebuilding year and was not clearly recovering, even though the team was contending.

A letter sent to the Mercury gave some idea of how the Bruins had spread the name of Estevan. Mr. Larry Eisler, a CN agent in Estevan, noted messages from different departments around the country were processed by a central machine before being routed to their destinations. In the case of Estevan the machine accepted either Estevan Saskatchewan or Estevan Bruins.

The first place race was tight. After the Bruins dropped a 6-5 home decision to Flin Flon, the Bombers, with scoring stars Chuck Arnason and Gene Carr in their lineups, moved to within four points.

On March 17/71, the Mercury and Estevan fans sighed a breath of relief. Taking games against Medicine Hat and Swift Current, while Flin Flon was losing, secured their first regular season division title since the WCHL was formed They ended up three points ahead of the Bombers.

Melfort's Lorne Henning secured third in scoring and took home the league's most sportsmanlike player award.

In the west Edmonton came out ahead of Scotty's Centennials by ten points. The playoffs had the potential to see old rivals Edmonton and Estevan face off once again. It didn't happen.

Round one was against third place Winnipeg, who had not even managed a plus.500 season and who were 22 points behind them. The Bruins were highly favoured to get revenge for last season's ouster.

It started with the Bruins tying game one in Bismarck and then going into Winnipeg to steal game two 3-2. The Jets came back to stun Estevan 4-2 at the Auditorium and then take their home game 3-0. Jets goalie Mike Schneider was making the difference as the Bruins outshot the Jets 46 to 34 before 6848 Jets fans in the 3-0 game. The Bruins regained form at home for a 6-4 win but then went down 4-3 in a wild Winnipeg game to face the prospect of elimination. The Bruins required police protection in the game which had Jets fans throwing beer on them. Down 4-0 their comeback fell just short.

Back on home ice for game seven, the team had its biggest paid fan turnout of the season. 1818 fans were hoping the club could stave off an upset elimination to go on against hated Flin Flon. Little did they know they were watching the last official game the team would play as the Estevan Bruins. The upset happened. The paper reported that well after the game had ended three or four Bruins were still sitting on the bench contemplating the upset.

The loss for the Estevan fans was even greater.

The great season came to a shuddering end and the team

looked to possibly lose six players for the coming season. Four players, Glen Irwin, Dave Bonter, Ed Sidebottom, and Yvon Bilodeau went in the entry draft.

Only seven days after the paper reported the end of the Bruins season, headlines flashed Ernie McLean had gone down in a light airplane crash.

He had been doing a job for Dome Petroleum at Lynn Lake, Manitoba and was on his way back, piloting his own plane, when he went down north of Roblin Manitoba near Madge Lake. Suffering damage to one eye, lacerations and a broken jaw, he stumbled several miles to reach a road near the farm of Peter and Steve Chypyha. Driven into Kamsack he was airlifted to Regina for emergency eye surgery.

Cards and letters poured in, at the rate of 30 to 40 a day , from across North America. It was a time to think. Ernie decided to move to coaching full time and get out of the construction business. He could not do it with the team in Estevan. The decision came to move west. When his buddy Scotty called to see how he was doing Ernie asked him to find a place to move the team.

Originally it was headed for Vancouver and the Pacific Coliseum but when word got back to local movers and shakers Nat Bailey and Coley Hall that option was shut off. Bailey eventually got a new team and named it the Vancouver Nats. The paths of the two teams were to cross as the Nats, playing horribly, were moved to Kamloops to become the Kamloops Chiefs. After four years and much more success the franchise shifted to Seattle where it remains. It is now the old Bruins/Indians franchise that plays out of Kamloops as the Blazers and battles the team that kept them out of Vancouver. Thankfully, for Blazers' fans

Fresh from that closed door Ernie, Scotty and Bill Shinske got a surprise call from Tom Fisher and Bill Hill, owners of the New Westminster Royals, seeking a meeting at the Astor Hotel in Burnaby. They asked them if they would be interested in moving to the 3900 seat Queen's Park arena. After seeing the facility, which was already home to the New Westminster Salmonbellies, the lacrosse dynasty rivalling the Montreal Canadians of hockey, Ernie and Bill went for it.

On June 16/71 the Mercury made it official. The headlines read **15 Year Love Affair Over - Bruins Shift Franchise to New Westminster.** Ernie was quoted "We have tried to keep the team here, but it just can't pay. I haven't received wages for the past two years and a group of people in New Westminster are very interested in having a team there but they do not want to operate it themselves..............I just feel sorry for the people who have supported the Bruins for so many years."

Ernie and Bill cited the 5200 fan capacity of Queen's Park and a draw of 1.2 million people. An agreement was struck with the other owners to buy out the remaining team stock over three years and prospects were raised about having an affiliation with Estevan similar to the ones with Weyburn and Chilliwack.

On June 23/71 the paper reported the move was official but added the team would retain the name Bruins rather than adopt the historical New Westminster name of "Royals."

Needless to say the local fans were stunned and disappointed, much as their Humboldt counterparts had been 15 years earlier, but the move was generally seen as logical. As long as hometown boy Ernie remained involved many fans still followed the team they called "Our Bruins".

A working relationship was arranged and a new Estevan Bruins team, that still plays in the SJHL, emerged for the 71/72 season. The baby Bruins joined a league with many rivals familiar to Estevan fans. Moose Jaw, Regina, Weyburn, Prince Albert, Melville, Notre Dame, Saskatoon and the Ft. Qu'Appelle Silver Foxes became their new opponents.

As for Ernie. Mr. Everything for the team and franchise, he never lost his connection to his home town, often visiting and turning up at Bruins games. There was some initial bitterness on the part of a few fans but that passed.

No one could claim to have accomplished all that he had. He had been a player, trainer, bus driver, coach, manager and owner along with taking on any other role that came along.

Norm Parks commented on how both Ernie and Bill Shinske took on parenting and counselling roles with the players. Both of them spent time with the players and helped them with issues unrelated to hockey; not unlike the stories told about Scotty Munro. It is no wonder former players still have a warm spot for Ernie and so many returned to Estevan for the funeral of Bill Shinske in 1995. Team reunions in Estevan continue to draw back the alumni.

In 14 years in Estevan the team had made the playoffs 13 times, had 10 plus .500 campaigns, taken the league four times in the regular season, been Saskatchewan Champs three times and been to the Memorial Cup once. They had been a powerhouse throughout the 60's. The franchise had improved upon its record in Humboldt; what would happen with the move to British Columbia?

The franchise left Estevan, as it had Humboldt, but the unbroken line of players and the Seventh Man remained. The roots of the ongoing story forever tied to Humboldt, Estevan and Saskatchewan; just as a family's genealogy is tied to its forefathers.

The Seventh Man moved to New Westminster and his shadow grew larger.

26

Part Three
New Westminster
Queen's Park Bruins________1971/72

New Westminster, the "Royal City" along the banks of the mighty Fraser River, founded in 1860, once hoped to become the capital of British Columbia. Though it lost that battle to Victoria and later fell under the shadow of burgeoning Vancouver it nonetheless kept an identity that still makes it stand out from all the other communities in the Lower Mainland.

It's professional hockey began on January 2, 1912 when the visiting New Westminster Royals defeated the Victoria Aristocrats 8-3 in the inaugural game of the Pacific Coast Hockey League. They proved the class of the league in the first year, beating out the Vancouver Millionaires for first place and remained in the league for three years before disappearing until 1945. They re-emerged, again as the Royals, in a new Pacific Coast Hockey League.

Later, with colourful coach Kenny MacKenzie, they began having training camps at Kamloops' new Memorial Arena and established close ties with the Senior A Kamloops Elks. Thus started a love hate relationship between Kamloops and New Westminster that persisted in differing forms for many years. They stayed with the league, which became the Western Hockey League in 1952, until the end of the 58/59 season. Their best years were from 1948/49 to 1950/51 when they were the league power. Ironically Kenny MacKenzie left the team to buy and operate the Kamloops Chiefs of the interior league, prior to the Royals folding.

When junior hockey came to the fore in the 1960's Queen's Park Arena became home to the junior New Westminster Royals, who battled the interior champion Kamloops Rockets five times for the Provincial Championship. During that time a member of Kamloops' Recchi family first made an appearance in New Westminster. Ron Recchi, uncle of future franchise star Mark, made his thundering presence known along the boards of the historic arena.

So the Estevan Bruins came to a new home with knowledgeable fans and high expectations. Natural rivalries with Vancouver and Victoria were to be complemented by historic hockey battles with teams from Portland, Seattle, Edmonton and Calgary. It was a natural environment for Ernie and Bill's entertaining brand of hockey.

They were joined on the coast by two new franchises; the Vancouver Nats and the Victoria Cougars. Animosity began quickly as the Nats were fined $1000 for tampering with other teams' players and then came back to accuse the Bruins of doing the same.

1971/72 New Westminster Bruins (C. NWMA) **Back Row - Left to Right-** Frank Hyndman, Les Jackson, Bob Bilodeau, Don Martineau, Barry Smith, Bernie Lukowich, Vic Mercredi **Centre Row** - Ron Lyon, Gord Henschke, Ron Kennedy, Roy Carmichael, Bob Craig, Emile Demoissac, Terry Richardson **Front** - Doug Sauter, Bob Stumpf, Bill Shinske, Lorne Henning, Ernie McLean, Ken Ireland, Brian Newbert **Also suiting up** Alex Kogler, Grant Williams, Ray Tyler, Greg Reid, Larry Sokoloski, Dave O'Dennell, Rick Kramp, Mike Bodnarik, Wally Allison, Keith Richards, Randy Elliott, Grant Casper, Bob Hesketh, Leland Houm

The season opener sported nine returning players, including Don Martineau who was being compared to former Bruin Ivan Prediger for on ice meanness. Other 19 year olds returning were Ken Ireland and Les Jackson. Budding star Dennis Sobchuk did not come west with the team. His mother was ill and he wanted to stay on the Prairies so Ernie engineered a trade that eventually brought Stan Smyl, Vic Mercredi, Wayne Dye, Bob Hess and Amil Bimnosica.

On a tragic note, Barry Smith, who so impressed as a 16 year old in Estevan, died in a freak car accident in New Westminster. Travelling with Bob Stumpf and Bob Craig they were rear ended by another vehicle. Smith was eating chicken at the time and choked to death when a piece got caught in his throat. For Ernie it was the hardest and most tragic thing he ever had to deal with while with the franchise. He accompanied the body back to Prince Albert to Smith's parents.

Attendance immediately improved over Estevan and Ernie had lost none of his flair which added excitement to the game. In a 5-4 overtime victory over the visiting Centennials he was ejected for throwing a garbage can on to the ice. Attendance routinely exceeded 2000 and on occasion topped 3500.

The Bruins were hoping to increase the presence of local talent on the team and in November brought up local goalie Terry Richardson, who soon showed he was no token call up. After a slow start they returned to .500 hockey by mid December. In January they added Alex Kogler, from Swift Current, and the turnaround got even better. They went on a 17 game winning streak putting them alone in second place in the western division.

Richardson, Bob Stumpf, Lorne Henning and Kogler, who got the winning goal in the game, went on to represent the Bruins in the all star game.

By seasons end, Bill and Ernie could look at the move and team performance with some satisfaction. The club ended up third with a 40-27-1 record and fan attendance averaging 1850 compared to 1100 in Estevan. Henning was their only player in the top ten scorers despite being the 6th highest scoring team in the league. On top of that they sported the third best goals against average.

Their first round opponent was second place Edmonton Oil Kings, led by Darcy Rota. Despite outshooting the Oil Kings in game one they lost 4-2 and followed it up with another close loss, 5-3, to go down two games to none returning home. The largest crowd of the season, 3729, was on hand to watch their club finally take a game, 4-2. The match had been tied at two until Stumpf fired a pass up to Roy Kennedy who fed it to Alex Kogler for the game winner. The Bruins charged out in game four and outshot the visitors 48-26 but came away with a 5-3 loss to face elimination in Edmonton.

The club battled hard in Edmonton; twice coming back to tie the game before the Kings pulled ahead 6-3. Ernie pulled his goalie and Lorne Henning got one back but the tilt ended 6-4 in Edmonton's favour. The first season in New West was over.

It was Hennings' last goal as a Bruin. After five years with the team he was off to the pros where he drank from the Stanley Cup four times as a New York Islander, twice as a player and twice as an assistant coach. Melfort's pride skated nine years in the NHL.

Edmonton went on to oust Scotty's Centennials, who finished first overall, and reach the Memorial Cup. It was the last Memorial Cup appearance by the remarkable Oil Kings dynasty.

New Westminster's two provincial rivals faired poorly but had been faced with starting a team from scratch rather than inheriting a contender. Vancouver's stumbling never ended.

The entry draft took six Bruins starting with Henning (New York Islanders) followed by Bernie Lukowich (Pittsburgh), Don Martineau (Atlanta), Les Jackson (Boston), Ken Ireland (New York Rangers) and Ron Carmichael (Boston).

The alumni's Dallas Smith picked up his second Stanley Cup with the Boston Bruins.

The Bruins had landed on the west coast and before they were through they reached the franchise's greatest heights.

27

Fit to be Tied_______________1972/73

72/73 proved a tougher year than the first at Queen's Park. The club won fewer games but also lost fewer as they racked up a league record 15 ties.

Word came before the start of camp that two key elements were lost to the pros. Surprise walk-on back in Estevan, Don Martineau, carried his intensity and enthusiasm into the NHL where he skated over parts of four seasons for Atlanta, Minnesota and Detroit. Bernie Lukowich, father of future Kamloops' Blazer Brad Lukowich, enjoyed a couple NHL seasons with Pittsburgh and St. Louis before hanging them up after playing for the Cranbrook Royals.

The season and home opener was no treat as former Bruin Fred Hyndman potted two goals against his old team mates to lead Victoria to a 4-2 win in front of 1234 disappointed fans. It was one of the few times the Cougars could gloat as they were only saved from the bottom of the heap by the dismal performance of Vancouver. Edmonton, Medicine Hat, Calgary and New Westminster battled it out for top spot in the west while Saskatoon ran away and hid from the pack.

Three former Bruins or players they once listed, Dennis Sobchuk (Regina), Blaine Stoughton (Flin Flon) and Boyd Anderson (Medicine Hat) all finished in the top ten scorers. Vic Mercredi grabbed 8th spot.

Mercredi starred on the first line with rookie Wayne Dye, who was also picked up in the Sobchuk deal, and Ron Kennedy. Terry Richardson was their standout in goal; who Medicine Hat reportedly offered $30,000 for early in the season. Bob Stumpf, moved to forward from defence, played his way to the team captaincy. Two big season acquisitions were Surrey's Barry Smith, picked up from struggling Vancouver and a Yorkton, Saskatchewan player who scout Larry Berg spoke highly of; Clayton Pachal. Both became key parts of a budding Bruins dynasty.

As late as January 24/73, after a 13 game unbeaten streak, they were tied for first. Despite entertaining play and a competitive team, attendance was suffering, sometimes dipping below 1000. Some games did garner the numbers as attested to by the 4087 fans for a first place battle with Edmonton.

The shenanigans of league coaches remained both creative and humorous. In Swift Current Ernie sent all of his players over the boards to celebrate the tying goal so the ref wouldn't notice there were too many men on the ice at the time. On another occasion Ernie and Scotty threatened to play the game without helmets to protest the Bruins losing two points for playing an earlier helmet less game (their helmets had been lost at the airport). They had a change of heart when they learned they would be suspended if they did. Fined $250 for stepping on the ice to give a referee a piece of his mind Ernie received a reprimand from league Commissioner Tom Fisher that it was conduct "unbecoming a coach". Ernie's response was a telex saying "Go jump in a lake." Remember this is the same Tom Fisher who enticed Ernie to move his team to New Westminster.

72/73 New Westminster Bruins **Front Left to Right** Dr. Wodynski, Ian McWilliams, Bill Shinske, Bob Bilodeau, Ernie (Punch) McLean, Ron Kennedy, Dr. Metler, Terry Richardson, Dr. Dave Lough **Middle** Kelly Pruden, Marty Kissel, Brad Rota, Ron Greschner, Bob Stumpf, Gord Lane, Denis Andersen, Vic Mercredi, Lawrence Gingras **Top** Rod Fagerheim, Wayne Dye, Barry Smith, Marty Matthews, Bob Hess, Sid Prysunka, Emile Demoissac, Clayton Pachal (C. NWMA) **Also suiting up** Marv Lank, Ken Widmeyer, Al Cameron, Lorne Brennan, Wayne Dye, Jerry Huff, Dave Sharples, Marcel Vanderfraff, Kevin Erickson, Rod Sleigholm, Doug Abrahamson, Don Harrison, Bob Hesketh

A verbal exchange between Ernie and Brandon coach Rudy Pilous (coach of the 1961 Stanley Cup Champion Chicago Black Hawks) had Pilous calling Ernie a "Poor man's Punch Imlach." The reply came back that Pilous should get a new fedora. 'He's been wearing it since 1955 and it's a disgrace. I wouldn't even wear it in Moose Jaw much less Brandon."

Even the fans got into the act. A particular section, endearingly called the "North Enders", were especially renowned. Primarily composed of bikers even the police would not go in to deal with them when they began fighting. Ernie had a unique relationship with the fans including the North Enders and on occasion needed it.

Back on the ice New Westminster was destined for 4th place when they faced off at Queen's Park for their final regular season game against first place Edmonton. 2109 fans saw their Bruins dump the Oil Kings 10-3 and take the season series four games to two. Given Edmonton was their first round opponent this gave some room for optimism.

Reality struck in the first two games in Edmonton as they lost decisively 9-2 and 8-4. Game three at Queen's Park saw the Bruins, sparked by the return of captain Bob Stumpf and a four goal outburst by Mercredi, win going away 10-4. It looked to be a homer series.

Game four was a back breaker. 4402 fans were on hand for a game which was tied 4-4 with 27 seconds remaining. Darcy Rota sent the Bruins fans home disappointed when he nabbed the winner. The game proved pivotal with the teams returning to Edmonton for game five. Edmonton took it 6-3 and the series 4-1.

A respectable season but Edmonton remained a stumbling block.

Bill and Ernie had to deal with the loss of Terry Richardson, Gord Lane, Bob Stumpf, Vic Mercredi and Ron Kennedy. Richardson was picked up by Detroit and had a few backup games with them and St. Louis over the course of five seasons. Stumpf put in some NHL shifts in 74/75 with St. Louis and Pittsburgh while Mercredi did the same with Atlanta of the NHL and Calgary Cowboys of the WHA. Gord Lane, who had been picked up from Brandon, enjoyed the most success earning four Stanley Cups with the New York Islanders during his 10 year NHL career. A franchise high eight players were taken in the NHL entry draft as Wayne Dye (Chicago), Dennis

Anderson (New York Islanders) and Bob Bilodeau (Atlanta) joined the parade.

They still had Barry Smith, Clayton Pachal and future NHL star Ron Greschner to lend excitement for the coming season. They were also to land a player with deep roots in Kamloops' hockey who was to become an integral part of franchise history.

28

Munro vs. McLean__________1973/74

The battle for first in the West pitted Ernie against mentor and longtime friend Scotty Munro. Family connections added to the battle as Bill Shinske's son Rick and Ernie's son Brian skated in Centennial colours. The battle did not stop the friends from helping each other out.

In the Bruins home opener before 1637 fans the teams skated to a 4-4 tie. When the Bruins next played they had three new players. Ken Dodd and Murray Beck were joined by a player whose connection with Kamloops ran deep and who was fated to play a role in the franchise none other than Ernie himself had ever experienced. Don Hay, a sterling product of the Kamloops' minor hockey program, brought a will to win that marked him and the franchise. Ironically Hay came indirectly from the Kamloops' Chiefs who cut him before the season began.

After three dismal seasons in Vancouver the Nats pulled up stakes and headed to the Interior where their fortunes improved dramatically. Kamloops was and is a hockey town and the Chiefs came to take on the colour of the community.

On October 29/73 the Columbian boasted the Bruins had shutout visiting Calgary 2-0 before 2198 fans at Queen's Park. Leading the team in scoring at that stage of the season; Don Hay. Though he didn't hang on to first he remained one of the team's top scorers. The Bruins later added Mike Sleep from Flin Flon. Gordie Laxton came along to fill the void in net and Ron Greschner came in to his own when he surpassed the old league record for points by a defenceman; at 85, by March 1/74.

The Bruins were unstoppable on home ice. When they beat Calgary 4-2 in front of 4330 fans in mid March they tied Estevan's league record of 30 straight home games undefeated in a season, although it is important to remember Estevan only played 30 home games. They set a new league record, at 34, later the same month when they took Edmonton; this time 10-1. The franchise again went undefeated at home for an entire season. The record eventually extended to 38 regular season games over two seasons.

By early March Scotty's Centennials had secured first overall but the teams were not done with each other yet.

The Bruins first round foes were last seasons' WHL champs, the Medicine Hat Tigers. The two clubs had split the season series evenly so it was a toss up with the advantage to New Westminster due to home ice. The Tigers came right in to Queen's Park and took game one 5-2 before 3504 fans to end the home ice streak. Not a good time to lose. Needing game two they got it, but in heartbreak fashion as they came back to tie and then win 3-2 in OT on Bob Hess' goal. Hess had just stepped out of the penalty box and picked up an errant Tiger pass to go in and score.

73/74 New Westminster Bruins **Front Left to Right** Doug Allen, Doug Sauter (asst. coach), Bob Hess, Ernie (Punch) McLean (coach), Ron Greschner, Bill Shinske (GM), Emil Demossiac, Dr. Peter Woydynski, Gord Laxton **Middle** Larry Dean (trainer), Brian Anderson, Bob McNiece, Al Cameron, Erik Sanderson, Don Hay, Mike Sleep, Brian Shymr, Barry Clarke **Top** Brian McLennan (stick boy), Kelly Secord, Murray Beck, Sid Prysunka, Barry Smith, Ken Dodd, Clayton Pachal, Reg Duncombe, Glen Howes (stick boy) (C. NWMA)
Also suiting up Eric "Jumbo" Sanderson, Bruce Rolin, Harold Phillipoff, Kevin Schamehorn, Mark Arnett, Wayne Jeske, Innes Mackie

Heading to Medicine Hat they faced a Tiger team trying to run them out of the building. Doug Allen starred in net as the Bruins were outshot 36-21 but went on to win 4-3 and take a 2-1 series lead. Game four again went to overtime with the teams tied at two. Bob Hess was the hero once more, nailing the winner; this time only 27 seconds into overtime. Game five went in The Hat as well. Down 5-0 before they became untracked the Bruins fell 7-3 but still had the opportunity to put the Tigers out at Queen's Park.

There were 3929 fans on hand hoping to see their Bruins advance. The Tigers played well and even outshot the home side 27-16 in the first two periods but it was Ron Greschner who sniped the winner and Don Hay who put away the insurance marker in a 5-3 series clinching game. Their next foe was fitting.

Calgary and New Westminster faced off in the semis and the right to go to the WHL final.

Game one in Calgary was a bruising match; in which the Columbian claimed the Bruins won all their fights. Calgary took the match 7-4 and Ernie had to contend with a 6-2 loss in game two to go along with a $1000 fine for his actions in the previous game. The league wanted to make a point with Ernie so it also made him post a $5000 performance bond for game two.

Back home the fans showed no love for Scotty; hanging him in effigy. This time it was the Bruins outshooting the Cents, 48 to 23 and skating away with a 5-3 victory.

Same as last season they needed to pull out the fourth game; at home. The Bruins dominated the first two periods and were up 2-1 going into the third. They took three penalties and the Cents managed to score on all of the them leaving the club down 4-2. Dodd scored at 18:18 to make it close but the final score was 4-3 heading back to Calgary.

The last match was no contest as the Cents put it to New West 7-0 and went on to play Regina. The Pats prevented Scotty from regaining a seat at the Memorial Cup as they advanced and eventually won the Cup. Munro never got close to a championship again but it was not because of the teams he had.

Don Hay, Bob Hess and Ron Greschner all moved on. WHL league all star Greschner starred his entire 16 years in the NHL with the New York Rangers and played in the 1980 all star game. Bob Hess, taken by St. Louis, lasted six years in the NHL with three different teams. Don Hay, drafted by Minnesota, skated for a few years in the minor pros before returning home to Kamloops. There he settled into working for the fire department and becoming player coach of the Senior B Kamloops Cowboys. When he stepped down from the position he mentioned how he was going to miss coaching. Epitomizing the Seventh

Man his return to the bench and the franchise marked one of the highest points in its history. But that comes later.

Four others joined the draft selection, Sid Prysunka (New York Islanders), Brian Anderson (Minnesota), Ken Dodd (New York Rangers) and Don Allan (St. Louis) took the total to seven.

Bruin alumni were busy in the NHL where Ross Lonsberry and Joe Watson's Philadelphia Flyers prevailed over Greg Sheppard's Boston Bruins in the Stanley Cup final.

Ernie and Bill had seen marked improvement in their squad, even if they had lost the season battle to Scotty. Yet it was nothing compared to what was to start next season.

29

Return to Glory_______________1974/75

"We're going to be in the Memorial Cup with this team."

So Ernie told the Columbian's Don Connors as the 74/75 season neared.

A tall order with the loss of key veterans and strong teams being iced in Saskatoon, Victoria, Medicine Hat and Kamloops. He still had a potent returning core complemented by star potential rookies Mark Lofthouse, Fred Berry, Brad Maxwell and Steve Clippingdale.

Paddy Ginnel, whose connection with Flin Flon rivalled Ernie's with the Bruins, took over in Victoria and turned them into a team more known for aggressive play than the Bruins. Part way through the season he even picked up Bruin tough guy Eric "Jumbo" Anderson for futures to add to his arsenal.

The Cougars, destined for first in the west, well ahead of the pack, were the opening act at Queen's Park. They did not impress as rookie Steve Clippingdale notched two for the Bruins in a 6-1 victory. Victoria then went on to take the Lion's share of wins in the season series, including a 12-4 thrashing of the Bruins in Victoria. They would meet in the playoffs.

A close season long battle ensued between Medicine Hat, New Westmister and Kamloops for the2nd, 3rd and 4th positions with Edmonton a trailer. Last years division champs, Calgary, had their worst season yet under Scotty. They had worse news coming.

In late November, with the team competitive at 9-7-2, the Bruins made a pivotal trade. Rick Shinske came over from Calgary, for Paul Enqvist, and joined his father. The stick boy of the Estevan Bruins now skated in their colours. His contribution was immediate

In the battle for third with Kamloops and avoidance of powerhouse Victoria in the first round it came down to the last few games of the season. Shinske's second straight two goal game led the Bruins to a 5-2 home ice win over Regina to secure third and a first round matchup against the Medicine Hat

Tigers. They had taken all five regular season games so far in the campaign but in their last match "The Hat" toasted them 6-2 at Queen's Park. Not a good omen.

The team improved marginally over last year and only scraped past Kamloops by one point but they did it with a lot of new faces. They also stole six shorthanded goals for a team record. Despite their reputation as the "Big Bad Bruins" they were 4th in the league in penalties.

Although they dominated the Tigers all season Medicine Hat still finished ahead of them and were buoyed by their recent win at Queen's Park. They proved it was no fluke as the Bruins fell 6-5 in the opener in Alberta. It was close though as the Tigers only pulled it out with Barry Dean's winner at 19:29. Game two was a gut check.

74/75 New Westminster Bruins **Top Left to Right** Kevin Schamehorn, Terry Hochstetter, Mike Sleep, Rick Shinske, Allen Fleck, Kelly Secord, Brian Shmyr, Larry Dean **Middle** Jake Mitchell, Al Cameron, Bob McNiece, Barry Beck, Harold Phillipoff, Steve Clippingdale, Mark Lofthouse, Brad Maxwell, Jack Patrick **Front** Clayton Pachal, Doug Sauter, Kerry Nesbitt, Ernie (Punch) McLean, Barry Smith, Bill Shinske, Gord Laxton, Dr. Dave Lough, Fred Berry (C. NWMA) **Also suiting up** Eric "Jumbo" Sanderson, Lyle Bradley, Sheldon Geary, B. McAlister, D. Davis

New Westminster entered game two minus their equipment, which had been stolen along with all their right handed sticks. But, buoyed by the return of injured Mark Lofthouse, they put out a stellar effort. At the end of two the teams were deadlocked at three despite the Bruins taking the bulk of the shots. They finally got their reward in the third as they notched three unanswered goals and evened the series with a 6-3 victory. The Tigers were outshot 44-25.

Game three, again in Medicine Hat, was close and controversial. Barry Smith put the puck in his own net during a delayed penalty but the goal was disallowed because the ref claimed a Tiger hit Smith's stick thus stopping the play. The Tigers were adamant and their fans enraged. When the Bruins took the game 3-2, on the strength of Allan "Buzzard" Fleck's tie breaker, the ref needed a police escort to get out of the building.

The Bruins were coming home up 2-1.

A total of 3137 fans were on hand Saturday to see Shinske nail down a shorthanded goal and New Westminster take a strangle hold on the series with an 8-6 win. Second place Medicine Hat was on the ropes.

Game six had the Tigers hanging on 4-3 in the third until Barry Smith's shorthanded goal tied the game to force overtime. Queen's Park was rocking. In OT the Tigers rifled a clear shot on the Bruins net but Laxton was there to stop it. Then it was the Bruins' turn and Fred Berry slammed shut the series with the winner at 2:11. The series went to New Westminster 4-1.

Victoria had to come from behind to finally oust Kamloops 4-2 in their series but they had home ice advantage.

The first game went at Queen's Park with the next two set for the Island. The Bruins thrilled over 3000 fans when, on the strength of Fred Berrys' two goals, they took game one 6-2. Berry took his act to Victoria and scored the winner as New West upset the Cougars 3-1. Victoria finally got untracked in game three to set the Bruins down 5-2. Game four had the Bruins up 5-0 before the Cougars launched their comeback. It was too little too late and New West took the night 7-5. The Cougars, who finished 14 points ahead, were on the verge of going out.

Back on home ice Victoria staved off elimination with a 7-4 victory. Now they had to try to even it up in New Westminster. They appeared to have the game well in hand at 4-1, despite the looming presence of 4339 fans, but the Seventh Man came alive. The Bruins roared back to tie it at 4-4. Mel Bridgman put the Cougars ahead again but Fred Berry's third goal of the game knotted it at five. The gold and black had them by the throat and the Cougars were not going to get another chance. Brian Schmyr fired the winner and Brad Maxwell put in the insurance marker. For the first time since coming to New Westminster the franchise was going to the Western Final.

The season series between New Westminster and Saskatoon was a 3-3 saw off with each team winning their home games. The Bruins got home ice advantage but in the form of the first two games in New Westminster, the next three in Saskatoon and the last two in New Westminster. It started badly.

Saskatoon broke the home ice jinx in impressive fashion. Over 3000 were on hand to see their Bruins stunned 5-3 in game one. Only 2300 turned up for game two and witnessed New Westminster beaten decisively 5-1. It looked bad going to Saskatoon down 2-0. They needed two of three just to stay alive and come home.

In unfriendly confines the Bruins pulled ahead 2-0 in game three on goals by Schmyr at 39 seconds into the first and Brad Maxwell at 6:22. From there on it was the Gord Laxton show as he steered his squad to a 2-1 victory. Game four had the Bruins down 3-0 before they mounted a comeback to tie 4-4 entering the final minute of the third. Shinske took the face-off on the Blades end and put it back to big Barry Beck. Beck rifled home the winner at 19:40 and the series was tied at two. They had their two wins. If they got the third the Blades were on the ropes.

Saskatoon showed they too could pull a rabbit out of the hat in the last minute. They took game five 3-2 on the strength of a goal with only 23 seconds left. It was the Bruins on the ropes coming home. Almost 4000 fans turned up for game six at Queen's Park. New Westminster took it 4-1 to force the seventh and deciding game.

Surprisingly, with a trip to the Memorial Cup on the line, only 2700 fans lined the seats. They saw history as the Bruins erased any doubts. They won 7-2 to take the hard fought series. Ernie and the franchise were on their way to their second Memorial Cup appearance and the start of an incredible run not since duplicated in the WHL. The franchise hex on Saskatoon held.

Their first opponent in the round robin in Kitchener was the Sherbrooke Beavers. Down 3-0 at the end of the first New Westminster came back with five straight goals to skate away with a 7-5 victory. Next came the famed Toronto Marlboros whose lineup included future NHLer's Mark Napier, Bruce Boudreau and Mike Kitchen. Laxton was sensational; stopping Napier on a breakaway. Clippingdale broke the 2-2 tie early in the second and the Bruins earned a bye into the Memorial Cup final with a convincing 6-2 win. They were within a win of taking junior hockey's biggest prize.

The Marlies took the semi final game over Sherbrooke to go up against the Bruins in the final. New Westminster started off where they left off and had a 2-0 lead early in the game. Then the Marlies came on and at 17:02 of the first they knotted the score at 2. In the second they went up 3-2 but Mark Lofthouse brought the Bruins back to tie. This time the Seventh Man took a seat in the stands as Toronto pressed on to earn a 7-3 victory and the Memorial Cup for the seventh, and last, time since 1929. Two of them coming at the expense of the franchise.

For the Bruins it was a bitter disappointment but they were just beginning to make an impression on the national scene. Barry Smith was voted the tournament MVP and joined Brad Maxwell on the tourney all stars.

Star goalie Gord Laxton was lost to Pittsburgh where he made brief appearances with the Penguins over four seasons. Defenceman Barry Smith went on to three partial NHL seasons with Boston and the Colorado Rockies. Defenceman Al Cameron carved out a six year NHL career with Detroit and Winnipeg. Bill and Ernie also lost core players in Mike Sleep (New York Islanders), Kelly Secord (Pittsburgh) and Brian Schmyr Vancouver). Also going in the draft were Rick Shinske (California), Allan Fleck (Vancouver) and Bob McNiece (Vancouver) taking the total number of draftees to nine; a franchise record.

Alumni were busy in the NHL where Ross Lonsberry and Joe Watson sipped from the Stanley Cup as Philadelphia Flyers while Brian Spencer of the runner up Buffalo Sabres looked on. Topping it all was goaltender Glenn Hall, Humboldt boy made good, being inducted in to the Hockey Hall of Fame.

The Bruins had some new stars coming up to join their impressive returning cast.

The beauty of sport is that today's loss can be overcome by tomorrow's victory. It can be a stepping stone in a determined battle for ultimate success. But there are some losses for which there is no recovery; just lifelong memories and a tear in the corner of the eye.

The godfather of the franchise never lived to see the

Bruins or his buddy Ernie McLean achieve what he never did. Scotty Munro played the game of his life against cancer and in 1975 cancer won. He passed away in hospital in Calgary.

He had been more than a general manager and coach to his players and colleagues. He had been a prominent and loved citizen in Moose Jaw, Gravelbourg, Lethbridge, Crows Nest Pass, Humboldt, Estevan, and Calgary. His lessons imparted as much about life as they did about hockey, and friend and foe alike honoured his shadow. The Scotty Munro Memorial Trophy became emblematic of the regular season championship of the WHL.

There is a hockey heaven and Scotty is there enjoying a beer with the Seventh Man.

30

A Special Trophy____________1975/76

Finishing first overall in the WCJHL brought with it prestige and home ice advantage. It also brought a special Trophy, the Scotty Munro Memorial Trophy. It could not mean more to anyone in the league than Ernie McLean and Bill Shinske.

Kamloops, Victoria and Medicine Hat were strong in the western division and the east had Bernie Federko led Saskatoon. The Bruins were good but were they good enough?

There were to be some big nights for the team and individual players, starting on opening night against Victoria. Fred Berry and Mark Lofthouse each got a hat trick in an 8-5 victory. Berry and Rick Shinske ended up the season as the Bruins' top scorers finishing 5th and 6th respectively. Brad Maxwell and Barry Beck turned eyes in the NHL and word came in October that an NHL team had offered the Bruins $100,000 each for the two stars. Ernie and Bill didn't bite.

One of the best prospects was young Stan "The Steamer" Smyl. He was only 14 when Guy Demossiac, brother of Bruin Emile, called Ernie about the St. Paul, Alberta native. The Steamer was on Regina's protected list but Ernie let him try out with their development team, the Bellingham Blazers. He liked what he saw. During the 74/75 season the Pats brought out a heavyweight, Bob Poly, but neglected to put him on their protected list. Ernie immediately claimed him and then traded him back to Regina for the rights to Smyl. The rest is history.

It wasn't the first time Ernie pulled off a steal and it got so bad other teams were reluctant to trade with him. Top scorer Fred Berry was another example. The Bruins had an American player who was coveted by Flin Flon. The Bombers got their man in return for heavyweight Kim Clackson who was immediately sent packing to Victoria for the talented Berry.

Clippingdale, Lofthouse, Phillipoff, Clayton Pachal and Kevin Schamehorn contributed big nights as the power house Bruins battled the new force on the block; the Kamloops Chiefs, for division honours. Despite playing well everywhere else the

Chiefs struggled against the Bruins and did not get their first point until a 3-3 tie in December. The flip side had been true for New Westminster up until late December and at one time they were eight points back of front running Kamloops.

By late January Kamloops was still breathing down their necks but the Bruins had their sights set on Saskatoon for first overall. They lost their first game to the Blades 7-5 in Saskatoon but then took the next at home 8-3. It looked to be a homer series until they skated into Saskatoon in late February and took the game 5-2. It gave them a seven point lead on the Blades and they went on to clinch first overall by 16 points.

75/76 New Westminster Bruins **Top Left to Right** Jack Patrick, Rob Anderson, Kevin Schamehorn, Rick Shinske, Miles Zaharko, Randy Betty, Don Hobbins, Allen Fleck, Kevin Krook, Larry Dean **Middle** Doug Sauter, Brian Young, Mark Lofthouse, Harold Phillipoff, Bruce Andres, Barry Beck, Steve Clippingdale, Brad Maxwell, Jake Mitchell **Front** Blaine Peterson, Dr. Peter Wodynski, Stan Smyl, Ernie (Punch) McLean, Clayton Pachal, Bill Shinske, Fred Berry, Dr. Dave Lough, Carey Walker (C. NWMA) **Also suiting up** Richard Martins (goal), Kerry Nesbitt, Lou Daley, Gary Hoium, Terry Hochstetter, Randy Rudnyk, Glen Rawdon, Fred Berry

It was only fitting that Ernie McLean and Bill Shinske should become the first holders of the Scotty Munro Memorial Trophy.

Ernie predicted the team would be high scoring and it came true with a vengeance. Fred Berry and Rick Shinske smashed Lorne Hennings's team scoring record of 113. The team eradicated the old league scoring record of 416 goals by popping in 463. To this they added a new league record 112 points.

They set records for most 50 goal scorers in a season at four, most 40 goal scorers at five and most 30 goals scorers at eight; the last record lasting for 11 years until it was broken by the Kamloops Blazers. They were also catching the eye of Greater Vancouver hockey fans. In their final game of the season 9654 fans turned up at Pacific Coliseum to see them defeat Medicine Hat 5-4.

To these accomplishments were added the coach of the year award to Ernie McLean, goalie of the year to rookie netminder Carey Walker and first all star spot and defenceman of the year to Barry Beck.

But history had shown dominating the regular season was no guarantee of playoff success. Take your opponent too lightly and you're playing golf. It was a lesson the franchise had experienced more than once in Estevan and Humboldt.

Their foe in the quarter finals was Brandon, led by future NHLer Glen Hanlon. Despite Hanlon the Wheaties were major underdogs having ended the season 26 points behind the Bruins.

In game one, before 3148 fans at Queen's Park, the Bruins fired 43 shots on the red head but only managed to squeak out a 3-2 win. After that they had Wheaties for breakfast, taking the next four straight by scores of 9-2, 5-3, 9-4 and 7-4 in the best of nine affair.

Victoria, with Ernie's son Brian in the lineup, was next. The best the Cougars could manage was a 2-2 tie in game three in Victoria. They were finished off at Queen's Park in front of 2986 onlookers. New Westminster was down 2-0 but put in five straight goals in the second to win going away 9-4. The league final came down to the Blades and the Bruins for a second straight year.

It started better than last year as the Bruins stormed out in front of almost 3500 fans to take game one convincingly; 7-0. Steve Clippingdale notched the hat trick. Game two went at Pacific Coliseum in Vancouver and drew out over 7300 fans. Despite being shorthanded 11 times compared to once for the Blades they still took the match 6-3 to go up 2-0 in the series. It was looking good going back to Saskatoon.

The Blades gained sweet revenge. In game one the Bernie Federko, Blair Chapman, Neil Hawryliw line netted 18 points as the Bruins were decimated 10-3. The ref helped out as the Bruins got 21 of the 27 penalties and the Blades got six power play goals. It didn't get any better in game two as the Blades whipped New Westminster again; this time 9-3. Ernie claimed goaltending was hurting them but he was sticking by Carey Walker, the league's best all season.

During the 9-3 loss Ernie reached over to tap a linesman on the head and had his toupee come off in his hands. He quickly dropped it to the ice protesting he had only intended to get the official's attention. He got the league president's attention as well. For the toupee incident he was required to post a $5000 performance bond for the next game. He was also suspended for questioning president Ed Chynoweth.

You couldn't blame Saskatoon fans for feeling a little confident after the last two games. Yet it was the Bruins who charged out in game five and had four unanswered goals in the first period. They were up 7-2 before the Blades managed a furious comeback that fell short at 7-5. They were headed home with a chance to wrap the series up.

Just over 3000 fans were on hand for game six. Rookie Carey Walker had a chance to take the Bruins to the Memorial Cup. Kevin Schamehorn put the home side up 1-0 at 7:26 of the first. The teams played a scoreless second period in which the rookie goalie stopped Federko on a breakaway. A Bruins power play in the third saw Clayton Pachal net the winner. Ron Anderson's slapshot goal at 9:13 added insurance and New Westminster secured the game 3-1. They were western champs for the second straight time and the proud holders of the Athol Murray Trophy.

Losing coach Jackie Macleod credited the Bruins' depth and the play of Rick Shinske as major factors in their success.

They were headed east for the Memorial Cup round robin. This time in the prestigious Montreal Forum. They picked up Glen Hanlon as a reinforcement.

Facing off against the Quebec Remparts in front of 7400 fans they were immediately hit by an injury, during warmup, to goalie Walker. Hanlon came in as backup. Up 2-1 in the first and playing two men short Clayton Pachal outraced Rempart's Gagnon for the puck and put them up 3-1. The Bruins finished their scoring with three seconds left in the first and cruised to a 4-2 victory.

It was the OHL champion Hamilton Fincups they faced next. Penalties proved devastating. The Bruins got seven majors in the first period and were two men short for ten minutes. Hamilton's power play hit for seven goals in an 8-4 victory. The

Fincups earned a bye into the Cup final while the Bruins had to go up against the Remparts again in the semi.

The 8262 fans who turned up had to be pleased when Quebec scored on their first three shots on Hanlon, but the smiles didn't last. The Remparts were blasted 10-3 and the Bruins went on to their second straight Memorial Cup final.

Ernie's squad went into the match trying to stay away from penalties and it took them off their game. The Fincups put on a strong forechecking game, particularly in the second where they outshot New Westminster 21-7, and skated away with a 5-2 cup clinching victory. Hanlon starred in net as the Bruins were outshot 37-22. Surprisingly it was a Bruin, Rick Shinske, who skated away with the tournament "Most Sportsmanlike Player Award." Beck and Harold Phillipoff landed on the tournament all stars.

Three times Ernie and Bill had been to the doorstep and come away with the Bridesmaid award. There were hopes of coming back again next year but they would be hard pressed to ice a team as strong as the 75/76 squad, especially with big player losses.

Five Players went in the draft and none returned. Clayton Pachal put in 35 games over three years with Boston and Colorado. Rick Shinske had three pro years with Cleveland and St. Louis. Fred Berry had a three game stint in Detroit. Steve Clippingdale managed 19 games over two seasons with LA and Washington. Harold Phillipoff enjoyed two solid seasons with the Atlanta Flames out of a four year NHL stint that also included another 23 games with Chicago. Kevin Schamehorn had ten games at the top. Between graduates and NHL call ups the losses were huge.

In the NHL former Estevan Bruins Lonsberry and Joe Watson reached the Stanley Cup final again but this time had to settle for the bridesmaid award as the resurgent Montreal Canadians took the Cup.

The player losses for the Bruins were deep but there remained a nucleus of talent and experience; not to mention the Seventh Man. He was getting tired of waiting on the doorstep.

31

The End of the Rainbow______1976/77

For thirty years the team had been chasing the chalice known as the Memorial Cup. Ernie McLean and Bill Shinske had it come within grasp three times only to taste bitter defeat. Last season they had taken one of the strongest squads ever and still come up short. Though they had lost premier players they remained strong and, should they make it that far, the Cup final was to be hosted in their own backyard at the Pacific Coliseum.

Deals and promising rookies stole the headlines as the season neared. Sheldon Geary and Kevin Krook were sent packing to Calgary for David Orleski, whom Bruin scout Peter Laxton rated as the best midget defenceman in Alberta.

In camp was a sparkling prospect John Ogrodnick along with hopefuls Derek MacDonald, Carl Van Harewyn, John Paul Kelly and Bruce Howes, a New Westminster product. Ernie was impressed enough to suggest the club could be chasing first place for the next five years.

Prospects for a divisional crown were improved with the restructuring of the league into three divisions. They shared the west with Kamloops, Victoria and the new kid on the block, Portland Winter Hawks. The storied Edmonton Oil Kings, purchased by Brian Shaw, pulled up stakes and headed south. Though destined to be a good franchise in their own right Portland never regained the historic hockey dominance the old Oil Kings had once known.

There were 1833 fans on hand for the opener at Queen's Park, where the Bruins decimated the new Winterhawks 10-3.

Next came Kamloops, coached by former Bruin Ivan Prediger. Known for his fiery temper as a player he got in to it with the fans and paid a price. They started bombarding him with paper and he draped a towel over his head in response. In goal for Kamloops was future Blazer assistant coach Brian Henderson. The franchise was not kind to past or future members as the Bruins waxed the Chiefs 11-3.

With highly touted Brandon coming to town in late October the Bruins were battling Kamloops and Victoria for first. They remained undefeated on home ice in the process. The Wheaties featured the outstanding trio of future NHLer's Bill Derlago, Brian Propp and Ray Allison to go along with star goalie Hanlon. The Columbian credited Hanlon and the officials as game stars as the match went 5-1 to the Wheaties. New Westminster took 11 of the 12 penalties.

Making matters worse the Wheat Kings came back to win the next game, also at Queen's Park, 3-2 on the face of Hanlon's 39 saves. It marked the first time the team had lost two home games in a row since April 1975. They fell to third. Tinkering went on. Randy Rudnyk was reacquired from Medicine Hat and in his first game against his old team notched a hat trick in a 9-1 win. The Bruins also reached into Manitoba to pick up prospect Ray Creasy.

In early December the club shutout the Victoria Cougars 6-0 at Queen's Park to take sole possession of first with a game in hand on Victoria.

Kamloops was still in the battle for first but disturbing rumours were spreading the team was to be moved, possibly to Edmonton. The rumours wouldn't go away.

In a late December break Ernie coached the WCJHL entry in a tournament pitting the OHL, Quebec Major League and a Soviet team against each other. The Western squad went undefeated to win the tourney and the LaBatts Cup. Barry Beck was voted the top player.

By mid January the Bruins were running away with their division. The only challenge was to catch Brandon for the overall lead.

Come late January they headed out on an eight game road trip featuring two games in Brandon. Ernie was not optimistic about catching a team that was 15 points ahead, even though they did have six games in hand. The road trip started poorly in Kamloops as Brian Henderson gave the Chiefs their first win over New Westminster, 5-2.

The first Brandon game was better. They went up 1-0 at the end of the first and 4-0 at the end of the second in front of 4750 disappointed fans as they took a 7-3 "upset" victory. Sweet revenge for goalie Blaine Petterson who had been traded last season by the Wheaties. Brandon saved face in the next match by taking a tired Bruins' squad 9-4. The loss all but clinched first overall for the Wheat Kings. The Brandon squad finished with 116 points and surpassed the league record just set by New Westminster the previous season.

On March 9 The Columbian boasted the Bruins had clinched first place in their division. With the season winding down the rumour-plagued Kamloops Chiefs came to town. They had a new coach but the background remained familiar. Former Estevan Bruin Harvey Roy guided his lads to a 4-3 upset win; marking the first time Kamloops had won at Queen's Park in three years and ending the Bruins' 16 game undefeated streak. They wrapped up second place in the process.

The Bruins foes in the first round were the Victoria Cougars; who came in as clear underdogs. Yet with Paddy Ginnel behind the bench there was little chance they would go quietly.

Although the Bruins easily took game one 10-2 Ernie complained Ginnel was using goon tactics. It took an OT goal at 1:06 by Mark Lofthouse to secure a 3-2 win in game two in Victoria. The Cougars never got any closer. The series ended 4-0 for New West when they went into Victoria and took game four 4-1. The fans left a reminder of their feelings for Ernie as he was hit by an egg. At least it was better that the bolt that struck Scotty years earlier in Regina.

They now faced the Portland team that sidelined Kamloops. The Chiefs played their last game in Kamloops and were on their way to Seattle. The Interior city still had a tier two squad, the Braves, but dark days lay ahead for hockey faithful along the banks of the Thompson Rivers. Harvey Roy remained in Kamloops and was not done with the franchise yet.

Over 4000 were on hand at Queen's Park to see their club squeak out a 5-3 win in game one. It was even closer in game two as the Bruins were down 1-0 until 3:26 of the third when Brad Maxwell tied it. New Westminster outshot Portland 14-5 in the third and were eventually rewarded when rookie John Ogrodnick got the winner at 17:34. Final 2-1.

Going into Portland for game three they were without Beck, Maxwell, JP Kelly and Ray Creasy. Doug Derkson, scoring shorthanded, gave them a 2-1 lead in the third but the Hawks tied it to force OT. Stan Smyl was the eventual hero as he put in a rebound from a Dave Orleski shot at 5:16. The Bruins were up 3-0 in the series.

Portland benefited by penalty calls in game four to stave off elimination in front of their home crowd with a 6-1 victory. Down 3-1 they returned to Queen's Park. 4045 fans saw a New

Westminster club that refused to be intimidated by the bigger, stronger Portland side. Mark Lofthouse's hat trick led his squad to a 5-2 series clinching victory and the right to face favoured Brandon.

Brandon twice went ahead in game one in Brandon but twice the Bruins came back to tie. It had to be settled in OT. At 3:22 Smyl stripped the puck from Ray Allison and passed, from behind the Brandon net, to Randy Betty who gave his side the upset 3-2 victory. It was the turning point of the series. Brandon bounced back to take game two 4-1 but the Bruins had taken the game they needed. Home ice advantage was now theirs.

76/77 New Westminster Bruins **Top Left to Right** Doug Sauter, John Paul Kelly, Carl Van Harrewyn, Doug Derkson, Don Hobbins, Randy Rudnyk, Ray Creasy, Larry Dean **Middle** Jake Mitchell, Miles Zaharko, Randy Betty, Jerry Bell, Bruce Andres, Dave Orleski, Mark Lofthouse, Brian Young, Dr. Peter Wodynski **Front** Blaine Peterson, Brad Maxwell, Ernie (Punch) McLean, Barry Beck, Bill Shinske, Stan Smyl, Carey Walker (C. Richard Lapp) **Also suiting up** John Ogrodnick, Louis Clarke, Mike Perovich, Garry Galloway, Roy Wheaton, Derek MacDonald, Steve MacDonald, Mike Wills, Jari Vitalli, Jari Lingren, Larry Lozinski (goal), Rick Greenwood, Greg Rayson, Gerald Mykituk, Frank Nagy, Tero Kapynen, Don Fraser

Over 4000 at Queen's Park saw Randy Betty get three assists in game three as New Westminster skated away 5-2. Game four was tighter and it took until 16:27 of the third, with the Bruins shorthanded, for Don Hobbins to pot the winner in a 6-4 victory. Remarkably the New Westminster Bruins were on the verge of going to the Memorial Cup for the third straight time. But they had to play their next game in Brandon.

On May 4/77 The Columbian headlines screamed "Bruins on Way to Memorial Cup Again". Barry Beck, who had been off most of March with pneumonia, scored the winner in the second after Brandon had initially gone up 1-0 early in the first. Ernie went with Carey Walker in net and could savour beating out the WCJHL coach of the year Dunc McCallum. McCallum complained that his side was intimidated by the Bruins but added they were tame by comparison to other years.

The trip to the Memorial Cup this time was a short bus ride to familiar confines. The Pacific Coliseum was the site for the round robin between the Sherbrooke Beavers, Ottawa 67's and New Westminster. It marked the first time the Cup final had been held in B.C.

Roughly 9160 were on hand for the first match against Ottawa. Ray Creasy, who had just returned from his father's funeral in Winnipeg, contributed four assists as the Bruins held on for a 7-6 victory after having been up 7-4 at one point. On the bad side Stan Smyl was reinjured and joined JP Kelly on the sidelines.

The Beavers took charge of the first period of game two and it was Carey Walker's time to shine. Down 1-0 to start the second the Bruins went to the offence and outshot Sherbrooke 48-14 over the final two frames. 10,154 fans saw Ray Creasy tie the score on a tip in from a Rocky Greenwood shot. 50 seconds later Dave Orleski put them up 2-1. Jere Gillis tied the game in the third but star defenceman Brad Maxwell netted the eventual winner ten minutes after. Doug Derkson got the insurance marker 13 seconds later.

In past years two straight wins would have put New Westminster into the final but the format had been altered. The teams played a double round robin. The Bruins faced the 67's again.

Leading 3-1 late in the third Steve Marengere, with assists from future NHL stars Doug Wilson and Bobby Smith brought the 67's to within one. Kilrea pulled his goalie to try to get the equalizer. They did it and forced overtime. Marengere was the hero again as he gave the 67's the victory at 2:45 of OT. The Bruins could get still to the final if they stopped Sherbrooke.

Beck was a one man wrecking crew. He scored two goals, set up another and broke the nose of Beaver Allen Demers in a fight. Fans got into the act with the Sherbrooke players and two youths had to be escorted from the arena. Lofthouse gave New Westminster a 1-0 lead in the second but the Beavers came back to tie. Walker and three goalposts kept the game tied until Jere Gillis put the Quebecers up 2-1 at 2:27 of the third. Then came "those black seven minutes" for Sherbrooke. Orleski tied it at 5:37 on a rebound from a Beck shot, Ray Creasy banged in the winner at 7:42 and Beck finished off the evening's scoring with a 60 foot slapshot that eluded Sevigny. The Bruins were going to their third straight Memorial Cup final game, a league record since round robin play started in 1972.

The 13460 fans were on hand for the rubber match between Ottawa and New Westminster. It looked good for the Bruins as Creasy and Lofthouse spotted them a 2-0 lead in the first. In the second Bobby Smith tightened the score but Ogrodnick came back to restore the two goal lead. Doug Wilson made it 3-2 but once again New West came back, on another goal by Lofthouse, to restore the bulge. When Zaharko made it 5-2 at 18:19 of the second it looked like the franchise was on its way to its first Memorial Cup.

With the Cup on the line the 67's found renewed energy in the third. Steve Payne made it 5-3 at 3:10 and then Warren Holmes brought them to within one at 4:46. The air went out of the homeside fans at 12:46 when Holmes then tied it on what looked like a routine shot. Shades of game two against the 67's.

But not this time. With just over six minutes left Brad Maxwell picked up the puck behind his own net, raced down the left wing and fired a hard wrist shot at Ottawa goalie Pat Riggins. The puck squirted between the goalie's pads and the Bruins were up again. Maxwell was mobbed by his team mates. This time they did not let the lead slip and the May 16/77 Columbian headline shouted out "Maxwell Lifts Bruins to Memorial Cup."

Thirty one years after the franchise made its first tentative steps in Humboldt, 26 years after Scotty and Ernie first came on board, 18 years after Bill Shinske had joined, nine years after the franchise as the Estevan Bruins made its first Memorial Cup appearance in 1968 and six years after coming to New Westminster the franchise had won it all. Its litany of accomplishments had included everything but the supreme prize and now they had it.

It was a season of honours both for the team and individuals. First in their division, division playoff champs, league champs and Memorial Cup Champs as the best junior hockey team in Canada. Barry Beck and Mark Lofthouse landed on the Memorial Cup all star team. Beck was named the tournament MVP to go along with his WCJHL MVP, Top Defenceman awards and selection to the WCJHL All Stars.

It all finally came together and the New Westminster Bruins etched their name into Canadian Junior Hockey History. With numerous player losses expected for the coming season it would have been easy to see the 76/77 Memorial Cup as the culmination of the dynasty's drive for the ultimate prize.

The twin oaks on defence; Barry Beck and Brad Maxwell, were lost to the pros. Beck's thundering presence in the NHL lasted for nine seasons before injuries cut it short. His stints with Colorado Rockies, New York Rangers and LA Kings saw him skate in the league all star game for five straight years starting in 1978. Brad Maxwell's career spanned ten years, primarily with the Minnesota North Stars, and saw him skate in the 1984 league all star game. Mark Lofthouse skated for five seasons with Washington and Detroit. Miles Zaharko suited up for all or parts of four NHL seasons with Atlanta and Chicago. Also not in the cards for the coming year was Ray Creasy, who was drafted by Vancouver. Randy Rudnyk, Bruce Andres and Carey Walker also went in the draft as the team matched its franchise high nine draftees of 1975.

Gregg Sheppard carried the franchise colours to the Stanley Cup final before his Boston Bruins lost out to the Montreal Canadians.

To think that the Bruins could challenge for another Memorial Cup would seem a bit optimistic; except to the Seventh Man.

32

Crowning Glory 1977/78

Sometimes in this age of super stars we forget hockey is a team game. More than a collection of athletes whose individual talents ensure success. It is the melding together of a group of individuals, coaching and support staff included, to form a cohesive unit whose abilities are more than the sum of its parts. Sometimes the type of team no one picks to be there at the end.

The 77/78 pre season looked to be the harbinger of dark days. Many a team in the WCHL had dreams of knocking off the three time league champs and avenging many a loss. The Bruins went 1-6 against WCJHL clubs and even lost to the BCJHL, Tier II, Penticton Broncos.

Trying to shore up the squad before the season began they had to contend with both Randy Betty and Brian Young lost to injury. They picked up 6'1" Kent Reardon from Billings and then grabbed defenceman Steve Zanatta from Seattle.

The gloating stopped quickly as the Bruins took Victoria 6-5 in the season opener in Victoria and then marched in to Seattle to beat them 5-2. When they played their first game in New Westminster, before a poor crowd of 1912 fans, Brian Young returned from injury and helped them take a 4-3 win over Victoria. After taking Flin Flon next by a convincing score of 9-1 Ernie expressed his pleasure at being in first after pundits had picked them for last.

Still, he and Shinske, saw weaknesses. They continued efforts to secure Bill Hobbins, brother of former Bruin Don, from Portland but Brian Shaw was reluctant to trade with Ernie. He openly stated "I've never made a trade with McLean before. I don't want to look bad the way others have looked after deals with Ernie."

The weaknesses began to show as the undefeated Bruins then went on a five game winless streak punctuated by a 10-3 loss in Seattle, despite the promising play of goalie Larry Lozinski. The return of Carey Walker from the pros gave more hope but the team was still in need of changes. The trades came.

Lozinski was left unprotected and picked up by Flin Flon, although his destiny was yet tied to the gold and black. Zanatta was sent off to Calgary for two players; Steve Savard and a player whose name Ernie was not sure of. He knew only that his nickname was "Candy" and it reminded him of an incident where Scotty lost a player, Derek Haas, to Victoria because he had not spelled his name right on their protected list.

Larry Melnyk, was bought up for a few games from Abbotsford but could not stay with the team in the early going. They added Bill Oleksuk, Neil Meadmore from Flin Flon (for Lozinski) and Terry Kurylic from Calgary.

The manoeuvrings seemed to pay off as the squad was fighting tooth and nail with the other three division teams for first place early in the season. By the time late November rolled around they were alone in first with a 12-7-3 record but facing a difficult eight game prairie road trip. Just like years before with Estevan, illness struck the team on the road. After starting well they went on a six game losing streak leaving them tied for first with Portland but with the Hawks enjoying five games in hand.

Playing their 9th game in 11 nights, the squad, bolstered by pickups from other teams, gave 6200 Pacific Coliseum fans something to cheer about as they beat the touring Moscow Selects 3-2. The Curt Fraser, Stan Smyl, Ryan Walter line accounted for two of the markers.

Back with the regular campaign the road got tougher as Ernie, Smyl and Brian Young were off to join the National Junior Team and Larry Melnyk was lost to injury.

With December winding down the Bruins were the only team in the western division playing under .500 hockey. Seattle and Victoria were close behind with games in hand.

Just before the trading deadline the Bruins managed to pry Bill Hobbins away from Portland and added Larry Jones from Medicine Hat. They promptly went out and beat the Hawks 4-3 at Queen's Park before the largest crowd of the season, only 2293. By January 16/78 they were back to .500 and Ernie was expressing pleasure with his acquisitions as well as promising the Bruins would be there for the Memorial Cup final. How many believed him was another story.

Concerns about Victoria and Seattle began to emerge after two straight losses to Portland saw the Breakers take over second. The Bruins once again fell below .500 and could only take pleasure in some renewed fan support in their 7-6 loss to

Portland in front of 3998 fans, the biggest crowd in two years. Matters got worse in their next game against the Winterhawks.

Playing in Portland Ernie was ejected in the first period after he was accused of punching referee John Fitzgerald when the ref was skating by the bench. He denied the claim and initially asserted it must have been trainer Larry Dean. Dean, for his part denied that he had done anything and added that he couldn't even reach the ref because he was too short.

"My arms are so short I have to jump up to brush my teeth." he claimed.

Portland won the game and the Bruins found themselves in unfamiliar territory. Playing two games under .500 they were now in last place, 4 behind Victoria and 6 behind Seattle. They were in danger of missing the playoffs for the first time in 18 years.

Ernie was given a 25 game suspension as the team looked forward to league leaders Brandon coming to town. Doug Sauter took over behind the bench. They turned around and surprised Brandon 4-2 but then lost their skating legs in an embarrassing 8-5 loss to Billings at Queen's Park. Ernie was moved to comment

"I may have to forbid our guys from watching the Canucks play, even on the tube."

A more than humourous remark given rumours Ernie may become Vancouver's new coach.

He was not one to let a suspension keep him out of the action and so he moved his act to the press box. In a crucial game against visiting Seattle he relayed instructions to Carey Walker who in turn relayed them to coach Sauter. With the Bruins up 2-1 and on the power play he called down to move Van Harewyn off the point and replace him with Smyl who was a better puck handler. The puck went back to Smyl whose point shot was deflected by Bill Hobbins for the winning goal in a 4-2 victory. The "North Enders" noticed Ernie and began chanting "Ernie, Ernie" much to the displeasure of the ref. Still, they were struggling in the basement.

When Randy Betty was released for being over weight and out of condition and Larry Jones was lost to a five game suspension it continued bleak. February brought another eight game road trip. Ernie claimed the team, which had struggled all season on the road, had to play .500 hockey on the trip to have a chance of making the post season. They pulled off a 4-3-1 trip to barely reach their objective but it was enough to pull in to the race.

After a 5-4 victory over Seattle at Queen's Park, despite being down 2-0 and being outshot 39-31, they climbed over Victoria by two points. Back in Seattle they were enjoying a 5-2 lead when the Breakers charged back to tie the critical match. Kent Reardon saved the day with the winner at 18:30. They were tied with Seattle but every game remained pivotal.

Good news came with the return of a better conditioned and motivated Randy Betty along with promising 17 year old Florent Robidoux from Estevan.

With the season coming to a close the last playoff spot, behind runaway leader Portland, was still up for grabs. Seattle had 73 points with three games left, Victoria 69 with five left and New Westminster 71 with six left. The Bruins had three games left with Victoria (who they had not lost to all season on Victoria ice) Medicine Hat and finally their last two games of the season against Portland. No easy road.

They sawed off against Victoria in the first two games but lost the rubber match. Bouncing back to swat Medicine Hat 11-3 at Queen's Park they were in position to determine their own fate. They had to do it in their last two games against Portland. If they could win either one they would be in. Seattle was finished for the season and had 76 points while New Westminster and Victoria each had 75.

The decision came at Queen's Park before 4319 faithful. It started poorly. Down 2-0 Stan Smyl was attacked by the Hawks' Yakiwchuk and bloodied. Goalie Carey Walker came to the "Steamers" aid was ejected for his efforts. Richard Martens took over in net. The Hawks then took four straight penalties. That was all the Seventh Man needed. Terry Kirkham brought them to within one and then Kent Reardon tied it at 8:07 of the second. When Reardon scored again at 15:36 on a breakaway the old barn was in an uproar. Portland came back to tie it and put the fans on their hands but the Bruins were not done. Smyl scored the next two goals, the second by going around star Hawk defenceman Blake Wesley, to give them the win. Doug Derkson added the insurance goal in a 6-4 victory.

The Bruins made it by their very nose hairs.

Portland walked away with the division followed by Victoria and New Westminster tied at 77, one ahead of Seattle. The Cougars were awarded second on the basis of more wins. Even if the Bruins didn't advance past the divisional round robin their season had been a heart stopping exercise in desire, commitment and teamwork.

Jack Shupe of Victoria was dismissive about them.

"With what they have I don't know how we ever lost to them."

His words were answered in game one at Queen's Park where Ernie returned to the bench after serving his 25 game suspension. Led by Scott MacLeod, they were up 5-0 at the end of the second and held on for a 5-3 victory. Game two saw them stop favoured but injury riddled Portland 5-2 before 4189 at Queen's Park. The roll continued as they took on the Cougars in Victoria. JP Kelly, back from an eye injury with a protective face mask, did everything in a 3-2 victory. He hit, killed penalties, played the power play and checked Victoria's big line. He also scored all three Bruin goals.

77/78 New Westminster Bruins **Top Left to Right** Doug Sauter, Terry Kirkham, Larry Melnyk, John Ogrodnick, Randy Irving, John Paul Kelly, Bill Hobbins, Scott MacLeod, Dave Bensmiller **Middle** Larry Dean, Carl Van Harrewyn, Kent Reardon, Larry Jones, Neil Meadmore, Dave Orleski, Boris Fistric, Florent Robidoux, Brian Young, Jamie Nash, Bill Smith **Front** Dr. Peter Wodynski, Richard Martens, Jake Mitchell, Stan Smyl, Ernie (Punch) McLean, Doug Derkson, Bill Shinske, Carey Walker, Jack Patrick (C. Richard Lapp) **Also suiting up** Larry Lozinski, Steve Savard, Bill Oleksuk, Terry Kurylic, Tom Semenchuk, Randy Betty, Ken Berry, Rick Greenwood, Bruce Howes, Evan Williams, Dean Pronyk, Terry Tattam, Jim Dobson, Rick Slawson, Greg Evans, Brad Gauvreau, Craig Williamson, Tom Chisholm, Mike Allison, Darrell Henry, Rob Miller, Ken Berry, David Speer, Randy Carson, Ed Cooper, Glen Johnson, Mitch McCormick, Mike Schamber, Don Stewart, Don Webeniuk

The Bruins pulled off the same magic in Portland despite attempts by the Hawks to intimidate them. They responded with four power play goals and a 5-3 win to go 4-0 in the round robin. Pacific Coliseum hosted the Winterhawk Bruin rematch. 10989 fans turned up. Facing elimination Portland came to play and were enjoying a 4-1 lead before New Westminster began their comeback on power plays. Fittingly, it was "the Steamer" who netted the 5-4 game winner at 9:21 of the third to put Portland on the golf course. Portland's great season ended quickly.

The last three games were meaningless but still saw the Bruins take one each from Portland and Victoria before surrendering the last game 7-3 to the Cougars. They now faced Victoria in a divisional showdown.

In game one in Victoria, despite outshooting the Cougars 50-35, they were shot down 4-3 with the winning goal coming at 19:09. Back at Queen's Park for game two they poured on the shots again, 50 to 25, but this time were rewarded with a 7-4 win. JP Kelly netted the shorthanded winner. They had been down 3-1 at one point. Similarly in game three at Victoria they came back from 4-3 to pull off an 8-4 win. Tom Semenchuk was guarding the net for both wins.

In game four at Pacific Coliseum Scott MacLeod led the way with one goal and four assists en route to an 8-3 win. Up 3-1 in the series they could wrap it up on the Island.

Back on home ice Victoria showed more heart and came from behind themselves to tie the game at three and then go ahead 4-3. David Orleski got the tying marker for the Bruins. Smyl put New Westminster up 5-4 and Terry Kirkham netted the winner at 3:26. The Cougars made it close at 15:57 but the final read 6-5. Shupe had to eat his words. The Bruins were division champs.

Interestingly none of the divisional regular season champs advanced, including power house Brandon. It remained for two second place and one third place teams (New Westminster) to battle it out in the league final round robin.

The home town Bruins faced former team mate Larry Lozinski in the Flin Flon net and fired 78 shots at him before Doug Derkson netted the OT winner at 15:43 in game one. The next match saw them outshoot Dave King's Billings Bighorns 43-33 but still come out on the short end of a 7-4 game. Don Nachbaur with five goals and five Billings' goalposts were the Bruin killers.

Bouncing back they took out Flin Flon before over 10000 at Pacific Coliseum 10-3 and then got revenge against Billings 7-5 at Queen's Park.

Billings eliminated Flin Flon to set up the league final. The round robin had been damaging to New Westminster who saw David Orleski and Florent Robidoux join Carey Walker and Larry Melnyk on the sidelines.

Game one, at Queen's Park, saw the home side take a 5-2 lead and then hang on to win 7-5. Doug Derkson contributed three assists. Game two went to the Bruins 4-0 at Pacific Coliseum and then the venue switched to Billings.

Tied at three going into the third in game three, before 6000 fans, Smyl potted the winner at 7:54. The Bruins won it going away 6-3. One more win and they were headed to the Memorial Cup for an incredible fourth straight time.

Before 3000 fans Billings managed to grab a 1-0 lead and hold it into the third period. New West finally got that one back on a goal by Jim Dobson. Randy Irvine netted the game winner on a pass from, WCJHL rookie of the year, John Ogrodnick. JP Kelly's goal was into an empty net to secure the 3-1 League Championship clinching victory.

The team many had counted out surpassed everyone's expectations except perhaps themselves. They once again hoisted the Athol Murray Trophy as League Champs. Their four straight championships remains unchallenged and the team that eventually came closest years later was to be the same franchise, reborn in Kamloops.

Goalie Larry Lozinski got the chance to put on the black and gold once again as the Bruins picked him up for their title run.

The Cup round robin was shared by Sault Ste. Marie and Sudbury. New Westminster drew the Peterboro Petes in game one, with Garry Green behind the bench. It did not look good. Taking too many penalties they fell 7-4 to a team Ernie proclaimed played a Bruins type of game. He cautioned media not to write the Bruins off just yet.

Game two against the Trois Riviere Draveurs was much better. Smyl enjoyed his most memorable game in his four Memorial Cup appearances with three goals and two assists as his Bruins fashioned a 6-4 victory at the Sault. He had been brought up as an extra from Bellingham during New Westminster's first appearance in 1975 and now skated as team captain.

Once again going up against Peterboro they were still without Florent Robidoux and Dave Orleski. This time they showed better.

They were up 3-1 at 2:55 of the third and it looked like they were on their way to the Memorial Cup final game for an unprecedented 4th straight time. The Petes had other plans and stunned the Bruins with the tying goal at 19:57 to force overtime. The shock was worse when Keith Crowder, on a play which Ernie claimed was offside, netted the 4-3 winner 20 seconds into OT.

A disappointed Bruins squad had to beat Trois Riviere to earn a birth in the final and try to crack the Peterboro armour again. They had come so close.

Instead of being down they came out with a fine effort against the Quebecers. Up 1-0 going into the second they burst out with four goals in 52 seconds starting at 5:49 and opened up a 5-0 lead. The Draveurs mounted a comeback but it was far from enough as New Westminster took the game 6-3 to make Memorial Cup history.

Just like the previous game the Bruins, although being outshot 39-28, were up 3-1 at the end of the first. The Petes began their comeback again and the second period ended 4-3 in favour of the Bruins. The next goal determined the match. Scott MacLeod netted the winner, his third of the game, at 5:38 of the third and the Bruins cruised to a 7-4 cup clinching decision. Smyl contributed one goal and four assists. The Petes argued the winning goal should be disallowed because Ken Berry was in the crease but their cries were in vain. It was poetic justice as the Bruins had their 4-1 goal called back, unfairly according to Smyl, in the previous match.

It was the greatest of accomplishments for a team that lost major stars from the earlier appearances, who had been dismissed at numerous points in the season and who had fought back from the brink of elimination to set an unparalleled WCJHL and CHL record. No matter what they did later in life that achievement would always be a source of pride for themselves and that which they were a part of; the New Westminster Bruins.

Brian Young and Stan Smyl were voted to the All Star team and Smyl added the tournament MVP to his trophy cabinet. Rookie goalie Richard Martins contributed to the victory, a feat later accomplished by the Kamloops Blazers Randy Petruk.

Six players went in the draft including Smyl, Van

Harewyn, Richard Martins, Doug Pearson, Brian Young and Randy Betty. Smyl was off to begin his illustrious career with the Vancouver Canucks. Ken Berry and Brian Young each got in a few games in the Bigs. Van Harewyn and Doug Derkson graduated while Florent Robidoux and Jim Dobson were destined to play in the wrong colours in a game pivotal to the history of the franchise. Both would eventually garner a cup of coffee in the NHL.

In the NHL Greg Sheppard carried alumni colours into the Stanley Cup finals before his Boston Bruins lost out to the Montreal Canadians.

Whatever the future held for the team, the franchise and Ernie nothing could ever diminish the accomplishments.

There were rumours Ernie would not be back. Talk was that he might be the next head coach of the Canucks or, heaven forbid, the Portland Winterhawks. No one could seriously doubt his coaching ability now.

33

The Game 1978/79

Sometimes change comes slowly and sometimes like a thunderbolt.

The 78/79 season started like any other for the Bruins. The euphoria of success still lingered while the job of maintaining a contender had to be done. A core remained.

Two who did not remain were Florent Robidoux and Jim Dobson. They went over to the Winterhawks as part of last years Bill Hobbins trade. Both they and the Portland side were to figure prominently in the Bruins' future.

Doug Sauter was off to coach the Calgary Wranglers, crediting his success to his mentor Ernie McLean, but word was Richard Martins may be back.

League changes had the once powerful Flin Flon Bombers pulling up stakes and becoming the reborn Edmonton Oil Kings.

Winning their first two games of the season the Bruins headed to the unfriendly confines of Portland. They were swacked 11-1 to start a difficult and hostile campaign against their arch rivals. In the early going the teams were running a homer season and vying for first but as the campaign progressed the Hawks pulled away.

Ernie got to enjoy some big nights. In mid December he saw his squad, bolstered by eight pickups, handily down the visiting Moscow Selects 7-2 before 12650 at Pacific Coliseum. He then went on to coach the Canadian Junior squad whose roster included none other than a phenom named Wayne Gretzky.

Back in the WCJHL things remained hot for the Bruins. Both Ernie and Bill were fined $1000 for a fracas at Queen's Park during a Portland game. Ernie's was going on the ice to admonish the Portland goalie and Bill's for doing the same to the ref.

Difficulties were beginning to show however as the

Bruins were even having trouble winning at home where they were running up their worst record in eight years. The greatest home highlight, though, had to be a 2-0 victory over the Brandon Wheat Kings who had iced one of the strongest squads to ever skate in the WCJHL. They racked up a still unbroken season record of 125 points and suffered only five losses all season.

Unfortunately they could not do the same against the Portland squad destined to run up 111 points. The Hawks were winning at every turn both in Portland and at Queen's Park. It all came down to a culmination in mid March at Queen's Park. The echoes of that evening reverberated for months and spelled the beginning of the end of the New Westminster Bruins.

For years there had been bench clearing brawls, in which neither Portland nor New Westminster had been innocent. The history of the league was full of players, coaches and even general managers getting suspended, fined and required to post performance bonds. Season long rivalries had often led to bench clearing brawls. This time it was different.

The last ten minutes of the match got ugly and a fight ensued. The Bruins jumped over the boards expecting, as had been the norm, the Hawks would as well. Not this time. Hodge, for whatever reason, held his players back and the fight became an ugly assault of a whole team upon the six Hawks on the ice. Both Blake Wesley and, of all people, Jim Dobson, were severely beaten and had to be taken to the hospital. Seven Bruins received majors and game misconducts.

The after effects echoed long afterwards. At first Ernie blamed the fight on referee Gregson and four years of not getting a fair shake from officials. He felt that the fight was inevitable but had no idea Hodge would hold his players back.

Sixteen years before a similar incident had occurred with Scotty behind the bench in Estevan when his Bruins charged over the boards but the Moose Jaw coach held his players back. It was different this time and consequences extended beyond the league.

A later interview had Ernie accepting the blame for what happened and asserting it was not the players' fault. The consequences began to follow.

Eight players received suspensions of from three to five games while Ernie was suspended indefinitely. The season closed with the Bruins in 3rd place going into a round robin versus Victoria and Portland. On a brighter note they still set a league record for straight plus .500 seasons at nine.

A sinister cloud hung over the club and Ernie. It was darker than ever before.

The playoffs started with criminal charges pending.

After making a public apology he mused " If I feel that I'm the cause of it, if I feel the players are doing it for me, because of my philosophy then my only recourse is to get out of it."

78/79 New Westminster Bruins **Top Left to Right** Bill Stewart, Rick Amann, Pat McGill, Todd Semeniuk, Kent Reardon, Anthony McMurchy, Larry Melnyk, Scott MacLeod **Middle** Jack Patrick, Larry Dean, Randy Wickware, Doug Hall, Bruce Howes, Dave Orleski, Neil Meadmore, Rob Roflik, Boris Fistric, Andrew Ristau, Rick Slawson, George Crookshank, Mickey Willgress, Jamie Nash, Bill Smith **Front** Tom Semenchuk, Dr. Peter Wadynski, John Ogrodnick, Ernie (Punch) Mclean, John Paul Kelly, Bill Shinske, Bill Hobbins, Les Jackson, Richard Martens (C. NWMA) **Also suiting up** Randy Irving, Terry Kirkham, Rob Clavette, Jeff Kirton, George Crookshank, John Dobson, Barry Hill, Ron Dunnville, Curtis Issell, Ian Ramsay, Raalph Krueger, Brad Mammel, Pat Masiuk, Duane Swanson

Game one went to Victoria 6-4 on the Island and game two was a 9-2 drubbing by the Hawks at Pacific Coliseum before only 3503. A total of 2136 fans turned up at Queen's Park to see the Bruins come to life with 5-2 win over Victoria but the next match, in Portland, saw them again handled easily, this time 8-3. They took nine of 12 penalties handed out.

Word came in The Columbian on April 4/79 that Bill and Ernie had put the team up for sale. They were both upset at the media for focussing on the Bruins when there had been 10 major brawls in the league that season and for holding Portland blameless in the incident.

Perhaps the word put a burr under the saddle of the players for their performance improved. They came back to take Victoria 4-3 before taking 16 of 20 penalties in a 4-3 overtime loss to Portland. The shades were coming down. They lost the next two and a dark cloud closed over them.

Five players went in the draft. John Ogrodnick moved on to a sensational 14 year career with Detroit, Quebec and the New York Rangers where he racked up over 400 goals, was picked to the first string all stars in 1985 and played in five all star games. Dave Orleski managed a couple games in the colours of the Montreal Canadians. Boris Fistric, Larry Melnyk and JP Kelly were all taken but hopes were that they would be back.

New Westminster grad Ron Greschner got to the Stanley Cup finals with the New York Rangers only to see the Seventh Man's favourite pro team, the Montreal Canadians, skate away with the Cup.

On May 8/79 the paper reported a trial date had been set for seven Bruin players and Ernie McLean. The implications were ominous.

34

Twilight________________1979/80

The Sun did not rise again. The 79/80 season proved the darkest in franchise history since its formative years in Humboldt.

Criminal charges led to conditional discharges but Bill and Ernie were faced with seven players suspended for the first two months of the season. JP Kelly never returned as he was picked up by the LA Kings and skated in their colours for seven campaigns. Boris Fistric was eventually traded to Brandon and Bill Hobbins ended up in Calgary.

Without his "Black Aces" and suffering a media feeding frenzy the team's on ice performance deteriorated to the point they were the league whipping boys. Were it not for the pathetic play of the Great Falls Americans, which had come over from Edmonton and who never even finished the season, they would have been dead last in the league.

Despite the dire straits it seemed the officials were continuing to take their pound of flesh from the humbled Bruins. Ernie's statements that some people would like it if he were drummed out of the league seemed to gain some credibility.

In their 10th straight loss former Bruin Florent Robidoux tallied three goals against his old squad in a 6-3 decision. Robidoux went on to play parts of three seasons with the Chicago Black Hawks. The drought went on for thirteen games before they finally got their first point. A 5-5 tie in Great Falls Montana.

By November attendance was hovering around 1600 when the team needed 2500 to stay solvent. Other teams circled like vultures trying to pick up members of the Black Aces at sale prices. Even the return of some of the suspended players did not help much.

February 1980 saw Tracy Pratt behind the bench while Ernie went back east on a scouting trip. Pratt noted the change in the Big Bad Bruins - no drive, no hustle.

Rumours abounded. Talk was offers had come in from Winnipeg and even San Francisco. A Winnipeg group headed by one time Regina Pat, Fran Huck, who had delighted Estevan fans when he joined the Saskatchewan champs in their battles for the Memorial Cup, was seen as having a 50/50 chance of grabbing the club and moving it back east.

Bill Shinske was expressing his displeasure with the team's treatment by the other owners since the Portland game and spoke about wanting to get out. The fans were none too pleased either. In one home game against Portland, where they were decimated 13-2, some 500 fans stayed afterwards watching the ref, Wheeler, skate around until he could get a police escort out of the arena.

Ernie was not above getting in a few laughs though. With Portland in a heated battle for first against Victoria, the Cougars were at Queen's Park. Portland had lost to Seattle and Shaw had called to see how the Bruins/Cougars game was going. Ernie

79/80 New Westminster Bruins **Top Left to Right** Al Nixon, Mark Didcott, Brad Yachimec, Marc Chartier, Rene Vandriel, Dave Bourne, Bill Smith **Middle** Larry Dean, Don Sylvester, Anthony McMurchy, Andrew Ristau, Rob Roflik, John Winter, Daryl Stanley, Randy Wickware, Rick Amann, Jack Patrick **Front** Tom Muc, Tracey Pratt, Pat McGill, Ernie (Punch) McLean, Larry Melnyk, Bill Shinske, Bill Hobbins, Jim Gardner, Geoff Murdoch (C. NWMA) **Also suiting up** Brian Harland (goal), Doug Kostynski, Bruce Howes, Jack Wright, Jeff Rupert, Jeff Taylor, Paul Mathews, Luc St. Mars, Mark Vinet, Darrel Leahy, Dan London, Colin Lundrigan, Mike Johnson, Petrie Kangerva, Doug Fomenko, Ken Duncan, Doug Allison, Jim Crosson, Rory Delouise, Dan Deschenes, Ron Dunnville, Larry Dyck, Dan Early, Larry Mollard, Steve Gagon, Brian Inkster, Curis Issell, Stu Orpen, Stu Robertson, Perry Soper told him that he had just thrown a trash can on to the ice and the Bruins had received a double minor. Of course it hadn't happened and the Bruins were in fact on their way to one of their few victories of the season; 3-2.

The season came to a merciful end. The Bruins had skated their worst ever campaign at 10-61-1 for 23 points. Needless to say they were out of the playoffs. It had not happened since the 1959/60 season in Estevan.

New Westminster players experienced the revenge of teams who had long suffered at their hands and who now enjoyed their dog days. One young rookie, Doug Kostynski, who only skated in 11 games, was to see the resurgence of the franchise and the beginning of the next coming. The Seventh Man was only on a holiday and he would be back with a point to make.

Only one player, Tom McMurchy, was picked in the NHL draft.

Franchise pride was carried in the NHL by Lorne Henning and Gordie Lane who hoisted the first of four straight Stanley Cups by the New York Islanders.

Ernie and Bill had had enough and the end of the season brought with it word Nelson Skalbania had bought the team for his 20 year old daughter, Rozanda, for the sum of $325,000. Tracy Pratt took over as General Manager and hired former Sault Ste. Marie coach Muzz MacPherson, who had gained fame as Wayne Gretzky's junior coach. Ernie remained involved scouting new players for the following season. Bill Shinske eventually found his way back to Estevan where he once again became involved with the Bruins; the Estevan Bruins of the Saskatchewan Junior Hockey League. He had come full circle but was to have one last handshake with the Seventh Man before he left.

One bright star in the season was Larry Melnyk, who went on to play all or parts of nine NHL seasons with four different clubs and get his name etched on the Stanley Cup with the 84/85 Edmonton Oilers. Former Bruin Doug Sauter earned WCJHL coach of year honours with the Calgary Wranglers.

Ernie remained in the Lower Mainland and continued to keep his fingers in the hockey scene. He even made a come back with the reborn New Westminster Bruins that had once been Scotty's own Calgary Centennials. It went on to become the Tri City Americans who in turn captured another ex New Westminster and Kamloops alumni, Don Hay, as their bench boss.

For now that same Don Hay was the player coach of the only major hockey act in Kamloops; the Kamloops Cowboys of the Interior Intermediate A hockey league. Kamloops had lost their Tier Two Rockets of the BCJHL in December of 1979; coincidentally to Revelstoke, the farm team of the New Westminster Bruins.

The franchise was in its darkest days and the hockey faithful of Kamloops were pining for top flight hockey. Their paths were soon to cross and in ways that no one would have expected.

It is darkest before the dawn.

35

On The Road Again________1980/81

It was truly a season like no other. There was no Scotty Munro, no Ernie McLean and no Bill Shinske and, so it seemed, no Seventh Man.

Ernie and Bill had shared the franchise's greatest heights and struggled at its lowest ebb. From team mates in Estevan to the powers behind a squad that set an unparalleled record for four straight Memorial Cup final appearances. Ernie had filled virtually every position on the team from player through trainer, assistant coach, bus driver, coach and owner. It seemed impossible but now they had moved on. What legacy there was skated in the players Ernie and Bill had scouted, including young Doug Kostynski.

And so the franchise began its 10th and last year in New Westminster. It shared the western division with the new Spokane Flyers, the former Flin Flon Bomber franchise.

GM Tracy Pratt promised a faster smaller team behind bench boss Muzz MacPherson. MacPherson was characterized as being very much like Ernie and in a Columbian article in November made the point of claiming Ernie had been persecuted in the WCJHL. Despite the comparisons it was not the same. The season played out like a death march save for a sudden twist of fate near the end and a surge showing the franchise, though down, still had character.

It opened well as the new-look Bruins stunned Portland 5-4 in OT at Queen's Park. Newly acquired John Neeld from Seattle notched three goals in the comeback from a 4-2 deficit and Trav Gibson nailed down the winner before 1695 fans. By Oct. 8/80 they were sporting a 3-1-0 record and things looked good. Then the wheels began to come off.

Later that same month they were humbled 9-0 in Portland and then 13-0 in Victoria. The Cougars, proving it was no fluke, came back and thumped them again 12-4.

On Nov. 13/80, after a 7-4 loss to Winnipeg at Queen's Park before only 750 onlookers, the paper claimed a fan leaned over to tell the coach they would be playing before 100 fans by February. Embarrassing losses continued as they struggled for the fourth and final playoff spot with Spokane. Attendance suffered. New Westmisnter fans were not accustomed to supporting a losing team, especially if it no longer had Ernie as a drawing card.

The final embarrassment came in two parts in late January 1981. Spanked 12-3 at Queen's Park by Doug Sauter's Calgary Wranglers they found themselves at 13-29-1 and hanging on to fourth. Even worse, it proved to be the last game the New Westminster Bruins ever played at the storied old arena. Talk a CUPE strike would shut down play in the barn became more than that. The suitcase-Bruins became gypsies as their home games ranged throughout the Province and even down to the States. One stop in particular took on unique meaning.

The Bruins were swatted 13-4 in Trail by Portland. Tracy Pratt was incensed at how the once intimidating Bruins were manhandled by the Portland Winterhawks. Three players had their noses broken and one lost four teeth. No Portland players or management faced criminal charges or suspensions.

Then came the game with a meaning none would have guessed at the time. The suitcase squad played their next home game at Memorial Arena in Kamloops. A venue that, from the early 60's, had been anything but supportive of New Westminster teams.

MacPherson's club, sporting thirteen rookies, took to the ice against Brandon before 900 fans, despite the fact the NHL all star game was on the tube. The Kamloopsians adopted their temporary team with unexpected fervour. Kamloops Daily News reporter Mike Reimer commented that

"Most encouraging was the fan reaction whenever the Bruins scored. No one in the Press Box could remember the last time a Kamloops' crowd cheered a New Westminster team."

Veteran CFJC announcer, Earl Seitz, who used to call the old Chiefs' games and who was now calling the game back to Brandon, added,

"I've never seen it nor has Adam."

It would have been storybook stuff if the young Bruins had taken a victory. As it was Brandon thumped them 12-4; scoring seven goals in the last period. Future Kamloops Junior Oiler Trav Gibson got two of the New Westminster markers.

The team packed up its suitcases and moved on with no suggestion the team was even considering moving much less considering Kamloops. Word had it Kamloops was in line for another team but eyes were turned towards Spokane, the Billings Bighorns and even a return by the Seattle Breakers. There was even serious consideration of the professional farm team of the Vancouver Canucks, the Phoenix Road Runners, taking their act to Kamloops. New Westminster was not in the cards.

The losing streak ran to 25 games and remained a league record until the hapless 1989 Cougars took over the dubious distinction. When it ended in a 7-4 win in Spokane the squad was forced to win a "home" game in Trail against visiting Seattle if they hoped to have a chance of making the playoffs. They had not played a home game in Queen's Park for eight weeks and the coach was lamenting the lack of practise time.

The character remained and the club stung Seattle 7-4. The season all came down to a tie breaker game against the Spokane Flyers at Trail.

There were 804 fans turned out to see the Bruins, who had been down 9-6, come back to tie the game three times before it was finally sent into overtime. The tying goal came on a power play after Spokane's Zemlak was caught with an illegal stick. The teams played tight until there were only six seconds left in the ten minute overtime. Doom struck New Westminster at 9:54. Spokane's Mark Sochatsky scored the winner.

It ended the season and the existence of the famed New Westminster Bruins.

They improved by 14 points over their dismal showing of a year before but they were still tied for last place overall in the league. It looked a long way up from where they were and the support in New Westminster was not enough to see them through. Skalbania was not going to hang on to a money loser.

When the ice chips settled the following season the franchise hung on to only five players from their final New West season. Trav Gibson, Ron Amyotte, Doug Thompson, Larry Bumstead and in particular Doug Kostynski, were to experience the rebirth. Bright prospects Daryl Stanley, who played six NHL seasons with Philadelphia and Vancouver, and goalie Mike Zanier, who managed three games in an Edmonton Oiler uniform, did not want to remain with the franchise and moved on.

No players were taken in the NHL entry draft and the

franchise had to content itself with its alumni Lorne Henning and Gordie Lane hoisting their second Stanley Cup with the New York Islanders.

The last three seasons had been little more than a foot note for the power that was. In its ten years in New Westminster it had won the league four times and captured the Memorial Cup twice while making the playoffs in all but its last two tumultuous seasons. It had carved its way into junior hockey legend.

The Seventh Man impressed himself in Estevan and New Westminster not just through the efforts of Ernie and Bill but also with a strong supporting cast. The scouting staff highlighted by Larry Berg, Jake Mitchell, Bill Proskiw and Peter Laxton had been part of a perceptive farm system that garnered both the talent and character necessary to build junior hockey dynasties. In the end it took external forces to pummel the franchise into submission after it had proven impossible for it to be done on the ice.

If the franchise had faded into mediocrity with the occasional run for the roses they would still have had a legendary past to harken back to. What was to, in fact, happen was beyond anyone's wildest expectations. The Seventh Man was to return like thunder.

80/81 New Westminster Bruins (Unfortunately no photo available) Roster included Daryl Stanley, Ron Amyotte, Trav Gibson,Mike Zanier, Doug Kostynski, Muzz MacPherson (coach), Tom Semenchuk (goal), John Neeld, Anthony McMurchy, Brian Ingram, Dennis Labbe, John Strait, Randy Wickware, Larry Bumstead, Mike Winther, Randy Slawson, Rick Amann, Duane Potekal, Chuck Taylor, Doug Thompson, Bob Becker, Doug Barnes, Marc Ducharme, Dan Hill, Rod Jamieson, Joe Lesuk, Pat Murray, Clay Nygaard, Gord Padalec, Rick Rivard, Rick Siemens, Rob Wheelans, Daryl Wouters, Wayne Frenette, Ron Dunville, Mike Fournier, Steve Gagon, Stu Orpen, Sandy Sullivan

36

PART FOUR
KAMLOOPS

Home, Home on the Range____1981/82

The history of the white man at the meeting of the waters is older than any of the previous homes of the franchise. In 1811 fur traders established a post at the confluence of the North and South Thompson, long the home of the Shuswap Nation. The community grew ever so slowly during the years of the fur trade, gold rush and ranching eras but with the coming of the railway in the 1890's things began to change.

One of those changes was the arrival of that eastern sport; ice hockey.

Kamloops' fickle winters made for inconsistent ice conditions which put it at a disadvantage with its neighbours. When word came in 1947 that artificial ice had a home at the old bull sale arena the Sagebrush City quickly made up for lost time.

Artificial ice brought Senior hockey, led by players who had come from the east or the Prairies. Ex Humboldt Indians Jimmy Van Buskirk, "Moose" McNaughton, Art Asleson, Al Pyatt, Larry Berg and even Dick Warwick of the famed Warwick brothers came to skate for the Senior Elks or Chiefs. More than a few stayed on and contributed their skills and knowledge to a burgeoning minor hockey system. One of these was Andy Clovechok, former member of the Edmonton Allan Cup Champions of the 40's.

Connections with New Westminster began at the outset when Kenny MacKenzie brought his professional New Westminster Royals to the new Kamloops Memorial Arena for training camp in 1949 and had the honour of his team playing the first match in the new building; a tie with the Seattle Ironmen. In less than a decade he was back as the owner and manager of the Kamloops Senior A Chiefs.

The minor hockey system began producing championship junior squads by the early 60's and, more often than not, the provincial battles were with the New Westminster Royals at Kamloops' Memorial Arena and New Westminster's famed Queen's Park. The 1963 Rockets sported Ron Recchi, uncle of present day NHL star Mark Recchi. Bert Marshall became the first local to make it to the NHL.

That talent pool found its way to the franchise in Estevan with the likes of Don Newman, Jim Letcher and most notably Jimmy Harrison; who carved out a stellar pro career and established a Guinness World Record for most points in a professional hockey game. Local teams coached by former Senior A players Kenny Stewart, Buddy Evans and Andy Clovechok grabbed provincial titles at every level.

The seventies brought a change in junior hockey as teams began adding imports to their squads. Scotty Munro purchased the Rockets as an affiliate for his Calgary Centennials. Future pros started to make their way through Kamloops with the likes of Bob Nystrom, Gary Howatt, Andy Moog, Curt Brackenbury, Wayne Bianchin, Tim Hunter and locals Randy Rota and ill fated Don Ashby.

The seventies also brought the first head to head competition between Kamloops and its future franchise when Ernie McLean's Bruins came calling. Kamloops connection with the franchise went as deep as family roots as both Ernie's son Brian and Bill Shinske's son Rick skated in Rocket's colours.

When Kamloops got its own Tier I team, the Chiefs, it drew future NHLer's Regg Kerr, Ryan Walter, Barry Melrose and Errol Rausse and even had future Bruins star Barry Beck put in a game in Kelly Green. The local flavour was maintained by NHL bound Tim Watters. One of Kamloops' favourite sons, Don Hay, was cut by the Chiefs only to turn up on the franchise he eventually coached; the New Westminster Bruins.

It all came crashing down when the team departed for Seattle and the community had to settle for Tier II hockey. With the likes of Andy Moog and a local star with two Stanley Cups in his future, Doug Lidster, there was clearly some good hockey being played. Yet even that failed and the team departed for Revelstoke part way through the 1979/80 season.

What was left was the Intermediate A Kamloops Cowboys with player coach Don Hay and a host of locals whose resumes included stints at varying pro levels, including the NHL. Despite talent and entertaining hockey they played to poor crowds. Kamloops' hockey faithful were still reeling from their fall from hockey's graces.

So came together a storied franchise suffering its worst years and a hockey town pining for top level hockey. It proved a marriage made in hockey heaven.

Ex-Estevan Bruin Harvey Roy was the prime mover in trying to recapture a junior franchise for Kamloops. The best hopes seemed pinned upon struggling franchises in Billings, Spokane and even Seattle. The Bruins were not in the picture. That all changed in June of 1981.

Peter Pocklington, owner of the Edmonton Oilers, purchased the franchise from Skalbania and was intent on moving it. Red Deer Alberta and Prince Albert Saskatchewan were high on his priority list until Roy and the sports media from Kamloops came calling. But it would take more than talk to convince Pocklington to consider Kamloops; it took money. Local interests were expected to come up with $110,000 to purchase 33% of the franchise.

Roy contacted Andy Clovechok and the wheels were set in motion by pulling together a committee of influential Kamloopsians. Gary Cooper, Colin Day, Ken Almond and Loy Hoffbeck joined Andy and Harvey. Together, with media fanning the flames of local enthusiasm, the team took on the challenge.

Volunteers hit the pavement and the phone lines and on July 2, 1981 it became official; Kamloops was back in the WHL; ironically with New Westminster and Edmonton figuring in its arrival, both communities which played big roles in the history of Kamloops hockey and the franchise.

Kamloops 33% ownership granted them three board members but little say in the club's operation. Still that 33% was to prove valuable in the not to distant future. Local lawyer Dennis Coates was a major player in putting the plan together and negotiated a key "shotgun" clause in the contract with Pocklington that had profound implications in the near future. His connection with the franchise ran deep as a long time close friend of both Scotty Munro and Ernie McLean.

Harvey Roy came on as GM accompanied by Joe Arling as Director of Hockey Operations, Gordie Hahn as trainer and former NHL'er Lyle Moffat as coach. Five former Bruins suited up for the reborn squad. Doug Kostynski, who had originally been scouted by Ernie McLean, was given the captain's C and witnessed the return of the Seventh Man.

Joe Arling sounded an odd note in writing off the franchise's tradition with training camp impending.

"For such a long time that black and gold represented a winning philosophy from Estevan to New Westminster to Memorial Cups. But the last two years it's really been lost. They once had an aura about them but now its lost. For the players that's a good point. They come here with the air clear."

Not words to sit lightly with the Seventh Man.

Its easy to understand how Arling saw the benefits from last season. They were tied for last place and earned first crack at available overagers.

The community was excited too as 500 seasons tickets were sold even before the official seasons ticket campaign of the Kamloops Junior Oilers began.

Locals Colin Meissner and Eric Samuelson made the initial squad and locals Robbie Kossan and Mark Ferner were later picked up in trades. Significant player moves were in the cards.

After falling 4-2 in their season opener they awaited their home opener, fittingly, against Portland. The favoured Hawks, who played an indirect role in the team coming to Kamloops and who last played at Memorial Arena in 1977, when they beat the Kamloops Chiefs 5-1 to end their season and existence, roared out to a 4-1 lead by 6:18 of the second before 2700 disappointed fans. It was not yet time for a full return but the Seventh Man was on the bench that night.

By 16:50 the Junior Oilers were back to within one and out shooting the Hawks. Pouring it on in the third David Kromm knotted the score to force overtime.

At 4:47 of OT the crowd erupted. Former Bruin Doug Thompson took a pass from former Bruin Ron Amyotte and rifled a shot from the right point beating Darrell May for the 5-4 victory. They outshot Portland 38-28 and former Bruins figured prominently. Kostynski netted two assists, Amyotte a goal and assist and Thompson a goal and an assist. It was shades of the Seventh Man in the opening game of the Estevan Bruins at the AA in 1957 against visiting Regina.

One win does not a season make and the team struggled to surpass last season's slight improvement.

On December 5/81 the Daily News reported the Spokane

Flyers had folded. Holding on to last place the Junior Oilers were given first dibbs on players. Steve Bull and Mark Sochatsky were acquired along with a player destined to etch his name on the franchise and Kamloops hockey history. Dean Evason became the jump start that exploded Kamloops into the junior hockey prominence that continues to this day. The Flin Flon franchise that had been the Seventh Man's greatest rival faded into history but left a parting gift for his rebirth.

At the time such prominence seemed anything but likely.

On December 9/81 Lyle Moffat was replaced by Ron Harris. It made little difference nor did a host of trades. It was tough to attract and keep players in a rebuilding year. A far cry from Scotty's comment in Estevan that everybody wanted to join the team.

On December 14/81 the paper noted the addition of Czech star Jan Ludvig. The first junior defector out of the Czech Republic gave the fans plenty to cheer about and helped to boost much needed attendance.

Good news was not totally lacking as Evason and Kostynski both landed on the all stars and the Junior Oilers gave front running Portland headaches. In their last three regular season meetings the Hawks fell three straight to a crew that finished 47 points behind them giving some hope for the playoffs; or so it seemed.

The hopes were in vain as Portland regained its form and swept the upstarts in four straight on their way to the Memorial Cup. The Junior Oilers had managed to improve on last season's point total by two.

At the teams' award dinner in April Doug Kostynski was awarded the Cyril Day Trophy as the teams' MVP; Trav Gibson the Rick Anderson Award as the unsung hero; 16 year old Richard Hajdu the Derek Black Trophy (named after the Kamloops player whose untimely death from cancer stopped his rise to the pros); Ken Goodwin the Elroy Sports award as the top defenceman; Jan Ludvig the Vern Seaman's Award as rookie of the year and Dean Evason the teams' top scorer award. Both the old faces and the new were well represented.

Promising Jan Ludvig was already off to the Wichita Wind in the CHL playoffs and not fated to return. His destiny gave him seven seasons in the NHL with New Jersey and Buffalo before he hung up his skates and returned to live in Kamloops. He proved to be one of many Blazers or Junior Oilers who made Kamloops their home.

Not a single player was drafted and the franchise had to content itself with former Bruins Gordie Lane and Lorne Henning (as assistant coach) etching their names on the Stanley Cup with the New York Islanders. Stan "the Steamer" Smyl got to the final round with Roger Neilson's "white towel waiving" Vancouver Canucks. A future Junior Oiler, Garth Butcher, then with the Regina Pats, also made his NHL debut in the same playoffs.

There was to be another contribution from the Regina Pats who was to be the next peace of the puzzle.

The bad years were coming to an end.

1981/82 - First Year of the Kamloops Junior Oilers (Unfortunately no photo available) Roster included - Doug Kostynski, Larry Bumstead, Doug Thompson, Ron Amyotte, Colin Meissner, Eric Samuelson, Bill Ansell, Mark Ferner, Robbie Kossan, Taylor Hall, Rob Beckner, Bill Vince, Jeff Fenton, Fred Ledlin, Darryl Murray, Richard Hajdu, David Kromm, Sonny Sodke, Bob Wensley, Gary Stewart, Calvin Boyle, Jim Vanderlee, Ron Propp, Brad Armitage (goal), KenGoodwin, Cam Sebastian, Steve Bull, Dean Evason, Jan Ludvig, Lyle Kjernstad, Barry Brigley, Mike McLea, Paul Cloutier, Tracy Chapman, Sean Oswald (goal), Mike Sturgeon, Gary Holoway (goal), Helmo Brandstatter, Lyle Moffatt (coach), Rick Harris (coach), Troy Taylor, Darcy Lepine, Mike Dreger

37

But for the Pros, Who Knows_1982/83

82/83 brought to an end three years of struggling and, save for two NHL squads, prospects the ultimate goal could have been reached.

It looked reasonably good from the beginning as returnees included captain Doug Kostynski, Ron Amyotte and rising star Dean Evason. They were joined by a host of bright hopefuls including Doug Bodger and Greg Evtushevski. In December hard working Dean Clark was added to the lineup. One of the most dynamic additions was the new coach and GM, former Regina coach, Bill Laforge. He was to leave a deep imprint on players and team alike.

Two important trades brought promise and disappointment.

Early in the season Gary Stewart was traded for the rights to former Saskatoon Blade and Edmonton Oiler draft pick Marc Habscheid. Though not keen at the prospect of returning to junior hockey, Habscheid had the star quality a team could build on. On the down side it made captain Doug Kostynski expendable and he was shipped, along with three others, to Brandon for Vancouver draft pick Bruce Holloway, goalie Jim Campbell and Francis Matechuk. A disappointed Kostynski was not through with Kamloops quite yet though.

Habscheid, reluctant as he was, exploded on to the scene as he garnered one goal and three assists in his first game; a 10-3 thrashing of the new Kelowna Wings team. Reporters raved the likes of his talent had not been seen on Kamloops' ice before.

By early November the team was rated # 1 in Canada and gazing back at all the others. It got even better as veteran Kostynski, disheartened in Brandon, nixed a move to Portland and was regained in a trade sending Ed Palichuk east.

With a season record of 15-1, a home record of 10-0 and a rejuvenated lineup the squad was set to face the season favourite Winterhawks at Memorial Arena in a pivotal match.

A 10-8 loss was bad enough but the loss of Habscheid, who was knocked unconscious by Portland's Doug Saunders, was much worse. In only six games he amassed 23 points with no sign he was likely to let up. A major cog in the Junior Oilers hopes to reach the Memorial Cup he never skated in team colours again. When he regained his health he suited up as an Edmonton Oiler and the "who knows what might have been" question was left unanswered.

The junior star still had Kamloops in his destiny. Years later he rejoined the squad as a coach and almost took them to the Memorial Cup himself before losing out to former team mate Dean Clark's Calgary Hitmen. In the interim he patched together an NHL career of ten years with four different teams.

82/83 Kamloops Junior Oilers **Top Left to Right** Brad Melin, Robin Bawa, Steve Bull, Jim Camazzola, Richard Hajdu, Tony Vogel, Greg Evtushevski **Middle** Vern Smith (Business Mgr.), Doug Saunders, Deno Vulpitta, Dean Clark, Doug Bodger, Gord Mark, Doug Kostynski, Todd Davoren (assistant) **Front** Bill Laforge (Coach & GM), Jim Campbell, Lyle Kjernisted, Mark Ferner, Martin Wood, Dean Evason, Bruce Holloway, Dave Ross, Ron Coleman (asst. coach & trainer) (C. Doris Rubel) **Also suiting up** Marc Habscheid, Garth Butcher, Ron Amyotte, Darryl Murray, Jeff Fenton, Stacey Wakabayashi, Kevin Plypow, Gary Stewart, Byron Lomow, Allan Tarasuk, Mike Sturgeon, Denis Leclair, Sean Oswald (goal), Jay Zeidel, Tod Ewen, Ed Palichuk, Francis Matechuk, Fritz Maieir, Ben Proskiw, Ron Viglasi, Ken Trousdel, George Crawford, Dan Latin, Gavin Shuya

With Habscheid's departure his co billet Dean Clark took his place on the roster. Ironically Laforge traded for Doug Saunders the day after he levelled Habscheid.

By mid-December Kamloops had fallen to third; much to the dismay of demanding coach Laforge. Despite being plagued with injuries and illness he was not satisfied with player output. That did not include rejuvenated Kostynski. In a late December game he contributed three goals and one assist in a 7-6 comeback win in Kelowna.

Struggles continued in the New Year but promise came in the form of the team picking up the rights to Vancouver Canuck defenceman Garth Butcher. The former Regina star had played under Laforge and reached the Stanley Cup final the previous year with the Stan Smyl-led Canucks. The problem remained that Butcher, like Habscheid, was spending too much time on the bench in the pros instead of getting ice time in junior. The trade cost the rights to Cliff Ronning.

Still the team was on the road to recovery. When Laforge headed east to Sherwood Park Alberta to check out a promising 14 year old prospect the squad was 13 and 2 for their last 15 games. The young prospect's name; Rob Brown.

With the playoffs looming, tough guy Tod Ewen joined the squad. His stay was brief though his destiny lay in the NHL.

On March 6/83 the team etched itself into the league record books with the fastest two goals in an 11-5 victory over Portland at Memorial Arena. It took only three seconds for Kostynski and Saunders to set the mark.

Despite setting a league record for improvement from the previous season, at 55 points, the squad settled for third, three points behind Victoria. Home ice went to the Cougars and proved costly. On the good side Vancouver contributed Garth Butcher to the playoff cause.

Though they stunned the Cougars 4-2 in the opener in Victoria the series went the full seven games and gave the Cougars home ice in the rubber match. With Bruce Holloway out to injury they lost Butcher to the Canucks for the deciding game. He had been a devastating force, producing 12 points in six playoff games. Forced to go with four rookie defencemen, Mark Ferner, Doug Bodger, Gordon Mark and Dean Clark, the team still came close to pulling it out before losing 4-2. Goalie Dave Ross was outstanding in the Oilers' net.

Had Habscheid and Butcher been in the lineup they would

likely have beaten the Cougars and had more than a fighting chance against Portland. It was not the first or last time pro teams discarded the interests of the franchise or its fans. It recalled the loss of Barry Gibbs for the franchise Memorial Cup run in 1968.

Butcher went on to 13 NHL seasons, primarily with the Vancouver Canucks, playing the 1993 NHL all star game, while Todd Ewen chalked up 11 with four different NHL squads. Richard Hajdu patched in five games over two years with Buffalo and Bruin/Junior Oiler vet, Kostynski, managed 15 games in the familiar colours of the Boston Bruins. The draft saw Gord Mark and Evtushevski picked up by New Jersey and local Mark Ferner by Buffalo.

Dean Evason garnered the league's Player of the Year Award and rookie Doug Bodger revealed his potential in being selected to the 2nd All Star team. He racked up 92 points as a rookie, just one shy of the league record.

Franchise pride was upheld in the NHL with Gordie Lane and Lorne Henning again getting their names on Lord Stanley's mug.

The Kamloops International Bantam Ice Hockey Tournament (KIBIHT) held special interest for Kamloops' fans. In a match between St. Albert Saints, featuring phenom Rob Brown, and Kamloops' own Syd Smith Chevies, Brown notched both goals in a close 2-1 Alberta win.

As for the Junior Oilers their star was still rising.

38

The Goal 1983/84

There are defining moments in the history of teams. Moments that are so singularly significant their legacy becomes a source of team identity. Each incarnation of the franchise had them. For Humboldt the upset playoff win over Regina, for Estevan the Harrison led run to the Memorial Cup and for the New Westninster Bruins their odds-defying second Memorial Cup to cap four straight years of Memorial Cup appearances. For Kamloops it was summed up in a goal.

It didn't look good at the start of the campaign as the team lost all five pre-season games. Hopes hinged on veterans returning from pro camps, some promising rookies and a few key trades. Team captain and leader Dean Evason returned from Washington's training camp as did Evtushevski and eventually Ken Daneyko from New Jersey and Dean Clark from Edmonton. Daneyko, who played with Evason in Spokane, rejoined him in a deadline trade from Seattle. The two were to make history together. Evtushevski had been picked up two years earlier in a trade which sent former New Westminster Bruin Randy Wickware to Victoria. A pickup from the Kelowna Wings, Ryan Stewart, had also caught the eye of the Seventh Man.

They joined locals Mark Ferner, Kelly Para and Rudy Poeschek to compliment star prospects Doug Bodger, Doug Saunders and Jim Camazzola. Initially it looked like the promising Camazzola's future lay elsewhere when he was traded to Seattle for goalie Rex Grant but he returned to the Oilers to play a major role in the campaign. Grant joined rookie goalie Darryl Reaugh in the contest for top keeper. Reaugh had been picked up in a trade with the reincarnation of the New Westminster Bruins after they relocated from Nanaimo. To this already impressive mix two remarkable 15 year olds were to grab the attention of fans and management alike.

Fiery Bill Laforge was back behind the bench; his Junior Oilers squaring off in a season long battle with his old team in

Regina.

The pre season was quickly forgotten as the squad won their first three games and headed out on the road. In Calgary they were joined by 15 year old defencemen Rob Brown and Greg Hawgood. Great years lay ahead for the talented tandem dubbed the "Gold Dust Twins" by Kelly Moore, the team's play by play man. In 1964 the Estevan Bruins similarly trotted out 15 year old future star Dale Hoganson; this time the Seventh Man was seeing double.

The dark days of the franchise were over as the team became more than good; it became dominant. On November 24/83 the paper boasted Kamloops had recorded its first ever victory over Regina; 7-6 at Memorial. Former Regina coach Bill Laforge commented

"Tonight we beat a team with a winning tradition and that is what we've got to establish here."

His words were prophetic both for the season and the years ahead.

The start of 1984 brought word Ken Daneyko was being sent down by New Jersey to rejoin Canadian Junior National team mate Evason, after the World Junior Championships in Sweden. By mid-February the Oilers were the top ranked WHL team. By the 29th they had secured the Western Division Pennant and were in a battle for first overall with Regina. To the winner went the Scotty Munro Trophy and home ice advantage should they meet in the league final.

The spoils of victory fell to the Junior Oilers with a 7-6 triumph in Victoria in March. Only two years after being a league punching bag the team and franchise were on top again.

The first round against Seattle went quickly as the Oilers disposed of Daneyko's old squad in five straight. In game four Robin Bawa only got two shifts but he scored on both in a 5-4 victory. On to arch-rival Portland.

Portland fared no better as they went out in five straight as well. In game two ex Winterhawk Doug Saunders scored two goals and then followed it up with four more in game three in the Rose City; a 10-5 win, setting records for the fastest three goals by a player in the playoffs, and the most goals scored in a period in a playoff game by one player, at three. Game four went in Portland with the Hawks battling to a 4-4 regulation time draw.

Their hopes were dashed at 1:46 of OT as Bodger whipped in the winner. His goal and stellar goaltending by Reaugh had Kamloops within a win of the league final.

With only 21 seconds remaining in game five at Kamloops the sides were knotted at seven. Portland was called for a deliberate delay of game infraction and the Junior Oilers were awarded a penalty shot. It went to none other than Dean Evason, who had already scored three goals. He buried it and the Kamloops' Junior Oilers were western division champs.

Laforge and Tony Vogel, former Regina Pat, were going up against their old squad for the WHL crown. It was to be one of the greatest league finals in WHL history. The young western division champs going up against the more experienced Pats. Their ace in the hole; home ice.

The Pats had a special place in franchise history. The defining moment for the Humboldt Indians and Jim Harrison's fastest three goal record had them as the too confident opposition.

It looked like another quick exit for Oiler opponents as Kamloops used home ice to carve out two convincing 7-4 and 8-2 victories, setting a league record 12 game playoff winning streak. Regina was at home for the next three games. The tables turned.

In front of their fans they proved their worth, taking the next three matches 7-3, 4-3 and 4-1. The Junior Oilers came home on the verge of golfing and needing a spark. A thousand noisy fans were at the airport to greet them and urge them to keep the drive alive.

Game six at Memorial Arena. The Seventh Man was dressed.

As the game was winding down the Regina Pats seemed all but assured of a trip to the Memorial Cup in Kitchener. They were full measure for their 3-2 lead built up around a two goal performance by Dale Derkatch. Goalie Jamie Reeves seemed unbeatable as he stopped three Evason breakaways in the last three minutes of regulation time.

Only 20 seconds were left with the teams lining up in the Regina end. Kamloops pulled Darryl Reaugh. Doug Bodger recalled how the cocky Pats were wishing them a good golf season.

He spoke a few choice words to the team captain before the faceoff.

"I said to Dean (before the faceoff) You're number 20 and there are twenty seconds left. Put it in the net."

It was all or nothing.

Off the draw Ken Daneyko shoved the puck in to the corner and struggled to centre it with time winding down. His first attempt was blocked but the second made it through a maze of sticks and legs. It found Evason's stick and with only 12 seconds left he whipped the puck under Reeves.

The arena erupted. The moment etched in the minds of players, management and fans alike. The game was tied. The Oilers were still alive and overtime awaited.

The teams struggled through 13 minutes of OT. Tension drew away the breath of the faithful. A rush here, a shot there, a save; every chance held fame or disappointment. Then Brian Bertuzzi and Mark Kachowski broke away on a 2-1. They were stopped but in the ensuing goal mouth scramble Ryan Stewart, following up the play, banged in the winner. 13:13 of sudden death overtime brought the fans to their feet and the Oilers to a seventh and deciding game.

Another win and, in only their third season, they were headed to the Memorial Cup.

Game seven left nothing in the tank for either team.

The third period once again had the squads battling neck and neck. A 2-2 tie did nothing for the nerves of 3112 fans jammed into the old barn. At 7:25 rookie Ryan Stewart once again came to the fore as he rang a shot off the Pats goalpost and then followed it up with the go ahead goal. The rink went wild. Fans littered the ice with beach balls, balloons and squids to delay the game for ten minutes.

Regina had been unable to hold their 3-2 lead in game six; could the Oilers hold theirs?

When play resumed Kamloops went back to the attack. Regina was not without their chances as Selmar Odelien's point shot beat Reaugh but then pinged off the goal post.

The end came at 18:20.

A point shot by Gord Mark forced Reeves to give up a rebound. It couldn't have bounced worse for Regina. It landed on the stick of Dean Evason who fired home the insurance marker and the fourth goal of the match. Evason and the Oilers had earned a private place in the heart of the Seventh Man and the city of Kamloops. The team has never looked back.

Ben Kuzma of the Kamloops Daily News caught the feeling in quotes from Dean Evason and Ken Daneyko.

"I can't describe how happy I am, There's no question the overtime victory in game six brought us up for this game. I believe that was the turning point in the series. Twelve seconds left, they had it wrapped up, they were going to the Memorial Cup. Now we're going." (Evason)

"Tomorrow I will wake up and think it's all a dream. This is something I will cherish the rest of my life. This team is simply amazing. I've never been on a team with so much character." (Daneyko)

83/84 Kamloops Junior Oilers **Top Left to Right** Vern Smith (Business Mgr.), Dr. Mike Wilson, Todd Davoren, Mark Ferner, Todd Carnelly, Rob Brown, Mark Kachowski, Stacey Wakabayashi, Mike Nottingham, Greg Hawgood, Greg Evtushevski, Tony Vogel, Jim Camazzola, Brian Bertuzzi, Rudy Poeschek, ?, ?, **Front** ? Ryan Stewart, Doug Bodger, Gord Mark, Rex Grant, Bill Laforge (coach), Dean Evason, Ron Coleman (trainer), Daryl Reaugh, Dean Clark, Doug Saunders, Robin Bawa (C. Doris Rubel) **Also suiting up** Ken Daneyko, Kelly Para, Derek Ruppel, Walter Shutter, Brian Powell, Mike Goodwin, Dean Gladue, Tim Brown, Russ Goglin

For the first time in Kamloops' hockey history it was going to the Memorial Cup. From its first meagre steps with the Kamloops Junior Rockets of 1962 (who sported future Estevan Bruin Jimmy Harrison) and 1964 through to its promising Tier one Chiefs of the seventies it finally beat down the last barriers. For Kamloops it was the first journey and for the Seventh Man the sixth.

The ultimate series had the Kitchener Rangers and Ottawa 67's representing the Ontario Hockey League and the Mario Lemieux led Laval Titan carrying the Quebec league colours.

Laforge was returning to his old stomping grounds. He had coached the Oshawa Generals in the 80/81 season and wound up suspended for 50 games after a playoff brawl involving Peterboro. He never served the suspension as he headed west to take up the coaching reins in Regina and eventually land on his feet in Kamloops.

The series started off with a cold slap for the youngsters from the west. Midway through the second period of game one the host Rangers had them down 8-0. It looked like a laugher, but it wasn't. The character Daneyko talked about showed itself and by 16:09 of the third they were knocking at the door 8-7. It took an empty net goal with seven seconds remaining for Kitchener to secure their 9-7 victory.

A 4-3 win over Titan put the Westerner's in the semi final against Brian Kilrea's Ottawa 67's. The boys from the capital had taken the round robin game 5-1 and were destined to sip from the Cup. Kamloops' fantastic season ended 7-2 at the hands of the team New Westminster had beaten for the Cup in 1977.

The cup eluded them this time; just as it had the first time New Westminster got to prime time. Jim Camazola carried the team's colours as a Memorial Cup all star team selection

The NHL entry draft saw Doug Bodger taken in the first round by Pittsburgh followed by Darryl Reaugh (Edmonton), Brian Bertuzzi (Vancouver) and Rex Grant (Vancouver). Former Oiler Tod Ewen was taken by Edmonton.

Evason and Bodger landed on the WHL Western Division first all stars while Darryl Reaugh, Gord Mark, Mike Nottingham and Jim Camazzola secured second all star positions.

Former Estevan Bruin Terry Simpson established a name for himself as a coach, taking home the WHL Coach of the Year Award.

Even with the loss of key stars the team had every reason to be optimistic. Sixteen vets were expected back including Doug Bodger. Reality proved otherwise as the talented rear guard took hold in Pittsburgh to begin a lengthy NHL career starring in both Pittsburgh and Buffalo before heading back to the west coast. His junior days were over after tallying 190 points in only two seasons.

Jim Camazzola went on to sprinkle three NHL games into his North American pro career before heading overseas to star in the Italian league.

Ken Daneyko's star shone on the eastern seaboard as he began a long term career with the New Jersey Devils. There he was destined to share in two Stanley Cup wins with a future Kamloops Blazer star.

The heart and soul of the team, Dean Evason, went to the Washington Capitals to begin a 12 year NHL career, primarily with Washington and Hartford. His hockey destiny saw him come full circle and follow in the footsteps of franchise alumni Ernie McLean, Don Hay and, former team mate Marc Habscheid.

The losses even reached behind the bench as combative Bill Laforge caught on with Vancouver. His tenure proved brief as he only lasted for 20 games into the 84/85 season. His coaching future did not include a return to Kamloops. Another figure was to take and dominate that position.

The team was excelling on the ice and the franchise had reestablished the mystique of the Seventh Man but a ghost from the past was lurking in the shadows.

The Junior Oilers would never take to the ice in Kamloops again. It was time for the hockey faithful of Kamloops to face a familiar challenge. A challenge they had lost before but were determined not to lose again.

39

The Birth of the Blazers_____1984/85

Twenty seven years earlier the Humboldt Board of Trade sold the Indians to Scotty Munro. The sale made it possible for the team to move. Once again the team was on the verge of moving. Gary Cooper was alerted by NL radio that Pocklington was talking to Paddy Ginnell about selling the team to Swift Current.

Up until that time the 33% local ownership had been offered little more than token involvement but they did have the right to first option to buy the remaining 66%, if they could come up with $180,000.

Kamloops had lost the WHL Chiefs in 1977 just when they were developing in to a contender. Two years later they could not even hold on to their BCJHL Rockets. Kamloops is a hockey town and did not take kindly to the losses. The community swung into action behind the leadership of a rescue committee and the encouragement of local media. Open line pledge shows were held on radio NL and business, labour, groups and individuals came together in the biggest show of support for a team Kamloops had ever seen.

A voice from the 1979 attempt to save the Rockets reemerged. This time he wasn't alone as he had the backing of the hockey faithful. Colin Day emerged as part of a group including Gary Cooper, Harvey Roy, Andy Clovechok, Loy Hoffbeck, Ken Almond and Dennis Coates who sought financial and vocal support wherever they could find it. Determination led to personal financial risks being taken by group members but in the end the Seventh Man put down deep roots along the Thompson River.

Radio NL sponsored a name the team contest that was won by nine year old Blaise Laveay. Once again the franchise belonged to the community and it wasn't going anywhere.

For many years in Estevan and New Westminster players had pulled the B-emblazoned sweater over their heads and grown a bit taller with team pride. And so it came again as the

Blazers were born and the tradition rekindled.

It was a community effort to hold on to the franchise and credit must go to Kamloops itself. Those spearheading it all were committed to staying with the cause in the difficult years to follow.

Colin Day grew up on hockey in Kamloops. His father, Cyril Day, one time mayor, owned the local bottling works and was directly involved in supporting the Senior A Elks and Chiefs of the 40's and 50's. Colin saw and knew the stars who graced Memorial Arena and battled for the Allan Cup. He eventually brought his business sense and love of hockey to the new Blazers and became its long standing president.

One of those stars he watched was Andy Clovechok. He came to the Elks in the 51/52 season, just when Ernie McLean and Scotty Munro teamed up in Humboldt. In one glorious season he shone on a line with Johnny Milliard and Bernie Bathgate to set an unmatched record. At season's end all three tied for the league scoring lead with 79 points apiece. When his playing days ended he, like many other senior players, began contributing to the development of the impressive Kamloops minor hockey system.

Gary Cooper, the first President of the Blazers, played some minor hockey and coached before becoming involved with the local ownership group. A member of the Cooper's family of local grocery store fame he brought a creative business acumen to the mix.

Ken Almond, who moved to Kamloops from Penticton in 1965, had earlier been involved with the Board of Directors of the BCJHL Kamloops Rockets.

Loy Hoffbeck, originally from the US, came to Kamloops in 1972 and got financially involved in supporting junior hockey.

Dennis Coates His hockey knowledge and negotiating skills were pivotal in getting and maintaining the franchise

Dennis Coates' deep connections to the franchise and Kamloops were a crucial element in putting together the deal and contending with the legal fallout that came afterwards. A lawyer with Mair, Jensen Blair his commitment and expertise were the glue enabling the committee of business and hockey people to pull it all off. His connections with the franchise and local hockey went back to 1968 when he helped Scotty Munro get ownership of the Kamloops Rockets and fend off the political ramifications with the BCJHL. They became close friends and through Scotty an equally close friendship developed with Ernie McLean. He had been president of the BCJHL for three years and played an active role in getting the Kamloops Chiefs earlier. His negotiating of the "Shotgun" clause in the original deal with Pocklington proved crucial.

Harvey Roy brought his own history as a player in Estevan and involvement with Kamloops hockey since the days of the Kamloops Chiefs. Long and deep connections rewarded with a dream fulfilled. He had been instrumental in getting the team to Kamloops and in saving it from departure.

Despite the influence and ability of prominent individuals they would not have pulled it off without the support of many. Fund raising efforts for shares sold at a $1000 each had the great and the small contributing. From school children giving money from piggy banks to well known Edmonton business and sportsman Vic Mah buying 10 shares outright, the cause was picked up. Many hockey fans then and now owe a debt of gratitude to that team of stars and their many backers who kept the franchise and made possible all that came afterwards.

Their home assured the team went about defending its western title.

GM Harvey Roy was joined by a figure who soon dominated the bench and the scene as much as Laforge. Ken Hitchcock had already established his hockey reputation in the hockey hotbed of Sherwood Park, outside of Edmonton. In eight years he had taken his midgets to the Air Canada Cup, the national final, four times and had run up a remarkable win loss record of 518-43. The Blazers under his guidance didn't skip a beat.

Another figure returned home to begin his long association with the team and a love affair with its fans. Greg "Spike" Wallace, after two years with the Victoria Cougars, came on board as the team's athletic therapist. Few individuals draw the spontaneous applause that greets "Spike" whenever he is introduced.

Player moves and developments brought groans and smiles as the season approached. Stacey Wakabayashi, Doug Bodger, Ken Daneyko, Dean Clark and Gord Mark were all seemingly lost but then came word the Blazers had snagged talented Brian Benning from Portland. St. Louis acquired his rights but there were reasonable hopes they could hang on to him.

The perceptive scouting that brought them Hawgood and Rob Brown came up roses again with promising 16 year old Rob Dimaio.

The season began, understandably, with uncertainty. Key players gone, others in NHL limbo and still others promising rookies or sophomores. A new, untried coach. One consistent remained. Greg Evtushevski was back and his value affirmed with the captain's C.

After a slow start the team went on a roll which removed any doubts. By December they were ranked number one in the country. Contributions were coming from all sources. Gord Mark, who had balked at going to the IHL returned along with fellow 20 year old Dean Clark to add stability. They closed the year as the class of their division.

One of their few losses came in Prince Albert at the hands of Terry Simpson's Raiders. The campaign came down to a battle between the Raiders, the Blazers and Medicine Hat. Early in the New Year Kamloops turned the tables on the Raiders by taking them out 4-3 at Memorial.

February 5/85 proved a special evening for former Junior Oiler Dean Evason. The player, whose goal raised the team to its greatest heights and who became its heart and soul, received the greatest honour a team can bestow. As he watched, his number 20 was raised to the rafters and retired. There it hangs still as an inspiration to all who would wear the blue, orange and white. Hawgood celebrated the night with four goals in a 9-4 thumping of the Kelowna Wings.

Shortly afterwards bad news hit with a season ending injury to Brian Benning, taken in to the boards on an icing call. Injury and illness were to be the lurking shadow of adversity the team had to battle. Dean Clark was lost to a shoulder injury and went behind the bench with Hitchcock; an experience that stood him in good stead as he eventually earned coach of the year honours with the 98/99 Calgary Hitmen.

At seasons end they were 22 points ahead of their nearest division rival, the second coming of the New Westminster Bruins, and placed third overall. Ex-Estevan Bruin Terry Simpson's P.A. Raiders took the Munro Trophy and home ice for any match up in the league final.

They surpassed last season's 100 points by six and took

the west division regular season title for the second year in a row. In so doing they matched the record for back to back 50 win seasons.

First round opponent, 4th place Portland, finished 51 points behind but won their last six games to enter the playoffs on a high note. In game one Mark Kachowski's three goals led the Blazers to a 9-3 victory while defence man Todd Carnelley

1984/85 - First Year of the Kamloops Blazers - Complete with the Community Rescue Team **Top Left to Right** Kelly Moore (Play by Play Commentator), Greg Hawgood, Kevin Weremy, Todd Carnelley, Rudy Poeschek, Jeff Frank, Gord Mark, Neil Pilon, Ryan Stewart, Rob Brown, Mike Nottingham, Jim Kambeitz, Pat Mangold, Greg "Spike" Wallace **Middle** Dr. Mike Wilson, Bob LaBrier, Brian Benning, Harvey Roy (GM), Gary Cooper, Loy Hoffbeck, Colin Day, Andy Clovechok, Ken Almond, Donna Barrett, Gary Stewart, Mark Thietke, Ken Hitchcock, Todd Struthers (stick boy) **Front** Rob McKinley, Will Anderson, Rob Dimaio, Mark Kachowski, BrianBertuzzi, Greg Evtuschevski, Dean Clark, Mark Ferner, Gord Walker, Len Mark, Darryl Reaugh (C. Kamloops Blazers) **Also suiting up** Shawn Green, Ken Jorgenson, Jason Phillips, Mike MacWilliam, Ryan Jackson, Darryl Krechuniak, Mark Kulak, Mario Desjardins

led the way in a 7-4 game two triumph. In Portland the Hawks stunned Kamloops 4-3 in overtime and then forced OT in game two. It was former Winterhawk Mike Nottingham who ended their upset hopes with his overtime marker at 1:27. The Hawks had nothing left and went out easily by scores of 13-3 and 6-1 to give the Blazers the series five games to one.

New Westminster fared no better. Going out in five straight; though two went to overtime.

The WHL final came down to Prince Albert and Kamloops. The Raiders, already blessed with home ice advantage, iced a healthy squad against the wounded Blazers. Darryl Reaugh, Hawgood, Evtushevski and Kachowski were all on the limp. It still looked good as Kamloops was close in their 4-2 opening game loss in Prince Albert. The promise wasn't realized as the team went out convincingly in four straight to the eventual Memorial Cup winning Raiders.

If there had been doubts about the team. coach or the organization they were put to rest. The squad tied the league record, set only the previous season by the Junior Oilers, of 29 straight home ice victories.

The junior draft had Ryan Stewart taken in the first round by the Winnipeg Jets. He was followed by Tod Carnelley (Edmonton) and Neil Pilon (New York Rangers). In one of the steals of the draft local product and team enforcer Rudy Poeschek went to the New York Rangers. He skated longer at hockey's pinnacle than a host of others taken long before him.

With success came the inevitable losses to graduation or the pros.

Brian Benning, made the NHL all rookie team for 1987, and went on to nine years with five different NHL squads. Dean Clark graduated after getting in one NHL game with the Edmonton Oilers in 83/84. Mark Ferner carved out a sporadic NHL career with four NHL teams over a span of six years backed up by a lengthy minor league resume. Gord Mark had parts of four seasons with Edmonton and New Jersey. Gord Walker eked out spot duty for four years with the New York Rangers and L.A. Kings. Goalie Darryl Reaugh saw backup duty over three seasons with Edmonton and the Hartford Whalers.

Reaugh, Carnelley, Mark Ferner, Gord Walker and Greg Evtushevski shared in the Blazers domination of the west division first team all stars.

The franchise alumni were not silent either. Former New West Bruin Larry Melnyk carved his name on the Stanley Cup with the Edmonton Oilers. Estevan Bruin Terry Simpson captured the Memorial Cup and another Bruin, Doug Sauter, took home the WHL Coach of the Year honours with the Calgary Wranglers.

The community owned team had soared in its first year. New faces replaced those departing and continued to build the dynasty.

Hardly noticed in New Westminster was a four game stint by Mark Recchi that produced one assist.

The Blazers were reloading.

40

Return 1985/86

In hockey, as in life, the past and future cross paths time and again, like the twining of a rope. In the 85/86 campaign the Blazers surged to great heights and crossed swords with one of the Seventh Man's best friends in the process.

Changes in the league saw the faltering Kelowna Wings become the Spokane Chiefs and a face, familiar to the franchise, emerge in New Westminster.

Paddy Ginnel, whose battles with the franchise began as a player in Flin Flon in the 50's and continued afterwards as a coach, took over the reins of the Bruins. He was quoted in the paper, as he stepped in to Queen's Park Arena: "I swear I saw the ghost of Ernie McLean." He may well have. Ginnel did not finish the season with the Bruins.

The Blazers hit the exhibition season with a new logo and a promising 7-1 record.

A trade brought Craig Berube from New Westminster to join an enforcer lineup including Rudy Poeschek and Mark Kachowski.

The season marked the return of one of Kamloops' favourite sons to the franchise. Local hero Don Hay earned his stripes as he skated his way up through the local minor hockey system. Known for his work ethic he, nonetheless, failed to make the cut with the Kamloops' Chiefs and was picked up by Ernie McLean's Bruins. After a brief stint as a minor league pro he returned to Kamloops and made his presence felt as a senior league player/ coach. He learned from the best over the years, being able to credit Joe Tennant, Scotty Munro and Ernie McLean as his mentors. He was to learn more under Hitchcock.

The squad pulled out of the gate strongly before being stood up 7-2 by a Portland team predicted to take the division. Greater concerns were coming from the attendance figures. The team needed an average 2000 per game but in the first two averaged only 1600. Needing between 1200 and 1400 season ticket holders they were stuck at 800. As historic as Memorial Arena was it's basic comforts did not help draw fans.

The organization had entertained making a pitch for the Memorial Cup Tournament but Memorial Arena and the lack of sufficient hotel rooms made it impossible.

Back on the ice Portland took the next encounter by a convincing 9-3 margin and appeared full measure for their favoured position. They were holding first when the two teams met at Memorial. This time captain Mark Kachowski's disputed goal at 2:53 of the third gave the Blazers a 5-4 victory. The regular season contest became a homer series as neither team could win on the other's ice.

The New Westminster Bruins were struggling; winning only four of their 23 games to date. Ginnel was fired and owner Ron Dixon called up a very solid looking ghost. Ernie McLean returned to Queen's Park .

He saw a solid nucleus in the team; including Kamloops' own Mark Recchi. Harvey Roy had left the Blazers and was back with Ernie.

The Blazers continued to manoeuver in their battle for first. The rights to Ryan Stewart, who was with the Winnipeg Jets were traded to Prince Albert while promising Rob Dimaio went to Medicine Hat along with David Mackey for Ken Morrison. Dimaio would not forget being moved.

The Blazers met the new look Bruins at Queen's Park and took a 4-1 decision. Rob Brown figured in all four goals while Mark Recchi got the lone Bruin marker. It didn't seem like anything had changed as they got ready for the rematch in Kamloops.

Ernie's boys stunned the front runners 7-5 to win their second straight win for the first time that season. Recchi earned a star in front of the home town fans. The Bruins did it to Kamloops again in their next match. Recchi spoke about how the team's discipline and system play improved once the legendary McLean took over.

Early in January the Blazers were again trailing Portland. A trade got the rights to Greg Evtushevski back from Medicine Hat; although they had to give up fan favourite Craig Berube to do it. Chevy had been playing pro in the minors. His return brought immediate dividends. He snared four goals and one assist in his first game back.

Musical goalies plagued the squad all season. To help shore up the last line of defence they reached into Victoria and reeled in Randy Hansch, who joined Rob McKinley. Hansch's roots were to sink deep into Kamloops and the organization..

The battle between the Hawks and Blazers finally took a turn as the season wound down. A 5-4 road victory in Saskatoon began a 15 game unbeaten streak that took Kamloops to the last game of the season and locked up first. Along the way they massacred Portland 12-3 and finished seven points on top in the west division. Medicine Hat locked up first overall.

Rob Brown's three points in the final game, a 10-4 romp over Spokane, gave him 173 for the season and the league scoring title. At 17 he was the youngest player to have ever won the title. Ken Morrison landed third in scoring and Hawgood 12th.

85/86 Kamloops Blazers **Top Left to Right** Robin Bawa, Peter Soberlak, Dave Marcinyshyn, Rudy Posechek, Troy Kennedy, Lonnie Spinks, Len Mark **Middle** Bob LaBrier, Todd Strother, Greg "Spike" Wallace, Doug Pickell, Chris Tarnowski, Greg Evtushevski, Ron Shudra, Mike Ragot, Barry Kress, Pat Bingham, Ken Hitchcock, Don Moores **Front** Rob McKinley, Don Schmidt, Rob Brown, Ken Morrison, Mark Kachowski, Mike Nottingham, Todd Carnelley, Greg Hawgood, Randy Hansch, Pat Nogier (C. Fedorak Photo) **Also suiting up** Craig Berube, Rob Dimaio, David MacKey, Sean Pass, Willie Popp, Mike Ragot, Trevor Hendry, Robert Oberrech

Round one against Seattle seemed easy pickings, especially after taking game one 10-2, but a hard fought double overtime win in game two suggested otherwise. Evtushevski potted the winner; deflecting a Tod Carnelley shot. Seattle seemed to fold back on their home ice as Kamloops whipped them 11-2 but then came game four.

The T-Birds had the Blazers down 7-0 by 10:56 of the

second period before Kamloops erupted for one of its greatest comebacks ever. Down 8-7 with time ticking away Hawgood notched the tying marker. It could not have been any closer. The time was 19:59. At 3:34 OT Rob Brown sealed the incredible comeback victory.

That was it for Seattle as they lost the next game and went out in five straight.

The predicted division final between Kamloops and Portland became reality. Expected to be a homer series it was going as expected in the first three games. It was Kamloops who broke the jinx in game four when Hansch stole the show in backstopping his squad to a 4-1 victory and a 3-1 series lead. The Blazers pounded the Hawks 13-2 in Kamloops and then threw the jinx out the window with a series- clinching 6-4 win in Oregon.

The Blazers went on against Medicine Hat for the right to represent the WHL at the Memorial Cup while Portland got rested up. They were already in the Memorial Cup as hosts. That had been how they had got to and won their first and only Memorial Cup in 1983.

The Hat had taken both regular seasons games and had home ice. Word had it they saw Kamloops as little more than a speed bump on the road to Portland. They threw out an all former Blazer line of Berube, Dimaio and Dave Mackey at the visitors enroute to a hard fought 5-4 OT victory in game one. Kamloops proved a hard speed bump to get over. It got worse for the Tigers in game two as the Blazers controlled the game and evened the series with a 5-2 win. Two goals by Brown and a 4-0 shutout by Hansch put Kamloops up 2-1. Game four was pivotal

Tied 4-4 in regulation the Tigers were forcing the play in OT. That all ended at 5:25 when Greg Hawgood's goal put Medicine Hat on the verge of the golf season. The Tigers had nothing left and went out 7-2 in game five. Kamloops were league champs for the second time in three years and headed to the Memorial Cup for the second time.

It started badly.

Despite having period leads of 1-0 and 2-1 they fell in game one 5-3 to the Guelph Platers and then lost an overtime heartbreaker to Pat Burn's Hull Olympics 5-4, led by Luc Robitaille. They had to beat Portland in their final match just to force a tie breaker and advance.

It looked good as the Blazers staked out a 4-1 lead but a

five minute penalty to defenceman David Marcinshyhn allowed Portland to notch two goals and climb back into the game. The Hawks eventually tied it up at five. But Portland's comeback was not to be. At 17:35 Ken Morrison put the game away. Tied at 1- 2 in the round robin the teams met again to decide who went on against the Olympics in the semi final.

This time it was no contest and even home ice didn't help the Hawks. Three goals and one assist by Hawgood and the puck stopping of Randy Hansch ended Portland's season 8-1.

A tired Blazer team, that had played close in every game so far, ran into a wall in the semi against Hull. They fell decisively 9-3. Ernie McLean had taken the franchise to the Memorial Cup three times before hitting pay dirt. Kamloops had been to the fountain twice now and still had not got a drink. Ron Shudra played himself on to Memorial Cup all star squad.

It had been an outstanding season as the team secured their third straight regular season division title and second league championship in three years. Evtushevski shone throughout the playoffs prompting Hitchcock to suggest his number should be retired on that performance alone. Rob Brown added the league MVP award to his scoring title, Ron Shudra took the rookie of the year award and Ken Morrison secured Most Sportsmanlike Player. Hawgood, Brown and Morrison all made the west division all stars.

The draft saw Shudra (Edmonton), Brown (Pittsburgh), Hawgood (Boston) and Doug Pickell (Calgary) taken.

Former Blazers Craig Berube and Rob Dimaio went on to stable NHL careers. Berube began with Philadelphia and worked his way through three others before returning to the Flyers. Dimaio earned two Memorial Cups with Medicine Hat before moving on to an NHL career with five NHL teams and suiting up for the New York Rangers at the end of the 1999/2000 season. Ryan Stewart, who was also traded, can point to three NHL games in his pro career. His role in the Junior Oilers dash to the Memorial Cup in 1984 can never be forgotten. Blazer team captain Mark Kachowski departed for the pros and put in 64 games over three seasons with the Pittsburgh Penguins.

Former Estevan Bruin Terry Simpson was once again league coach of the year.

Few players were being lost this time and Hitchcock had proven he was more than capable of producing championship teams at the major junior level. There was room for optimism they could be contenders next season too.

Don Hay was to have company in the "Home town boy makes good" department next season. Once again New Westminster was to figure prominently in Kamloops' hockey fortunes.

41

Brown Out________________1986/87

With the new season on the horizon it seemed there was no end to the success of the Blazers. Again they iced a squad capable of challenging for league honours and a Memorial Cup birth. The word dynasty began to creep into descriptions of the team and organization. The measure would be on the ice and in battles against adversity.

Nottingham, Evtushevski and Morrison were definitely gone but hopes were they could get Randy Hansch back. The hopes weren't realized and Rob McKinley nabbed the number 1 spot.

Evason, Evtushevski, Mark Ferner and Darryl Reaugh all turned up for the first annual pro am game and proved too much for the new guys who fell 11-0.

Pre season developments punctuated the sports pages.

Gary Cooper stepped down as team president and Colin Day began his long and influential tenure in the position. Assistant coach Bob LaBrier, who had been with Hitchcock for 15 years going back to Sherwood Park, left the team. Darcy Norton came over from Swift Curren. Efforts to get Ryan Stewart back from Prince Albert were dashed and the former Oiler eventually made his way to the Winterhawks.

The biggest news came September 26/86. Ernie McLean was still up in Atlin, working on his gold mine, when the Bruins' John Olver made a blockbuster trade. Troy Kennedy, Pat Bingham and two others went to the coast while rookie G.M. Bob Brown, father of Rob, reeled in a true home town star. Mark Recchi came back to his roots. Ernie was not pleased when he heard about the deal. Mark was the most recent of the Recchi family to earn acclaim on the ice. His father Mel and uncle Ron had both earned local and provincial accolades at both the junior and senior levels. Younger brother Matt eventually got on board to keep the family tradition alive.

Don Hay was back as assistant coach being joined by

former Kamloops Chief Donnie Moores. A special item in the paper honoured Doris Rubel, the pre eminent hockey mom in Kamloops since the days of the Tier II Rockets. Epitomizing the local support behind the Blazer organization she had many years left being substitute mother to the hoards of young teenagers who left home for the travails of junior hockey.

After all the changes and accolades it was time for hockey.

Ernie McLean's Bruins were the first visitors, including disgruntled ex Blazers Pat Bingham and Troy Kennedy. Feelings ran high and when the duo potted a pair of goals each they tossed the pucks to an enraged Hitch. Going the other way Recchi made his presence felt in a Blazer uniform by garnering one goal in an 8-7 victory.

86/87 Kamloops Blazers **Front Left to Right** Stacey Nickel, Len Mark, Steve Nemeth, Robin Bawa, Rob Brown, Don Schmidt, Greg Hawgood, Rudy Poeschek, Dean Cook **Middle** Colin Day (President), Jim McQueen (trainer), Don Moores (asst. coach), Todd Strother (stick boy), Darcy Norton, Rich Wiest, Mike Needham, Kelly Para, Mark Recchi, Glenn Mulvenna, Doug Pickell, Ken Hitchcock (coach), Bob Brown (GM), Don Hay (asst. coach), Greg "Spike" Wallace **Top** Garth Premak, Casey McMillan, Dave Marcinyshyn, Warren Babe, Steve Weinke, Ron Shudra, Devon Oleniuk, Bill Harrington (C.Fedorak Photo) **Also suiting up** Peter Soberlak, Jason Proulx, Wayne MacDonald, Dave Whistle, Jason Mager, Curt Brennan, Serge Lajoie, Calvin MacDonald, Casey MacMillan, Scott Daniels

The season was still young when word came Rob Brown had inked a deal with the Pittsburgh Penguins and the Blazers had pulled off another trade with Swift Current to pick up Mike Needham. Both were destined for the Penguins but in 1986/87 they were all Blazer. The Swift Current connection continued in November when Bronco Warren Babe came west for local product Peter Soberlak and Jason Proulx.

On the ice Rob Brown was spectacular. By mid November he had amassed 43 points in only nine games. He was unstoppable in Gretzky like proportions. His sidekick Greg Hawgood was impressing in his own right and pulled down a spot on the Canadian Junior National squad.

Brown proved he could score clutch goals as well as go for volume. In the battle with Portland a January 87 match saw the team struggle to their fifth straight overtime game. Down 6-3 they battled back to tie and win it on Brown's marker just 29 seconds in to OT. It was the fifth straight OT loss to Kamloops by Portland and there was one more waiting in the next game. The Blazers were pulling away.

Sentiment took the ice in February as Ernie McLean was on hand to present a plaque to long time friend and coach Joe Tennant; honouring his contribution to hockey in Kamloops. An integral part of Kamloops' hockey history he had been a link in the franchise's Munro/McLean/Shinske connection since the days of the Estevan Bruins. Ernie took the opportunity to praise the Blazers as the best team in the WHL and one of the best in the country.

More honours were given out that same month as Hitchcock's suggestion Evtushevski's number be retired, was realized. Chevy was on hand as his number 26 rose alongside former team mate Dean Evason's.

Brown's record breaking pace had him in New Westminster for the opportunity to break Cliff Ronnings season point record. He needed three points to tie. He got four points. The honours rang down. Ronning telegrammed congratulations, a plaque was presented to him and, in a class act, Ernie brought his entire team on the ice to honour the Kamloops star.

Next on the line was Brian Propp's career record of 514 points. It fell in short order only a few days after Ronning's. Notching six points in a 9-4 win in Victoria he surpassed the former Brandon star by three points.

Propp's response took a little of the edge off when he responded that he was unaware his record was being chased or who Rob Brown was. Not to worry, the greatest of them all took notice. Wayne Gretzky took time to praise the accomplishment.

It all came to an ominous conclusion in the last game of

the season. Already missing injured Recchi they lost Brown for at least the first round of the playoffs, with a severe ankle injury. They still had four other 100 point players in Shudra, Hawgood, Norton and Bawa and were clear favourites over first round opponents Seattle.

The team took home the Scotty Munro Trophy for the second time; finishing 17 points ahead of Portland and securing the divisional crown for the fourth straight time. No team in franchise history had matched their 113 points. The 75/76 Bruins came the closest at 112..

Brown was followed in the top ten league scorers by Hawgood, Shudra and Bawa taking positions seven through nine. Bawa and Hawgood also joined him on the west division all stars.

The sharpshooter was further honoured with the league MVP, player of the year and top plus/minus player to go along with his league scoring title.

The team had shown they could still win without him as they sent Seattle packing in five then turned to face second place Portland. Brown rejoined the team for the Winterhawk series after receiving word that he had won the Canadian Hockey League MVP.

Though not fully recovered his presence was clearly needed as the underdog Hawks came into Memorial and stole game one 8-6. The Blazers took game two but when they returned home from Portland they were down 3 -1 in the series. Brown did his bit in game five, contributing 5 points, but it was not enough as Portland took it 9-5 to put Kamloops on the verge of elimination going back to Portland.

Goalie Stacey Nickel stole the show in the Rose City as the Blazers stayed alive with a 6-5 thriller.

Some 2959 fans packed Memorial Arena for game seven; their Blazers once again on the edge. The players added their own pizzaz with multi coloured hairdos. The clear winner in that department was Rudy Poeschek who sported a blue Mohawk cut. The cliff hanger went to overtime before Darcy Norton brought the fans to their feet with the winner at 12:07. The final 7-6 and the Blazers were headed back to Portland.

This time there was no recovery. It ended in a 7-3 loss. There was no Memorial Cup appearance for one of the best teams the Blazers ever iced.

Portland did not survive the next round against Rob

Dimiao's Medicine Hat Tigers who were on their way to their first Memorial Cup.

Regardless of the disappointment acclaim fell on the Blazers. They set a record for most goals in a season at 496 and for having the most 30 goal plus players at nine. Hitchcock won coach of the year and Dean Cook took home the top goalie award. Brown's records included the most assists (136) and most points (212) for a centre ice man as well as a forward. Even with his injury he had managed 11 points in five games against the Winterhawks.

The draft saw Darcy Norton go to Minnesota, Devon Oleniuk to Washington and Don Schmidt to Minnesota.

This time the team had to brace itself for significant losses. Brown was gone to Pittsburgh where he ran up 115 points in 88/89 as well as skated in the league all star game. His pro journeys eventually brought him full circle as he once again skated for Pittsburgh in 99/2000. Popular Rudy Poeschek battled his way in to a long term NHL career starting with the New York Rangers and placing him in St. Louis for the 99/2000 season. Scott Daniels, who was traded to New Westminster, after time in the minors made his way to the NHL where he suited up for the New Jersey Devils in 1998/99. David Marchinyshyn saw NHL spot duty with three teams while Steve Nemeth and Ron Shudra each got in a few games at the highest level before joining the Sheffield Steelers of the British League. Robin Bawa garnered NHL spot duty with four different NHL squads and found a home in the minor pros.

A great season came to a disappointing end. It looked like next season would be a rebuilding year. Or so it seemed.

42

Drive for Five________________ 1987/88

Kamloops had finished first in their division four straight times and prospects for an unprecedented fifth title were more than a mere possibility. True, they had some big player losses but then they had some promising players on the rise as well as Hitchcock returning to the bench. Remarkably, hopes of another Memorial Cup appearance were attainable.

Pundits were picking Kamloops to repeat in the west and Medicine Hat in the east. More than a few saw the Tigers capable of taking home the Memorial Cup for the second straight time.

Ernie McLean left the New Westminster Bruins but his legend remains undiminished.

Dean Cook was back as number one goalie and Greg Hawgood took on the captain's C with a team icing eight rookies for the season opener. Recchi returned to join promising rookies David Chyzowski, Pat MacLeod, Phil Huber and Scott Loucks. Norton, Needham, Babe and Mulvenna all eventually returned from their pro camps.

They blasted out of the gate to show they were still a force without Rob Brown. His buddy Hawgood opened up with five points in the 7-5 season opening win over Victoria at Memorial. It took ten games before anyone could stop the Kamloops juggernaut.

Though all was going well on the ice the perilous financial picture was not made any better when the projected 5000 seat waterfront arena complex was narrowly voted down. Despite its charm and history Memorial Arena constantly had the community team struggling at the gate. Bob Brown commented, later in the season, the 2569 seat arena could not support a $600,000 budget on attendance alone. Praise was heaped on the Booster's Club, which raised $40,000 the year before, and the 170 volunteers. The city contributed $10,000 and Mayor John Dormer commented on how the team contributed financially with its $70,000 ice rental and through the positive advertising throughout the hockey world.

By the end of December Kamloops was pulling away from the pack and eyeing Medicine Hat and Saskatoon for first overall. Their journey into Tiger Territory in November saw them suffer a 4-1 setback but they returned the favour when their Alberta rivals came visiting. Behind the Tiger bench was former Kamloops Chief star Barry Melrose.

The rivalry with Medicine Hat had special meaning for a couple ex Blazers in their lineup. 20 year old Jim Kambeitz looked back fondly on his time in Kamloops while Rob Dimaio had a point to make. He felt he had not been given a good enough opportunity while in Kamloops.

"It was just a matter of them (Kamloops) not giving me enough time to develop."

Yet for one brief exhilarating moment Dimaio united with Blazers Babe, Hawgood, Recchi and former team mate Rob Brown, under the watchful eye of Ken Hitchcock, to take the World Junior Championship. Their accomplishment over, they resumed their WHL battles.

On March 17/88 the Daily News made it official. A 5-4 victory over Portland, put them out of the playoffs for the first time and secured the Blazers fifth straight divisional crown.

First overall was surrendered to the Saskatoon Blades with Medicine Hat managing to finish three points up on the Blazers in second. It meant home ice to the Tigers if they met in the final.

Recchi showed his big league potential finishing third in scoring only six points behind Theoren Fleury and Joe Sakic. Hawgood topped all defencemen and came in number eight overall.

Their first round opponent was a tough New Westminster Bruin squad threatening to pound the smaller Blazers into submission. It didn't as Kamloops took the first two at home and the next two at Queen's Park. In game three an irate Bruin goaltending coach tossed a chair on to the ice in protest to a call. Bruin fans responded with a chant of "Ernie, Ernie". Despite playing the Blazers close in every match the Bruins were swept with a 2-1 loss in game five at Memorial

Second place Spokane, with Troy Gamble in net, felt they had a genuine chance of taking Kamloops out. They even had the better record during the regular season series at 5-4-1. The

Blazers crushed them in game one 15-3 and took match number two 6-3. Former Blazer Doug Pickell was the Chief's best player in game two.

Just as in 82/83, when Garth Butcher was called up by the Canucks, a parent NHL club threw a spoke in the wheel. The Boston Bruins called up Hawgood. Without their point man the Blazers suffered a 3-0 setback in Spokane. It was the first time the team had been shut out in 456 games. Hawgie was still out for game two and the Chiefs carved out another win, 7-4, to tie the series up going back to Memorial Arena.

87/88 Kamloops Blazers **Top Left to Right** Mike Haertel (stick boy), Todd Decker, Mike Needham, Greg Rogalski, Sean Crowther, Paul Checknita, Kim Deck, Phil Huber, Pat McLeod, Mark Recchi, Orry Roberge (stick boy) **Middle** Jim McQueen (PR marketing), Don Moore (asst. coach), Don Hay (asst. coach), Garth Premak, Steve Kloepzig, Bill Harrington, Greg Davies, Casey McMillan, Dave Chyzowski, Willy MacDonald, Bob Brown (GM), Ken Hitchcock (coach), Greg "Spike" Wallace, Colin Day (President) **Front** Calvin MacDonald, Darcy Norton, Doug Pickell, Greg Hawgood, Don Schmidt, Glenn Mulvenna, Devon Oleniuk, Dean Cook (C. Fedorak Photo) **Also suiting up** Scott Loucks, Russ Churla, Jeff Cox, Curt Lehner, Kelly Ross, Alex Sheflo, Cecil Vaughn, Mike Rickert, Marty Prazma, Joel Dyck

Game five had Hawgood back in the fold and present for a special celebration. The 2845 fans were on hand to see Rob Brown's sweater retired. In an emotional moment Hawgood, who broke in with Brown four years before, gave his former team mate a hug just before his number began to rise to the rafters. The Chiefs did not participate in the ceremony, much to the dismay of Colin Day, choosing instead to remain in their dressing room.

Glen Mulvenna was the star of the show as he netted two goals and an assist in a 5-3 Blazer victory. Returning to Spokane, 4914 fans were not enough to put the Chiefs over the top as former Chief Tony Horacek notched the winner at 9:20 of the third. Final 3-2 Blazers.

The "Cookie Monster", goalie Dean Cook, was the difference in game seven at Memorial Arena as Kamloops put an end to the upset prospect. Taking the series 5-2 they were west division champs for the fourth time in five years. The next obstacle, Rob Dimaio's defending Memorial Cup Tigers.

Two years before the Blazers went up against a favoured Tigers team and earned their way to the Memorial Cup. There was no clear edge this time around but Medicine Hat again had the all important home ice advantage plus star goalie Mark Fitzpatrick.

Goaltending was a factor in the first two games as the Tigers secured 4-1 and 5-1 victories respectively. Kamloops had to use their home ice to advantage as well.

In game three, at Memorial, they were up 3-0 before the Hat began its comeback. They moved to within one goal at 5-4 before Recchi netted the insurance marker.

Game four was another tight affair with Dimaio starring for the Tigers. The winner came off of the stick of Blazer Greg Davies with his one handed deflection of a Don Schmidt shot with less than four minutes remaining. They needed it as Dimaio brought his side to within one before the 4-3 victory was secured. Cook did his part stopping Dimaio on a penalty shot. Feelings were running high and with ten seconds left the Tigers got into a stick swinging brawl with some fans. There was no lack of intensity for the last game in Kamloops.

It was pivotal and it was devastating.

Dimaio was a one man wrecking crew. Two goals and four assists were the difference in a convincing 8-2 victory before a silenced Blazer crowd. Three years after being traded it was as much a joy to Dimaio as it was a disappointment to his former fans.

"It's such a great feeling. It was the last time I'll ever play here. I wanted to go out with a bang and show how they maybe made a mistake by trading me."

It had been closer than the score suggested as Kamloops outshot the Tigers 37-36

The Blazers were in game six at Medicine Hat until the end when Trevor Linden got the 5-2 insurance goal into the empty net with 13 seconds left. Hawgood gave the ultimate compliment to former team mate Dimaio, claiming he and goalie Fitzpatrick were the difference in the series. Kamloops had no reason to hang its head. The Tigers were on their way to their second straight Memorial Cup; a feat not be repeated until 1994 and 1995 by the Blazers themselves.

Dimaio had company as the top playoff scorer in the person of Mark Recchi. Hawgood was close behind in third followed by Darcy Norton in 7th. Norton joined Hawgood and Recchi on the west division all stars.

The season's achievements for Greg Hawgood did not end there as he picked up the WHL's top defenceman award and went on to join the Boston Bruins in the Stanley Cup final against Gretzky's Oilers. He had one goal in the debut of his two game stint.

Recchi skated off with the top plus/minus award and was selected #67 by the Pittsburgh Penguins.

Neither player returned. Hawgood began a career which saw him flit back and forth between starring in the IHL and getting in regular NHL time, suiting up for the 99/2000 campaign with Vancouver. Mark Recchi went on to be one of greatest players ever produced by the franchise, team and Kamloops itself. He became the first Kamloopsian to get his name carved on the Stanley Cup and has been a keystone player with every team he has played for. On December 28/99 he was declared Kamloops' greatest athlete of the century and had a portion of Lorne Street, near Riverside Coliseum, renamed Mark Recchi Way.

Warren Babe got in three years with Minnesota before concussions ended his career. Glen Mulvenna got a couple games in with Pittsburgh and Philadelphia before finishing his career in Europe. Tony Horacek has skittered between the NHL and the minor leagues getting, in playing time over five years with Philadelphia and Chicago.

Five straight regular season division championships, four WHL league finals and two Memorial Cup appearances in five years. An incredible run but now there was a price to be paid. Would they collapse like the Portland Winterhawks last season and end up out of the playoffs or would the Seventh Man ensure they remained a team none could take lightly?

43

Reload 1988/89

This time there was no call for a first place finish or a run for the Memorial Cup. The season was to be a measure of the team's depth and character as well as Hitchcock's coaching..

Don Schmidt pulled on the captain's C but was not destined to be wearing it when the season came to an end. The organization began pulling in new faces. Cal McGowan came up from Merritt after the Blazers got his rights from Seattle and was joined by hard rock Paul Kruse. Corey Hirsch was the rookie backup to Dean Cook and 16 year old Darryl Sydor suited up on defence. Zac Boyer was added in early March. Mid way through the campaign the squad picked up stellar defenceman Geoff Smith from the college ranks and former Blazer Pat Bingham.

Only eight veterans lined up with the 17 rookies that started on the road in Spokane. Phil Huber notched four goals and Chyzowski two as the team took the Chiefs 6-3 for their 7th straight season opening victory.

The campaign proved a see saw of success and struggle. By early January 89 they were in unfamiliar territory playing sub .500 hockey. Yet when the season began winding down in March they had hiked up their boots to close to within five points of division leading Portland. The bloom fell off the rose with an 8-2 loss to the Hawks at Memorial and a three game losing streak to end the season. They finished one game above .500, to keep the plus .500 streak alive, and out of first for the first time in six seasons; three points behind Victoria and 13 back of Portland.

Only Phil Huber cracked the top ten in scoring when he secured the 10th spot.

Wayne Naka's Cougars had reason to feel confident. It looked even better when they had the Blazers down 4-1 in the first game. That confidence tumbled when Chyzowski netted two power play goals within 12 seconds and Kamloops fought back for a 6-5 upset victory. Zac Boyer nabbed the winner. Although Victoria took game two they had relinquished home ice to Kamloops.

In game three Zac Boyer again rose to the occasion potting the winner in a 5-3 victory. Huber was the hero in game four with two goals and the Blazers were up 3 -1 in the series. The Cougars did not lose again on home ice but they could not solve the puzzle at Memorial.

Down 4-3 in the series they faced elimination in Kamloops. The Blazers were looking at the prospect of going to the division final for the 6th straight time. Pat MacLeod, the starring Blazer defenceman, was still suffering the effects of a vicious slash behind his knee by Cougar standout Len Barrie. Only days before he couldn't even walk but he was there for the pivotal game. Injury or not he stole the show with two goals and two assists. The rookie laden Blazers took the game 5-4 and the series five games to three; a testament to coaching and character.

88/89 Kamloops Blazers **Top Left to Right** Kelly Moore (play by play), Dave Chyzowski, Steve Yule, Kim Deck, Zac Boyer, Paul Kruse, David Linford, Corey Crichton, Brad Heschuk, Cal McGowan, Randy Keller **Middle** Greg "Spike" Wallace (trainer), Don Moores (asst. coach), Don Hay (asst. coach), Corey Anderson, Ed Bertuzzi, Ryan Harrison, Brian Shantz, Darryl Sydor, Taylor Harding, Trevor Buchanan, Bryan Dicken, Len Jorgenson, Darwin McClelland, Ken Hitchcock (coach), Pete Friedel (asst. trainer) **Front** Mike Haertel (stick boy), Corey Hirsch, Bob Brown (GM), Pat McLeod, Mike Needham, Don Schmidt, Phil Huber, Colin Day (President), Dean Cook, Orry Roberge (stick boy) (C. Fedorak Photo) **Also suiting up** Pat Bingham, Geoff Smith, Kevin Hoffman, Darryl Kruse, Brian Shantz, Darwin McClelland, Corey Anderson

The Rose City awaited and was not kind. After losing game one 6-5 and seeing their 5-0 lead in game two evaporate in to a 6-5 loss it looked like a quick exit. A tight 5-4 loss at home in game three seemed to seal their fate.

They could easily have cashed in their chips and gone out quietly to the highly favoured Hawks. With their impressive season showing and upset playoff victory they could already boast of their accomplishments.

The young guns clung to the edge by taking the next cliffhanger 8-7. Corey Hirsch guarded the net and defenceman Geoff Smith returned to the ice after a three week recovery from a broken jaw. Boyer broke a 7-7 tie with the winner. He wasn't done yet.

He returned in game five at Memorial to notch the 5-4 OT winner and send the series back to Portland with the Blazers more than alive. The Hawks rode home ice to a 5-3 victory and put Kamloops on the edge of elimination. Even to stay alive they had to take the next game and it was also on Portland ice.

Cinderella wasn't ready to go home yet as Kamloops kept it close and went in to the third tied 4-4. When the final buzzer went the 6-5 score favoured the Blazers. Huber's hat trick and two goals by Trevor Buchanan proved the difference. The boys were coming home.

On home ice the "never say die" Blazers built up a 2-0 lead but saw it turn in to a 4-3 deficit entering the third. Eleven rookies, including goalie Corey Hirsch, sore legged captain Pat MacLeod and Geoff Smith playing with a wired jaw finally succumbed 6-4.

No one expected them to be there and or do as well as they did. Except perhaps the Seventh Man.

Huber, MacLeod and Chyzowski all figured in the top ten playoff scorers.

It was also the last game Portland won as they fell in four straight to the Swift Current Broncos. The Broncos sporting former Blazer and Kamloops' native Peter Soberlak along with future Blazer Trevor Sims were on their way to taking the Memorial Cup.

The team had shown character and promise despite its youth. Hitchcock had demonstrated his ability to draw on raw talent and foster a competitive edge. There was much to work with but also some losses to make up for.

David Chyzowski was the only member to crack the west

division first all stars. It wasn't surprising either as he was also taken number 2 in the draft by the New York Islanders. Not since Estevan Bruin Barry Gibbs at #1 in 1966 and New Westminster Bruin Barry Beck at #2 in 1977 had a franchise player gone so high.

Pat MacLeod was taken by Minnesota, Needham by Pittsburgh, Huber by the Islanders and Trevor Buchanan by Hartford.

MacLeod, who landed on the second all stars, went on to star in the minor pro leagues and pick up spot duty in the NHL with four different clubs. Geoff Smith, who also landed on the second all star squad, enjoyed a lengthy NHL career that earned him a Stanley Cup ring with the Edmonton Oilers in 1990 and a regular spot on NHL rosters until he returned to Kamloops in the Fall of 1999 to retire.

Franchise alumni Glenn Hall got to touch the Stanley Cup one last time; as the goalie coach of the champion Calgary Flames.

The Blazers had passed a test of fire. They had not collapsed after the build up to a Memorial Cup challenge and a long run at the top. They defied the norm and were bouncing back.

The season to come had great promise and a former on ice enemy was to be a big part of it.

44

Familiar Road 1989/90

Throughout the 80's Kamloops dominated the western division of the WHL and was a major force in the league itself. The challenge was to get beyond that.

Seattle was chomping at the bit to get the season started with their new star Czech, Peter Nedved. They felt it was their year and Kamloops was the primary obstacle in their path.

Kamloops had their own star on board. Once hated Len Barrie, who committed the heinous slash on Pat MacLeod in last season's playoffs, came over from the Cougars to begin the season of a lifetime in blue, orange and white. Loyal fans were stunned but soon learned to see him in a new light. Promising rookie defenceman Scott Niedermayer made the roster but the return of David Chyzowski looked unlikely. Greg Hawgood was gone but not forgotten as his sweater number rose in retirement to the rafters joining "Gold Dust Twin" Rob Brown. There it remains.

Local hockey heroes Ed Dempsey and Brian Henderson joined Don Hay as assistant and goalie coaches respectively. Dempsey had risen through the minor hockey system while Henderson had starred with the old Tier I Chiefs and then settled down along the Thompson.

The regular season promise suggested by the 7-1 exhibition record began on the road. Len Barrie returned to his old stomping grounds and enjoyed the 10-5 Blazer victory this time; their 8th straight season opening win.

In the home opener former public enemy number one was the hero as Barrie piled up six points in a 7-0 whitewash of Portland before 2530 fans. The team went on to win its first eight. Portland G.M. Brian Shaw called them the best team he had ever seen come out of Kamloops.

If Seattle heard they ignored the claim as they battled the Blazers all season long for first in the division and league. By mid-December Kamloops was sitting at 25-5, they were 13 points up on Seattle and ranked #1 in the country.

Personal achievements had Needham, Hirsch and Chyzowski (who was still with the Islanders) suiting up for the junior nationals. The squad went on to win the World with Chyzowski finishing third in scoring behind Czechs Robert Riechel and Jaromir Jagr.

Len Barrie, joined later in the season by former Cougar line mate Clayton Young, earned his 100th point in a 9-2 win at Memorial over Portland. The man the fans once loved to hate got a standing ovation. He also inked a new deal with the Philadelphia Flyers.

By the time March rolled around Seattle closed to within five points but time ran out on them. When the clock stopped ticking the Blazers returned to their familiar position of first in the division and also secured the Scotty Munro Trophy for first overall. They finished the campaign with David Chyzowski back in the lineup and ready for the playoff run.

Barrie's 185 points, including a franchise record 85 goals, gave him the league scoring title which he added to the plus/minus award with a league record plus 87. Huber landed fourth in scoring and Needham 15th. Those three were joined on the west division all stars by Darryl Sydor on defence.

Fourth place Spokane, 47 points behind, seemed to offer little challenge. Chiefs goalie Jeff Ferguson stunned the 2796 fans at Memorial as his 38 save performance led his underdog squad to a 4-2 upset win in game one. The loss woke up the sleeping giant.

Barrie grabbed five points in the following 8-5 Blazer victory and former Chief Murray Duval notched three goals in a 4-1 win in Spokane. The next three games went to Kamloops and Spokane bowed out 5-1.

The divisional final pitted number one ranked Seattle against number two Kamloops.

Trevor Sim had a little something to prove against the team that traded him a year earlier and earned two assists in the series opening 6-3 Kamloops victory. After taking game two at Memorial they were off to the unfriendly confines of Seattle's home ice.

The "Birds of Prey", as they had been calling themselves, brought out their claws in game three to win going away 8-4. It looked like a homer series. The thought ended quickly as the Blazers took the next tilt 4-1. A tight 2-1 victory back at Memorial Arena with Needham scoring the winner, sent 2969 fans home knowing their boys were within one game of putting Seattle out.

To do it they had to win in Seattle.

In game six the T- Birds had Kamloops on the ropes leading 5-4 in the third but Barrie tied it up with 4:26 remaining to force OT. The first overtime period settled nothing though Kamloops was carrying the play. The second did not last long.

Trevor Sim picked up the puck in the neutral ice zone and went around Seattle defenceman Brent Bilodeau. Unleashing a shot on net the puck bounced off the post to the waiting stick of Murray Duval. He made sure of it and Kamloops was on its way.

89/90 Kamloops Blazers **Top Left to Right** Cal McGowan, Zac Boyer, Craig Bonner, Todd Harris, Lance Johnson, Murray Duval, Shea Esselmont **Middle** Brian Henderson (asst. coach), Mike Haertel (stick boy), Ken Hitchcock (coach), Dean Malkoc, Todd Esselmont, Clayton Young, Darryl Sydor, Paul Kruse, Trevor Sim, Jarrett Bousquet, Steve Yule, Jason Bilous, Pete Friedel (asst. trainer), Greg "Spike" Wallace, Don Hay (asst. coach), Ed Dempsey (asst. coach) **Front** Jeff Watchorn, Dale Masson, Jim McQueen (PR/marketing), Len Barrie, Brian Shantz, Phil Huber, Mike Needham, Bob Brown (GM), Joe Mittelsteadt. Corey Hirsch, Scott Niedermayer (C. Fedorak Studios) **Also suiting up** Tommi Virkunnen, Brian Shantz

The boys were in the WHL final for the fifth time in nine seasons.

The Lethbridge Hurricanes, coached by ex Blazer scout Bob Loucks, who finished six points behind in the overall standings, offered an equally daunting challenge. When they came in to Memorial and stole game one 5-4 in overtime a tight series seemed assured.

In a must win in game two Clayton Young scored the biggest goal of his career. With 6:10 left in the third he knocked down a clearing pass by Ron Gunville and went in to score on Dusty Imoo. Duval got the insurance marker at 18:28. It was a comeback win as the Blazers had been down 3-1 and had to fight off eight straight power plays in the second.

Game three was no less important. The McGowan, Kruse, Boyer line picked up three goals in a 6-3 victory putting the Blazers up 2-1 in the series going to Lethbridge for the next three.

Game four looked good to start as Kamloops built up a 3-0 lead before 4994 fans but the Hurricanes charged back to tie. Enter the Seventh Man. At 18:57 a falling Phil Huber broke the tie and with 18 seconds left Barrie got the insurance. The Blazers regained home ice advantage and could advance to the Memorial Cup with one more win.

Lethbridge did not go down easily. Still, it appeared Kamloops was going to the Memorial Cup when play entered the last minute of the third and they were holding a 5-4 lead. Shades of Dean's Evason's goal against Regina appeared when the home side sent their fans into ecstasy with the tying goal at 19:28. Momentum appeared to swing.

The teams entered overtime. There was only one shot on net.

Phil Huber skated in alone on Imoo but elected to pass to Needham instead of shooting. The puck deflected off of Needham, over the net, off the boards and back to Huber. He banged it home. The Blazers were off to Hamilton for the Memorial Cup, for the third time, and this time they were the favourites.

The Blue Thunder line of Huber, Needham and Barrie garnered seven points and Chyzowski played his best game of the series netting two goals. Hirsch had been stellar all series.

Being the favourite is not always a blessing.

Game one against the Kitchener Rangers was a heartbreaker as they fell 8-7 in OT after blowing a two goal lead in the second. In game two they dominated the Oshawa Generals, outshooting them 50 to 21, but it was the Generals who skated away with the 7-6 overtime victory at 3:55 of OT. The Blazers had been down 6-2 entering the third but at 19:30 they completed the comeback on Chyzowski's goal that sent the game into overtime.

Still, if they beat the Laval Titan they could fight their way back in.

The disappointment was complete as they fell 4-2 to Laval. The dream season ended in disappointment. The rookie goaltending of 16 year old Hirsch that led them through the regular season and the playoffs let them down. For Hirsch and the team it was a hard pill to swallow. They had been the favourites, they had the other teams on the ropes but they had gone winless in their third Memorial Cup appearance.

But lessons had been learned and the Seventh Man would soon be back seeking redemption. Ernie McLean had taken the franchise to the Memorial Cup final three times without a win but eventually hit pay dirt the fourth time.

Though it was tough to recognize at the time the team had an incredible season. Their 3rd Munro Cup, their 6th regular season championship in seven years and their 3rd WHL crown.

Graduation and the pros raided the larder.

Chyzowski was gone for sure as he headed for the Islanders and a pro career seeing him star in the minors and put in NHL appearances. Paul Kruse went on to NHL duty with the Flames, Islanders and now Buffalo with whom he reached the NHL final in 1999 against his old Blazers' coach. Mike Needham earned a Stanley Cup with Pittsburgh in 1992 during his two years at the NHL level, a career cut short by back injuries. Trevor Sim put in three games as an Edmonton Oiler and has parlayed his skills into a minor league pro career. Len Barrie has flitted up and down between the minors and the NHL having his best season in 94/95 with the Pittsburgh Penguins.

The biggest loss was the mentor himself. Ken Hitchcock, the 1990 WHL coach of the year, went on to assistant coaching duties with Philadelphia before turning to head coaching in the IHL. He left with a WHL record winning percentage of .699. His fortunes lay in the NHL though. He was joined by two other Blazers in the 1999 playoffs where he coached the Dallas Stars to their first Stanley Cup. The Memorial Cup may have eluded him but he eventually took home the grand daddy of them all.

Heading the list of successful alumni was Geoff Smith earning a Stanley Cup ring with the 1990 Edmonton Oilers. His opponent in the final series was Greg Hawgood in Boston colours.

The team set a record for most home wins as they took 33 of a possible 36.

The draft had Sydor gone # 7 in the first round to Los Angeles. He was followed by Cal McGowan (Calgary), Paul Kruse (Calgary) and Dean Malkoc (New Jersey).

In nine seasons during the 80's Kamloops had seen the re-emergence of the Seventh Man. Team and player accomplishments abounded. They had more than matched the regular season accomplishments of the franchise's time in New Westminster but the same post season success still eluded them.

That was to change in the 90's.

45

The Never Ending Story______1990/91

If ever there was an excuse for a poor year 90/91 could have been it. Gone were Hitchcock, Len Barrie and David Chyzowski. A new coach, respected but untried at the Tier I level, came on board. Tom Renney needed to prove himself, especially after promising a Memorial Cup during his first interview with NL's Rick "The Bear"Wile.

Spokane, with Bryan Maxwell at the helm, looked like the team to beat.

The Blazers started off as usual by winning their ninth straight season opener, 7-4 over Portland at Memorial Arena. Niedermayer showed his potential netting four goals and two assists.

In October Joey Mittelsteadt, who had been released as an extra overager, came back. A trade sending Dean Malkoc and Todd Esselmont to Swift Current for Ed Patterson provided an overager opening. He was reunited with Niedermayer as the talented D man had slumped without his old linemate. Malkoc's road was to take him on to the NHL where he has toiled for Vancouver and Boston. Being sent down was goalie Joaquin Gage whose pro career took him to Edmonton.

By mid December the surprising Blazers were eight points up on Spokane. Sydor and Niedermayer earned spots on the Canadian Junior National squad that brought home the gold.

January 91 opened with a convincing 8-2 victory over Spokane and a national ranking of #3 compared to the Chiefs' # 10. Even with newly acquired star goalie Trevor Kidd in net the Chiefs dropped the next match 6-2. It looked good despite the fact Spokane continued to tailgate the Blazers in the standings.

A new presence joined the side in February. The strong silent type. "Digger", a fluorescent dog in Blazer colours began his crowd rousing career that became as much a part of Blazer hockey as the flaming logo. Exciting and entertaining the crowds hockey as the flaming logo. Exciting and entertaining the crowds he became the special favourite of every youngster who has ever taken in a Blazer game.

When they met the Chiefs again Spokane still held the season series lead at six to five. A 4-2 Blazer victory suggested they were for real. Spokane would not make up the difference.

On March 18/91 the Kamloops Daily News boasted "Blazers add Chapter to Storybook Season". Not only did they win their division for the 7th time in eight years they also won the league and the Munro Trophy for the 4th time. It was their 9th straight plus .500 season and tied them with the record set by the Estevan/New Westminster Bruins from 1970 to 1979. Cal McGowan finished 3rd in scoring followed by Murray Duval who was 13th.

First round rival Tri Cities finished 26 points behind them and looked to be an easy out in round one. Somebody forgot to tell the Americans as they outshot the Blazers in every game but the series ending match. Even then they made it close before losing the game 7-5 and the series 5-2. It came down to #3 ranked Kamloops against #6 ranked Spokane.

Spokane ruined the party. The Chiefs came right into Memorial to take the first two games 4-1 and 3-2. Hirsch kept the matches close but Trevor Kidd barred the door on the Blazers. It was no better in Spokane as injuries and lack of scoring had Kamloops facing elimination in game five at home.

It ended ingloriously with a 3-2 loss before the hometown fans. Down 3-0 with less than two minutes remaining they pulled to within one before the final whistle. Zac Boyer, with 45 seconds left on the clock, scored the last goal of the season for Kamloops. He would do the same next year.

They had won the regular season honours and could hoist another banner but the loss to Spokane stung. The Chiefs did not lose another game as they road their bandwagon to a Memorial Cup. As for the Blazers the expression "Wait until next year" was not a hollow promise.

Adding to the team honours was the selection of Hirsch, Sydor, Niedermayer and McGowan to the first string west division all stars. Sydor took home the WHL top defence man award, Niedermayer the scholastic player of the year, Bob Brown executive of the year and rookie coach Tom Renney coach of the year. He had proven himself in the regular season but the Memorial Cup promise remained unmet.

Franchise alumni also earned accolades. Kamloops local Mark Recchi became the first Kamloopsian to etch his name on the Stanley Cup with Pittsburgh.

The NHL entry draft saw Scott Niedermayer go # 3 overall, to New Jersey. He was followed by Boyer (Chicago), Patterson(Pittsburgh), Steven Yule (Hartford), Hirsch (New York Rangers) and Shane Green (Minnesota).

Their regular season success in the WHL had been unprecedented and their three Memorial Cup appearances had earned them national recognition. Yet without a Memorial Cup they were all bridesmaids awards. They needed the ultimate victory if they were to shake the "almost" label.

90/91 Kamloops Blazers **Top Left to Right** Greg Shukin, Mike Mathers, Todd Esselmont, Jarrett Deuling, Jeff Watchorn, Scott Loucks, Jiri Kloubcek, Pete Friedel (asst. trainer) **Middle** Terry Bangen (asst. coach), Kelly Moore (play by play), Brian Henderson (asst. coach), Scott Niedermayer, Jamie Barnes, Corey Stock, Fred Hettle, Craig Bonner, Lance Johnson, Shea Esselmont, Jarrett Bousquet, Brian Gourlie, Craig Lyons, Chad Berezniuk, Joaquin Gage, Greg "Spike" Wallace, Ed Dempsey (asst. coach), Don Hay (asst. coach) **Front** Dale Masson, Dean Malkoc, Tom Renney (coach), Ryan Harrison, Colin Day (President), Cal McGowan, Bob Brown (GM), Zac Boyer, Murray Duval, Darryl Sydor, Steve Yule, Corey Hirsch (C. Fedorak Photo) **Also suiting up** Joey Mittelsteadt, Ed Patterson, Dan Blasko

46

Attainment 1991/92

To be the best. To reach the ultimate in your sport in the company of your team mates. It is the goal of every player who pulls on his team's jersey. Without culmination it is not achieved.

The franchise had been to the trough eight times and had taken home the Memorial Cup twice. Kamloops itself had been there three times but returned empty handed; just as the Bruins had done before they took the chalice.

If all the pieces fit together in 91/92 a return to the ultimate series was a possibility.

Terry Bangen took over as assistant coach from Ed Dempsey. New faces emerged in the lineup including Darcy Tucker, Tyson Nash, Chris Murray, Rod Stevens and Scott Ferguson. Rookie Aaron Keller joined fellow Kamloops product Ryan Harrison. The big question was who they were getting back from the pros.

Even with some of the pieces of the puzzle missing the Blazers began the season the usual way. They won their 10th straight season opener; 7-3 over Victoria. Two games in and word came Corey Hirsch was back. In November New Jersey returned Scott Niedermayer. By the time early December rolled around they were holding first and sending Renney. Niedermayer and Sydor to the junior nationals. Five points ahead of Spokane they were ranked #1 in the country as the squad went under the care of Don Hay for Renney's absence.

Early in January came even better news as Darryl Sydor was returned by the L.A. Kings. The pieces of the puzzle were fitting together.

An early showdown for a possible WHL final came with the Prince Albert Raiders visit. Riding a 14 game winning streak they were holding down first in the CHL rankings ahead of #2 Kamloops. PA appeared full measure for their ranking as they stormed out to a 5-0 lead. Then the Seventh Man stepped on the ice for one of the greatest comebacks in team history. At 19:17 of the third Sydor fired in the tying goal. Shayne Green capped the remarkable comeback with the winner in OT.

On Feb. 7/92 the team tied a 25 year old record, set by Estevan, for the most goals in a period. They potted 11 markers in the second period in a 13-1 win over the expansion Tacoma Rockets to match the 1967 record. Craig Lyons notched an individual record with six assists in a period.

Hirsch wasn't left behind in the individual accomplishment field. A 9-0 whitewash of Seattle in February gave him a career high 13 shutouts, breaking the record of Edmonton Oil King Ian Wilkie who played from 1967 to 1970. He almost added another as he came within 24 minutes of tying the 67/68 season record of Chris Worthy of the Flin Flon Bombers who had gone 265 minutes without being scored on.

First place in their division, for the 8th time in nine years, was already secure as the battle for first overall, with Prince Albert, came down to the wire. On March 16/92 the Daily News proclaimed Kamloops the regular season league champs for the 5th time. They set a record for being the first WHL team to win over 50 games for three consecutive seasons. Despite being the third highest scoring team in the league they only placed one player in the top 15 scorers. Zac Boyer landed in 7th place.

Their first round opponent was the expansion Tacoma Rockets. It was a costly sweep as Craig Bonner was lost for the rest of the playoffs.

While waiting for their next round opponent word came Hirsch had been named league MVP and top goalie. He secured a 2.72 goals against average, a save percentage of 92% and five shutouts.

Seattle emerged from the Washington State battle with Spokane, a credit to them as they were already assured of a Memorial Cup birth given they hosted the tournament. The T-Birds had never beaten Kamloops in a playoff series and when they lost the first two games it looked like they were in for an early exit. They turned it on at home to take the next two and show that they were for real. The Blazers were back on home ice for game five but were now minus Ed Patterson to injury as well.

As expected they won 4-1 but had to face Seattle ice for game six. The homer series ended convincingly as the awakened Blazers skated into Seattle and waxed the Birds 8-1. They were off to the league final for the sixth time.

Now came the Saskatoon Blades, upset winners over

Prince Albert in the east. The franchise undefeated playoff streak, dating back to Humboldt, looked to be in danger at the outset as the Blades came into Memorial and stole game one 3-2 in overtime. They grabbed home ice. Though the Blazers took the next two they now faced three straight games at Sask Place. Over 10000 fans came out to cheer their Blades but had to suffer through a 6-3 Kamloops victory that regained home ice for the Blazers. They needed it as Norm Maracle back stopped his side to the next two wins. Game seven went in Kamloops.

It was the last game the Blazers played at Memorial Arena. The barn had seen them open with a win in their first game back in 1981 and witnessed the convincing 8-0 victory over Saskatoon that put them in to the Memorial Cup for the fourth time. The new Riverside Coliseum was rising along the Thompson River.

Hirsch and nine others had a point to make in the Memorial Cup after the disappointment of 1990. Eddie Patterson returned from injury. The WHL playoffs saw Boyer finish atop the scorers followed by Niedermayer in third and Shayne Green and Craig Lyons tied for seventh. Jarrett Deuling was voted playoff MVP.

Game one in Seattle against the Sault Ste. Marie Greyhounds brought back that sinking feeling. Dropping the match 6-3 they were reminded that in seven tries they had never beaten an OHL team in the Memorial Cup. They bounced back from 4-0 to make it 4-3 before Niedermayer gave up the puck for the Soo's fifth goal. Shayne Green joined Bonner on the injured roster.

Hirsch was awarded the CHL goalie of the year award but nothing short of a Memorial Cup was going to satisfy him or his team mates. He came back to stone Verdun 4-0 and set up a two game series with Seattle to determine who was going to the final against the 3-0 Greyhounds. Game one determined who got home ice advantage for the semi final matchup.

Niedermayer redeemed himself in game one scoring once and setting up two others in a 3-1 victory. Game two left no doubt as Kamloops erased the T-Birds 8-3. Mike Mathers scored one and set up five. They were in the Memorial Cup final for the first time. A one game crap shoot.

There were 7500 fans, including Ken Hitchcock, on hand; 3000 of whom were loyal Kamloopsians rocking the joint with chants of "Lets go Blazers, Lets go" and "We want the Cup."

They were filled with elation as their boys roared out to a 3-0 lead but lapsed into nervous tension as the Soo came back to tie it in the second. Again in the third the Blazers went ahead and were outshooting the Greyhounds 3-1. The air escaped the balloon when gritty Chris Simon knotted the score again at 15:33. It looked like overtime.

With time winding down Eddie Patterson was speared behind the Greyhound net. As he struggled to the bench four Greyhounds charged towards the Blazer end. No sooner had Patterson reached the bench than goalie Dale Masson pushed Boyer on to the ice. Scott Niedermayer grabbed an errant pass from the offence minded Greyhounds and feathered it up to the home free Boyer. Hodson came out to face the on rushing Blazer. Boyer deked to the goalie's left and then went right to stare in to the open net. He fired the puck and the light went on. There were only 14.6 seconds left.

91/92 Kamloops Blazers **Top Left to Right** Scott Niedermayer, Todd Johnson, Darcy Tucker, Tyson Nash, Scott Loucks, Rod Stevens, Len Forshener, Chris Murray **Middle** Stu MacGregor, Trevor Elliot, Terry Bangen, Pete Friedel, Brian Henderson, Mike Mathers, Jeff Watchorn, Jarrett Deuling, David Wilkie, Len Johnson, Jarrett Bousquet, Craig Lyons, Ryan Huska, Scott Ferguson, Craig Bonner, Don Hay, Greg "Spike" Wallace, Kelly Moore **Front** Dale Masson, Shayne Green, Colin Day, Darryl Sydor, Bob Brown, Zac Boyer, Rob Lelacheur, Tom Renney, Steve Yule, Corey Hirsch, Adam Clark (stick boy) (C. Fedorak Photo & Brian's Photography) **Also suiting up** Ryan Harrison, Fred Hettle. Jarrett Zuliwsky Dan Blasko, Michel Sup, Roland Ramoser, Antti Boman

Pandemonium swept the crowd and the faithful watching the match on TSN. No more bridesmaids awards. The Seventh Man was bringing the Cup home. The puzzle had come together. No more team “almost”. The Blazers were the Champions. Tom Renney delivered on his promise.

Parading the Cup around the ice the Blazers took it over to their screaming home section to share the moment. Almost forty years after the Rockets made the community’s first tentative steps on the road to the Cup Kamloops had attained the ultimate goal on the national stage.

Adoration poured upon the homecoming heroes as they paraded the Cup through to Riverside Park. Ironically gathering at the bandshell near where the first recorded hockey game in Kamloops occurred back in 1902; they shared the moment with their fans.

Four years later they gathered again as the 91/92 Blazers were inducted into the B.C. Sports Hall of Fame.

Niedermayer, Mathers and Hirsch ended up on the Memorial Cup all star squad. Boyer set a record for most winning goals in a Memorial Cup at three. Hirsch was awarded outstanding goalie and Niedermayer tournament MVP. Sydor had earned a spot on the WHL west division alongside Niedermayer and Hirsch.

There were no "buts" at the end of the season; only accolades.

The draft saw David Wilkie go to Montreal followed by Deuling (New York Islanders) and Mathers (Washington).

The franchise alumni turned up in the Stanley Cup finals. Mike Needham got his name on the mug with the Pittsburgh Penguins while Rob Brown looked on as a member of the finalist Chicago Black Hawks.

After the party came the partings. There would be no forgetting though.

Corey Hirsch took his act to the New York Rangers to start his pro sojourn taking him to Vancouver and Nashville. It included a stop with Tom Renney’s 1994 Canadian World Championship team. Boyer and Patterson skated off to minor pro careers with spot duty in the NHL. Niedermayer had Stanley Cups in his future with the New Jersey Devils along with former Junior Oiler Ken Daneyko. Sydor made it to the Stanley Cup final with LA in 1993, played in the 1998 all star game along with Niedermayer and joined Ken Hitchcock, Brad Lukowich and Kamloops local Doug Lidster in Dallas on the 1999 Stanley Cup Stars. Tom Renney went on to the international stage with the 1994 World Championship Canadian team, leaving a WHL league coaching record of .731 surpassing the old one so recently set by Ken Hitchcock. His brief two year stay with the underachieving Vancouver Canucks ended in 1998 with serious questioning as to whether he had been given much of an opportunity. He carried himself throughout with the same class that characterized him as the Blazer bench boss.

For many teams the Memorial Cup was a singular achievement followed by a fast fade for many years to come. Were the Blazers of that mould or were they the stuff of a dynasty?

47

Native Son _______________ 1992/93

The mountain had been climbed and the standard set. For those remaining and those coming on board the tradition was imbedded and the measure by which they would be judged established. Renney was gone and his replacement embodied the team, community and the franchise.Native son Don Hay played as a Bruin under Ernie McLean, Scotty Munro as a Calgary Centennial and worked with the Blazers as an assistant coach under the tutelage of Hitchcock and Renney. The Seventh Man could not have picked better himself. The last franchise player who came back to coach the squad won two Memorial Cups. It would be a tall order to match the accomplishments of Ernie McLean himself.

Ed Dempsey rejoined the team as assistant coach along with Terry Bangen.

Despite player losses the Blazers were still haled as a force in the WHL. Even before the season began CHL rankings had them listed as #3 ahead of # 7 ranked Portland. Bob Brown didn't agree and prophesied the Winterhawks were the team to beat.

Promising rookies arrived in the persons of Bob Maudie, Hnat Domenichelli, Shane Doan and Nolan Baumgartner. Local Aaron Keller was back for a full, rookie, season this time around.

.

The side opened the season in the usual manner; with a win; their 11th straight season opening victory. Dustin Green, brother of Shayne Green, got the winner in OT in Spokane.

The season home opener was the event everyone was waiting for. The Memorial Cup appeared, the banner was raised and the sound system replayed Kelly Moore's broadcast of Boyer's winning goal. The atmosphere was electric. What an opening for the new Riverside Coliseum and its capacity crowd; the largest to ever see a home game.

Unfortunately the Winterhawks spoiled the show by

trouncing the home side 8-2. It was clear this season was not to be a cake walk.

As 1992 came to a close the squad was battling for fourth place and playing sub .500 hockey at 17-18-2. Attendance at the Coliseum even dipped below 3000 for one January game.

1993 brought new life. Beginning with a 7-1 victory over visiting Moose Jaw followed by an 8-7 win over front running Tacoma. Tucker stole the show with five points. Their next match was a 4-1 win over Spokane that put them over .500 for the first time since October.

On Jan. 22/93 news came they had swung a deal for Steve Passmore, the stellar goalie of the long suffering Victoria Cougars. He wanted a trade to a contending team. The price was Dale Masson; a heart breaking deal for a Blazer who went all the way to the Cup in blue, orange and white.

When the teams met for the first time Masson came out the winner in a 5-4 decision but these were two sides going in different directions. Kamloops fans quickly adopted the colourful Passmore and he began to make a difference.

By early February they were second. They crawled to within three points of the Hawks with a 4-2 win but fortune turned against them when leading scorer Craig Lyons was injured in the next match. He was gone for six weeks. Domenichelli moved up to the Mathers/Tucker line as a replacement and the team kept rolling. Winning their last three games of the season landed them in third, seven points behind number one Portland.

Passmore, Mathers and Lyons all made the west division all stars. Mathers finished 10th in scoring followed closely by Lyons in 12th.

The first two matches against Seattle at Riverside were tight affairs. Mathers got the winner in game one in overtime and former Tbird David Wilkie notched two goals in the 3-0 game two victory. Seattle took one game on their home ice but returned to Kamloops facing elimination in game five. Down 3-2 in the third the Blazers tied it up to force overtime. It took two extra periods before Darcy Tucker salted away the game and the series.

Next came Spokane while Portland enjoyed a bye.

Down 5-2 in game one at Riverside they charged back to tie and force overtime. It only took ten seconds for “Rocket” Rod Stevens to fire home the winner. The bad news was David Wilkie was lost to concussion and Passmore with mono. The

Chiefs fell in three straight as Kamloops took the best of five. They were in the west division final for the 10th straight time.

They had gone 2-5-1 against the bigger Winterhawk squad so they were in tight. Despite taking 2-0 leads in both games in Portland they ended up on the losing end and returned to Riverside down 2-0 in the series. It was made worse by the loss of rookie defence man Aaron Keller.

Character showed in game three. Down 4-0 they climbed back with four goals in the third to take the game 6-4. Lyons and Tucker each struck for two goals. Again in game four they came back to tie the game in the third but this time the Hawks got the winner at 18:07. Down 3-1 they were facing elimination. They boarded the bus for the Rose City while Portland flew home in comfort. The end came with a 6-2 loss in Oregon.

92/93 Kamloops Blazers **Top Left to Right** Bob Maudie, Jason Holland, Shane Doan, Dustin Kelley, Bob Westerby, Brad Hammerback, Dustin Green, Nolan Baumgartner **Middle** Greg "Spike"Wallace, Pete Friedel, David Pirnak, Chris Murray, Scott Ferguson, Mike Josephson, Tyson Nash, Rod Stevens, Darcy Tucker, Aaron Keller, Hnat Domenichelli, Ryan Huska, David Wilkie, Terry Bangen, Kelly Moore (play by play) **Front** Andy Gagnon (stick boy), Rod Branch, Craig Lyons, Jarrett Deuling, Don Hay, Colin Day, Craig Bonner, Bob Brown, Mike Mathers, Jarrett Bousquet, Scott Loucks, Don Larsen, Dale Masson (C. Brian's Photography) **Also suiting up** Steve Passmore, Mark Bell, Fran Defrenza, Brad Lukowich, David Benard, Lee Grant, Chris Josephson, Shane Kuss, Steve Parsons

Their performance had made it clear they were not about to take a tumble after winning a Memorial Cup, like so many other teams. Hay had done more than a credible job and they were coming back stronger next year. Mathers, Lyons and Bonner were their major losses.

The bullet that was dodged was not on the ice. The arrival of the new coliseum was more crucial than anyone realized. Blazer President Colin Day confirmed the team was on the verge of financial ruin and it would have been gone without Riverside Coliseum.

It had been a battle to get the franchise to come to Kamloops, another to save it from being sold to Swift Current and then to build the facility necessary to keep it. The Seventh Man was as much in evidence with the team of individuals who made the Blazers a reality and gave them a permanent home. Despite success on the ice Humboldt, Estevan and New Westminster were not able to hang on to the franchise. This time the crisis was looked in the eye and stared down. Without that off-ice team the franchise would have moved on and perhaps, this time, the mystique would have been lost forever. Every hockey fan in Kamloops owes a debt of gratitude to all those who took part making the team a part of the community and keeping it.

The new coliseum offered even more to the community as the Blazers began piling up surpluses which they used to develop the Blazer Foundation. Drawing on interest from its 1.5 million dollars they have turned around and made donations throughout Kamloops for worthy causes. In word and deed the Kamloops Blazers are a responsible contributing part of the community.

So the feared eventuality did not come to pass and the team proved solid on and off the ice. The 92/93 squad even tied a 25 year old franchise record for consecutive home ice victories at 21. In doing so they matched the 1967/68 record set by the Jimmy Harrison led Estevan Bruins.

The draft had Ryan Huska go to Chicago and Montreal pick up a steal with Darcy Tucker.

Franchise alumni Darryl Sydor reached the Stanley Cup final, along with Kamloopsian Tim Watters, with the LA Kings against the Montreal Canadiens.

It had been a fine season and a warm welcome for the native son.

48

Hay Ride to Heaven__________1993/94

Two years before, the Blazers reached the Cup final and brought back the hardware. The question remained. Would they be one Cup wonders or would they remain a force? The 93/94 campaign provided a resounding answer.

Training camp brought a combination of youth and experience coupled with a sound defence. Newcomers to watch were Jason Strudwick, Jarome Iginla and Jason Holland. Wilkie, Tucker and Scott Ferguson returned from the pro camps. As good as they looked none of the local sportswriters were calling for them to challenge for first. That was given over to either Portland or Spokane with Kamloops being called to garner either second or third. Talk was the team was more likely to contend next season when there were hopes Kamloops would host the Memorial Cup.

The season started with the Blazers winning their league opener for the 12th straight time. This time 7-4 over Spokane.

Playing at .500 in early October word came Quebec was returning Steve Passmore. He could have gone to the minor league pros but a quote in the local paper revealed his feelings about his old team. "I wasn't going to win a Memorial Cup ring in the East Coast Hockey League".

Meanwhile Portland was still undefeated.

Little seemed to change until mid-November. Sitting just below .500 they were 15 behind first place Portland with the Hawks coming to town. The White Lightning line of Deuling/Tucker/Stevens erupted for nine points as the Hawks were roasted 9-0.

Offsetting good and bad news didn't stop the newly motivated team. The good news was Kamloops had won the right to host the 1995 Memorial Cup. The bad news was Passmore was injured and out. Backup Rod Branch got the call. When the Mark Recchi sweater retirement night rolled around nine games later the resurgent Blazers were riding a ten game undefeated string.

Local hero Mark Recchi lived out the Canadian dream. Standing at centre ice in his home town, with friends, family and fans surrounding him, he was given the ultimate honour. His number rose to the rafters to join Evason, Evtushevski, Brown and Hawgood. He symbolized the strength and success of the team, the franchise and the Kamloops Minor Hockey Organization all rolled in to one.

His words thrilled the crowd. 'This means more to me than any single accomplishment I've won".

The evening celebration continued with the streak going to 11 at the expense of Swift Current. It did not end until the team reached 16 games straight unbeaten; surpassing the club record set in 1985/86. In the absence of Passmore Branch had carried the team. They were now battling Portland for first and thinking a shot at the Memorial Cup was not out of the question.

93/94 Kamloops Blazers **Top Left to Right** Kelly Moore (play by play), Doug McLeod, Greg Hart, Shane Doan, Chris Murray, Jason Strudwick, Jarome Iginla, Nolan Baumgartner, Jason Holland, Mike Krooshoop, Don Larsen, Pete Friedel **Middle** Greg "Spike" Wallace, Ed Dempsey, Louis Dumont, Bob Maudie, Tyson Nash, Rod Stevens, Mike Josephson, Aaron Keller, Brad Lukowich, Hnat Domenichelli, Dion Hagan, Brian Henderson **Front** Rod Branch, Stu MacGregor, Ryan Huska, Colin Day, Jarrett Deuling, Bob Brown, Scott Ferguson, Don Hay, Darcy Tucker, Steve Passmore. Stick boys - Allan Mitton, Kevin Harris (C. Brian's Photography) **Also suiting up** Scott Loucks, David Wilkie, Jarret Bousquet, Jason Becker, Craig Swanson, Bob Westerby, Sean Matile

January 6 brought sad and exciting news. Four year vet Louis Dumont was unhappy in Regina and wanted out. So too did Blazer rearguard David Wilkie. It seemed all sides would be happy with the deal except it also included fan favourite Scotty Loucks travelling east with Wilkie. In Dumont Kamloops got a power play man, face-off man, penalty killer and proven scorer.

The run continued and on January 10 the Blazers owned first place. The Hawks were still holding the #1 national ranking with the Blazers right behind at #2.

An eastern road trip took them to Regina for an emotional match. Loucks was at his best as he got two goals and an assist while Wilkie added one goal. Dumont did his bit by contributing a goal and an assist in the close fought 6-5 OT Blazer victory.

By the time February rolled around it was the Blazers holding number one in the country followed by Laval Titan in second. Portland fell to 6th place. When the Branch led squad took Spokane 10-4 the goalie in the shadows ran his season record to 15-1-1.

March brought news they had lost talented Shane Doan for the season but that didn't stop the blue, orange and white. With a 4-3 victory at home over the Victoria Cougars Kamloops set a new record for straight home ice victories, at 25. They eventually ran the record to 29. The same night, in a class act, the Blazers Booster Club honoured former Blazer goalie Dale Masson; once a Blazer always a Blazer.

The Daily News proclaimed the Blazers west division champs on March 14/99, for the 9th time. They went on to take the league title and Scotty Munro Trophy for the 6th time in ten years.

The joy was dealt a blow in the final game of the season as Chris Murray was suspended and Passmore was facing the same prospect after a melee in Portland involving a fan. The Hawks poured it on winning 7-0 in the Rose City to serve notice they were still a force.

Tucker landed 2nd in scoring and joined Passmore on the division all stars. Bob Brown took home the Lloyd Saunders Memorial Trophy as executive of the year. It was no wonder that they were big favourites over Seattle.

On the home front the Kamloops Jardine Blazers under coach Mickey Fritz busied themselves winning their own prestigious Kamloops International Bantam Hockey Tournament over Detroit; 7-2. Skating for Jardines were John Bradley, goalie Jeff Blair, Derek Paget and AJ Baines who had netted two goals and two assists. The future held another Blazer Detroit game at the

Coliseum in its crystal ball.

The underdog T-Birds, with nothing to lose, stunned Kamloops 4-1 in the opening game of the series, then forced the hosts to double overtime before Louis Dumont whacked in the winner for Kamloops in game two. When the teams returned to Kamloops for game five Seattle had proved they were no fluke as the series was knotted at two apiece. Despite finishing 39 points behind Seattle was threatening. Kamloops regrouped and won 8-5. Game six, a 5-3 victory, in Seattle sealed the series for the Blazers but they lost Dumont for three weeks in the process with a separated shoulder.

Portland was next and motivation was no problem. Chris Murray had revenge in mind against the team that physically pounded and eliminated them last year.

Local sportswriters still favoured Portland over the home side despite the great season. They had been wrong before and hopes were they would be again. It looked like it as the Blazers took both home games but the season long Rose City jinx held. They returned with the series tied 2-2. Adam Deadmarsh had demolished them in the 4th game with four goals and two assists as Kamloops fell 9-3.

On home ice the Blazers returned the favour with a 7-2 win while holding Deadmarsh pointless. Just like last season Kamloops boarded the bus for the long trip south while Portland sailed in comfort by jet. It didn't save the Hawks this time.

The battle was tough and not finally settled until 19:55 of the third. Rookie Jarome Iginla, who had scored the Blazers first goal on an assist from Scott Ferguson, set up Ferguson for the 2-1 game and series winner. Revenge on a tight rope but revenge nonetheless.

They now faced a Saskatoon side that had won eight of their nine playoff games and had WHL goalie of the year Norm Maracle between the pipes. This time the local sportswriters threw their hats in the Blazers ring. They looked like prophets.

The Blazers were leading the series 3-1 and playing their third game in Saskatoon with the prospect of a win sending them to the Memorial Cup. Their own history should have told them to be wary and remember how Regina had thought themselves headed for the Memorial Cup ten years earlier. The Blades didn't fold and grabbed a heart stopping 3-2 victory with only 29 seconds left.

Back on home ice the Blazers found themselves smashing up against the stone wall that was Norm Maracle. The Blades goalie performed the miracle despite Kamloops dominance. The Blades won 2-1 to force a seventh and deciding game. Was it possible they could finally break their jinx against the franchise?

It was not even close. The jinx held and Saskatoon was throttled 8-1. Kamloops was going to the Memorial Cup for the 5th time. Steve Passmore, who had lost out to Maracle as the league's top goalie, took home the AirBC award as the WHL playoff MVP.

League President Ed Chynoweth was quoted as saying "I have never seen an organization or team work so hard."

There was reason to feel proud.

The Memorial Cup went in Quebec where the Laval Titan played host in their "House of Pain". The pain all belonged to the Titan in game one as Kamloops took them 5-4. Laval served notice they had character though as they charged back from a 4-2 deficit and missed the tying goal in to an empty net with only 65 seconds left.

The Chicoutimi Sagueneens fell 5-0 before the shutout performance of Passmore and three goals from Tucker.

The early tourney favourites North Bay had a 1-0 lead in their game and were more than holding their own until Chris Murray's battle with Centennial tough guy Steve McLaren stopped them taking liberties. The rink tilted and Kamloops ran away with the game 5-1. At 3-0 they earned a bye to the final. Darcy Tucker earned first star for the third straight game.

The Titan powered their way to another shot at the western reps. Just like two years before Kamloops roared out in front. The second period ended with the Blazers enjoying a seemingly secure 4-1 lead. Laval clawed back in the third and carried the play. At 13:09 they made it 4-2 and followed that up with another at 14:06. There was one more goal left to be scored.

The Blazers and their fans erupted in joy at 19:08 when Bob Maudie fired home the empty net goal that ended the Titan's hopes. For the second time in three years the Kamloops Blazers were Memorial Cup Champions. The question was answered. They were no one cup wonder.

Tucker took home the Stafford Smythe Memorial Trophy as tourney MVP and joined Aaron Keller and Rod Stevens on the all stars

They had taken the Hay ride to the ultimate prize. Don Hay had put his personal stamp on the team from his home town.

The accolades rained down and there remained the prospect of the team earning back to back Cups with their free ride to the tournament in 1995.

They would have to do it without Passmore, Deuling, Ferguson or Murray. All four headed to the pros. Deuling flitted between the minors and the New York Islanders while Ferguson grabbed some spot duty with Edmonton and Anaheim. Chris Murray caught on regularly with Montreal and moved on through Ottawa and Chicago before landing with Hitchcock in Dallas for the 99/2000 season. Passmore battled through career threatening illness to star in the AHL and move on to be a crowd pleaser in Edmonton and Chicago before being traded to LA.

Former Blazer David Wilkie moved up to the Montreal Canadians and then Tampa Bay.

The NHL certainly noticed and reached down to draft a franchise record tying nine players; matching the 1975 crop from the New Westminster Bruins.

Baumgartner went #10 to Washington, Holland to New York Islanders, Chris Murray to Montreal, Strudwick to New York Islanders, Hnat Domenichelli to Hartford, Lukowich to New York Islanders, Josephson to Chicago, Westerby to Buffalo and Tyson Nash to Vancouver.

The alumni had their share of glory with Corey Hirsch backstopping the National squad to an Olympic silver in a game settled in a shoot out. Behind the bench was Tom Renney who also went on to share the joy with Hirsch and the National Squad as it won the World Championship for the first time in 33 years in 1994.

Kamloops proved they were not willing to sell the farm to win a Memorial Cup and fade in to oblivion afterwards. The Blazers were for real and were coming back next year.

The question now was, would they be back in as the host city to earn a tarnished victory or would they get there the honest way through the front door.

49

Perfection______________1994/95

There are moments in a team or franchise's history when all the stars align. When the ultimate achievement in the ultimate setting come together. Such was the 94/95 season.

Training camp had the promise of returning vets but also laid bare the losses of key parts of the squad. Colourful and incredible Steve Passmore moved on leaving big skates to fill. Rod Branch came forward as the number one man while local Jeff Blair vied with 16 year old Randy Petruk for backup. Rob Skrlac came along as the best new tough guy prospect while rookie hopefuls Shawn McNeil, Don Kinney and Cam Severson showed promise up front. Hopeful locals Ajay Baines and Dion Hagan failed to make the cut.

Don Hay remembered his own experiences as a local player not making the home team.

"I can remember being cut from Kamloops. I was a 19 year old player that was cut because they (Kamloops Chiefs) probably had too many 19 year olds or whatever. You feel like it's the worst day of your life. It makes you feel like nobody wants you and you have no place to go."

Of course Hay went on to play that very season with the New Westminster Bruins and finished 3rd in team scoring. His accomplishments after that made him a compelling model for any player going through that disappointing experience.

There was no under dog role this time. The Blazers were picked #1 by the CHL and were expected to do well; sometimes a harder task than starting with lower expectations. Brandon was picked #3 and expected to battle for the league honours. Traditional foes Portland were ranked # 9 and called to nab second place. They faced Kamloops in the season opener.

A bright new season. The fans had a new play by play announcer with NL radio as Jeff Patterson replaced the ever popular Kelly Moore who had gone to greener pastures in Winnipeg.

They also had a young backup goalie who had made the grade as a 16 year old. By season's end the name Randy Petruk was on every Blazer fan's lips.

They opened like thunder. The Winterhawks were stunned 11-1 as Hay enjoyed his first home opener win in three years before an adoring Kamloops audience. For the 13th straight time the Blazers opened the season on a winning note. Hnat Domenichelli led the way with a "Hnat Trick".

Four games later they were undefeated and giving Petruk his first start, against visiting Prince George. He stopped 28 of the 29 shots as his teammates rolled out a 7-1 victory over the Cougars. The P.A. system thundered out the tune "Wild Thing" when the rookie netminder made the outstanding saves. The rookie had a theme song with his first game.

A perfect record to date did not stop Blazer brass from tinkering and early October brought the news Merritt's Mike Josephson was on his way to Lethbridge for Ukrainian goal scorer Ivan Vologjaninov. Josephson's place in Blazer history was assured and he had a future Memorial Cup appearance ahead of him with the Hurricanes in 1997.

When #2 ranked Brandon came to town the Blazers were in a divisional battle for first with Tacoma. They needed the win to set the tone between the league favourites. Keeping Wheaties star Marty Murray in check they accomplished the task with a 4-1 victory.

On November 5/94 the boys were first overall and on a roll. Returning from their 4-0 road trip they dropped second place Tacoma 5-1. The battle was for first overall as the Blazers stared at their divisional rivals through the rear view mirror.

With December came news Darcy Tucker and Nolan Baumgartner were off to join the junior nationals. They returned with a gold medal.

With New Years on the horizon the Blue, Orange and White were sitting in a first overall tie with Brandon and carrying a game in hand in to the New Year.

By late January they were pulling away and continuing to hold on to their #1 CHL ranking. Spokane coach Mike Babcock, after watching his team fall 3-2 , gave the team and organization one of the nicest compliments a team can receive.

"I wonder how many games they win before they even get in the rink. They work hard and have talented players but there is this awe factor that comes with the Kamloops Blazers."

February brought the usual jockeying for position through trades. Brandon loaded up with star defencemen Bryan Mccabe and Brendan Witt. Kamloops answered by acquiring forward Ashley Buckberger and steady defenceman Keith McCambridge from Swift Current. In doing so they got proven ability and Memorial Cup experience yet they had to pay a price in futures. Promising prospects Cam Severson and Jeff Henkelman went the other way. Severson was destined for his own Memorial Cup appearance in 1998 with Spokane.

February 15/95 ran news that hit those close to the franchise's history. Bill Shinske, aged 64, passed away in Estevan. The silent partner in the triumvirate with Munro and McLean, he had been a big part of the glory years in Estevan and New Westminster. The Seventh Man joined the host of ex Bruins who made the journey to Estevan to honour his memory. The Blazers did not forget their history and paid their own homage to the hockey pioneer.

Don Hay spoke of the former GM fondly "Bill did a lot of work behind the scenes in administration. He should be remembered for doing a lot for junior hockey..... for giving guys like myself the opportunity to play pro hockey.....He was one of the pioneers of the WHL."

Originally from Brandon Bill became a Coca Cola salesman after finishing his Senior A hockey days. He got on with the team by helping Scotty Munro keep the books in Estevan. Eventually he and Ernie, his former hockey team mate, bought the franchise. Colin Day recalled he even had a brief role with the Kamloops Blazers when he was brought in to help with team scheduling.

From the loss of one life to the saving of another. The very next day the Daily News carried the story about Blazer Bob Westerby pulling a man from a burning car. The only down side; it occurred at three a.m., well past Bob's curfew. Catch 22?

In February they played the pivotal game in their eastern road swing as they skated into the Key Arena in Brandon. They emerged 6-2 winners to sweep the season's campaign against their strongest rival.

On February 27/95 they secured their 5th division title in six years. Six days later they garnered the Scotty Munro Trophy as WHL regular season champs, also for the 5th time in six years. Topping it off they became the first team in CHL history to hold on to its number one ranking from season beginning to end. They added a new league record for fewest goals against in a season.

The only race left was Darcy Tucker's pursuit of Tri City's Damon Langkow for the scoring title. It went down to the wire before Langkow secured the title by three points. The difference; Tucker played eight fewer games as a result of the World Junior Championship. Domenichelli finished in 6th place.

Their playoff reward for finishing first. Nothing.

The league decided the western division would have two round robin tournaments to eliminate two clubs with the remaining four then getting home ice advantage for their regular season standing.

The Blazers went up against 3rd place Seattle and 6th place Portland. Questions hummed about who would get the starting goaltender role. Petruk had been the backup at the start of the season but his play had earned alternating games with veteran Rod Branch as the season came to a close. Branch for his part led the league in Goals Against Average. Kamloops added overage scoring star Jeff Antonovich from Langley of the BCJHL.

The Round Robin didn't help the opposition any as Seattle went golfing. Kamloops now faced 6th place Portland with home ice advantage. The Hawks had disappointed those calling for a second place finish.

Showing grit they skated in to Riverside Coliseum and stole game one 5-3 despite being outshot 39-17 with Branch in net. Hay didn't lose faith in his goalie and had him back between the pipes for game two in Portland No doubt this time as the Hawks fell 4-1. Again Hay went with Branch and had nothing but praise for his backstop as the Blazers eked out a 3-2 overtime win in the Rose City. Iginla grabbed the winner at 9:25. Back on home ice the Blazers left nothing to question in game four. The pesky Hawks were batted aside 7-2. Iginla earned raves as the best player in the series.

The divisional final put them up against Langkow's 4th place Americans. Hay again went with Branch who rewarded him with two close fought victories in game one and two at Riverside. Game one ended 4-2 Blazers with the last goal in to an empty net and game two was even tighter. It took a goal by Ashley Buckberger, in the second overtime frame, to secure the match. The win was critical as Bob Louck's Americans turned it on at home. Trailing 5-2 they stormed back to win 7-6 in overtime despite being outshot 54-39. Branch was in again in game two as his team outshot Tri City but came up on the short end of a 4-3 overtime score.

Back on home ice Kamloops regained its form to trounce Tri-City 6-2. Tri City was on the ropes but it was going home for game 6. It didn't help as Randy Petruk made his first appearance and led his side to a convincing 7-1 series clinching victory. Buckberger chipped in with two goals and an assist in the one sided match which saw the Blazers outshoot Tri City 60-24.

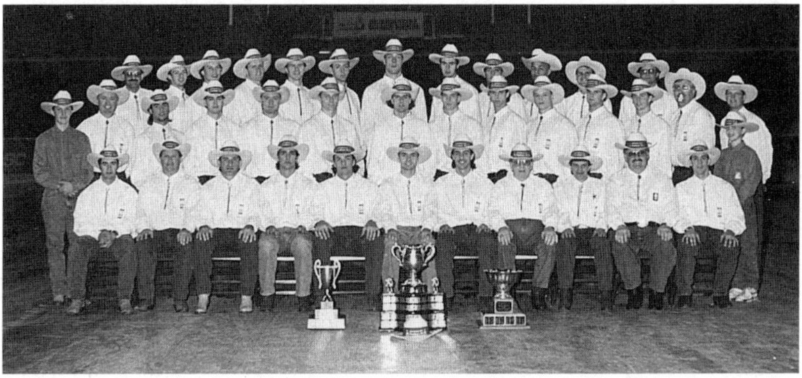

94/95 Kamloops Blazers **Top Left to Right** Doug McLeod, Donnie Kinney, Shane Doan, Jason Holland, Keith McCambridge, Ashley Buckberger, Rob Skrlac, Jeff Oldenborger, Bob Westerby, Jarome Iginla, Randy Hansch, Brian Henderson **Middle** Allan Mitton (stick boy), Ed Dempsey, Jeff Antonovich Aaron Keller, Ivan Vologjaninov, Bob Maudie, Tyson Nash, Hnat Domenichelli, Brad Lukowich, Greg Hart, Jeff Ainsworth, Shawn McNeil, Don Larsen, Pete Friedel **Front** Rod Branch, Stu MacGregor, Don Hay, Nolan Baumgartner, Jason Strudwick, Darcy Tucker, Ryan Huska, Bob Brown, Greg "Spike" Wallace, Colin Day, Randy Petruk (C. Brian's Photography) **Also suiting up** Mike Josephson, Cam Severson, Jeff Henkelman,

The Blazers were division champs for the 8th time and facing a Brandon squad that had not made the WHL final for 16 years. Both teams were assured of a spot in the Memorial Cup at Riverside Coliseum. It was a question of whether they backed in or earned the tarnished entry. The stars seemed to favour Kamloops with its season long dominance, regular season title and home ice advantage. Yet it never pays to forget history. Way back in 1970/71 the franchise, then the Estevan Bruins, had earned first place in its division well ahead of 3rd place rivals the Winnipeg Jets but were stunned in the first round.

The Daily News predicted a close fought series calling

for Kamloops to prevail in seven. The fans gathered at the Coliseum expecting a victory.

Brandon coach Bob Lowes had been captain of the Regina Pats team when it was ousted years before in Kamloops, thanks to The Goal" by Dean Evason. He recalled his disappointment and hoped to see the tables turned this time.

Despite outshooting Brandon 35-27 the Blazers were kept off the sheet and suffered a 3-0 setback. It got worse. In game two Branch gave up the first two goals and was pulled for Petruk. He never played as a Blazer again. The seventeen year old rookie let in the next three as Kamloops fell 5-4 despite a 51-22 shot advantage. Kamloops was heading to Brandon down 2-0 and thoughts of not getting a clean entry in to the Memorial Cup were on the minds of many.

The Blazers turned the tables in game three as Petruk outshone Elder in a 4-1 win.

Game four went to overtime tied at two as Petruk again starred. Vologjaninov notched the winner at 2:01 to tie the series and ensure the Blazers at least one more home game. It got better. Petruk again starred in a 5-4 victory at the Key Arena silencing the expectant crowd. Their Wheaties had been up 2-0 coming home for three games. Now, thanks to a seventeen year old rookie, they were going back to Kamloops down 3-2 and facing elimination.

The Kamloops fans were ecstatic but nervous. Brandon showed its character by not folding their tent. The Wheaties had the hosts down 4-3 going into the final two minutes and it looked like there was going to be game seven with home ice being more of a disadvantage. Darcy Tucker rewrote the script at 18:18 when he sent the fans into an uproar with a power play goal, his third of the game. This one was doomed to OT. A charged up Blazer squad hit the ice flying and outshot the visitors 10-3. A battle in front of the net between Huska and Kevin Pozzo saw the Blazer forward dig out the puck and beat Elder on his stick side at 6:03.

The Coliseum erupted. The comeback was complete. Kamloops was going to its 6th Cup appearance with a chance to set a record with three cups in four seasons.

Nolan Baumgartner, the series MVP, summed it up "That's the way we wanted to go in. We proved everybody wrong. A lot of people doubted us (trailing 2-0) going to Brandon and we won three straight."

It was the chance of a lifetime. The Memorial Cup was being hosted in Kamloops and the city was wild about it. Their boys could achieve the ultimate with an unblemished Memorial Cup victory on home ice in front of the home crowd. The whole tournament was electric and caused one visiting reporter to christen the city Blazerville. Shades of Estevan's Bruinville in 1968

Masses of white towels, placards, painted faces and Halloween attire greeted the teams as they stepped out on to the ice. Proof positive even cement can vibrate.

The Hull Olympics came on first and fell 4-1 before a cheering full house. Outshooting the visitors 49-19 the Blazers were carried to victory by Iginla's two goal performance. Home town boy Aaron Keller snatched the winner.

Game two had the OHL Detroit Junior Red Wings led by star defenceman Brian Berard lacing up against the home side. The game proved tight and with Kamloops up 3-2 Tucker took a stick in the face from Berard. Despite losing a tooth in the incident there was no penalty. Three minutes later he got his revenge as he netted the 4-2 goal. When Doan made it 5-2 it looked to be all over. Instead the Blazers found them themselves hanging on to the end before skating off with a 5-4 victory.

Their familiar foe Brandon was next. The third had the Blazers hanging on to a one goal lead courtesy of Iginla until Tyson Nash, who had irritated and bashed all game, netted the insurance marker with 1:28 remaining. The final score 6-4 Kamloops. They were in the final. Winner takes all.

It was their fifth straight tough win against the Wheaties and Brandon did not get another chance. It was Detroit which skated out for the final matchup. The tension in the building was electric. Save for the Hull game there had been no easy matches. It turned in to a celebration.

The first ended 1-0 favour the Blazers but Detroit had already shown problems maintaining discipline as it fell time and again to penalties. In the second the roof caved in as they amassed more penalties. Six unanswered markers had the Blazers up 7-0 entering the third. In their past Cup wins they had built up leads and seen their foes storm back but when Antonovich got number eight at 2:32 that seemed impossible. Even when Detroit managed two late goals the most anxious Blazer fan was confident the ultimate prize was going to be won before their very eyes.

The Thompson Valley echoed to an eruption of screams and hollers as the seconds ticked down. The Blazers had reached perfection. Three Cups in four years with the latest on home ice.

On and on the cheering went as the song "We are the Champions" rolled over the P.A.

In the stands were many of the alumni. Hometown hero Mark Recchi, Darryl Sydor, Rudy Posechek, Rob Brown, Scott Ferguson, Louis Dumont, Craig Bonner and Mike Josephson.

Don Hay's emotions spilled out as he spoke about Josesphson and the Blazers.

"He's still a Blazer, I think deep down he feels he's a Blazer right now. He wants to share in the victory and I think its great everybody welcomes him back with open arms. That's what this organization is all about."

The Seventh Man was dancing on the ice, his presence growing even greater as the franchise lived the moment. The team tied a record with back to back Memorial Cup wins with five other teams including the New Westminster Bruins, set the record for most Memorial Cups since 1972 for a team at three and franchise at five and the most Memorial Cup appearances by a franchise at ten.

The awards were handed out. Shane Doan was proclaimed MVP after garnering nine points while Iginla, who had gone without a penalty throughout the tournament was awarded the George Parsons Trophy for Sportsmanship. For Doan it was especially pleasing as he was injured the year before and did not feel he contributed the way he wanted to.

Huska, Tucker and Nash joined Robert Savard as the only players to ever win three Memorial Cups while Hay tied a record with eight others for winning two Memorial Cups; including Ernie McLean. Doan, Tucker and Baumgartner landed on the Memorial Cup all stars.

Baumgartner, the WHL's top defenceman, was joined on the west division all stars by Tucker.

The team had set a new record for consecutive home ice wins over overlapping seasons with a new mark of 33 games.

Doan was drafted # 7 by Winnipeg, Iginla # 11 by Dallas, Hart by Montreal, Maudie by New York Rangers and Rob Skrlac by Buffalo.

The franchise alumni saw Scott Niedermayer and Ken Daneyko sip from the Stanley Cup with the New Jersey Devils.

The personnel losses were deep; beyond the expected departures of Tucker, Vologjaninov and Antonovich. Tucker skated in the colours of Montreal and Tampa Bay before donning a Maple Leaf in Toronto in 2000. Strudwick started with the New York Islanders and landed in Vancouver. Huska enjoys cups of coffee in the NHL and a minor league career. There was to be another, unexpected, loss.

Forty-nine years after it had all started in Humboldt the franchise hoisted its fifth Memorial Cup after eleven appearances. An astounding achievement.

The shadow of the Seventh Man stretched across the country.

50

A New Era 1995/96

Player losses were expected and few were surprised when Don Hay obtained a coaching position in the NHL with Calgary but no one expected the departure of GM Bob Brown. Perceived as the architect of the Blazer dynasty he was a key figure in five of their Memorial Cup appearances. The team never posted a sub .500 season under his guidance and developed an unsurpassed record of success. In a hockey town like Kamloops the debate over what happened became the topic of the day. Neither Brown nor the Blazers organization elaborated in detail and time was left to take care of the rumblings and rumours.

Bob Brown's place in franchise's history was secure. The Blazers now had the daunting task of sustaining the magic despite personnel losses. They had to do so facing Bob Brown in the eye. Within a week of his departure Brown re-emerged as GM in Tri-City.

In his wake Stu MacGregor took over as GM. The long time scout chose to stay with Kamloops rather than head off for prospects in Regina. Hay's position was taken by long time friend and assistant coach Ed Dempsey.

Dempsey, a local hockey product, played his junior hockey in Penticton and was with the 72/73 squad that ousted favoured Kamloops Rockets, led by Don Hay, from the Provincial Championship. The Broncos went on to the national final and play in the Centennial Cup. His playing career took him to Michigan Tech where he skated in three NCAA championships winning one in 1975. The following year he set a school record for points surpassed, ironically, the next year by fellow Kamloopsian Tim Watters. Ed enjoyed a few AHL games before returning to Kamloops and teaming up with Hay again; this time with the Senior B Kamloops Cowboys.

For the past three years he filled the position of assistant coach and now had a two year head coach contract in his pocket. To say it was a challenge was an understatement. His charge was to take over a squad hard off the heels of three Memorial

Cups, satisfy a demanding fan-following expecting nothing but success and follow in the footsteps of local hero Don Hay.

In his own words "I'm taking over from a living legend"

Joining him behind the bench as assistant was Al Glendenning, former captain of the Calgary Centennials under Munro himself. Brian Henderson stayed on as goaltender coach.

At least on the ice he had more than a few assets to work with as Baumgartner, Iginla, Domenichelli, Lukowich, Holland and goaltending sensation Randy Petruk returned. Hopes were Doan would return from Winnipeg. Rod Branch was claimed by the expansion Calgary Hitmen.

Wheeling and dealing brought a third player with NHL bloodlines as Steve Gainey, whose roots were in eastern Canada, obtained special permission to play in the WHL. Kamloops obtained his rights from Calgary and he joined Blair Rota and Chris St. Croix as players whose fathers had toiled in the bigs.

The pre-season started well with an 8-5 victory over Seattle on the strength of Doan's three goal, six point performance as he prepared to head off to Winnipeg. With Doan in the lineup and the other returnees' a fourth Memorial Cup was not an unreasonable goal. It was not to be though as Winnipeg eventually signed the promising 18 year old and brought back memories of the losses of Habscheid and Butcher in 1982/83. Key players who could have made a difference. Hopes for his return lasted the entire season but were never realized.

The season opened with team captain Hnat Domenichelli leading his side to a 7-6 victory in Kelowna, the new home of the Rockets. The 14th straight season opening victory by Kamloops. Despite the strong returning core of players the Blazers did not rate in the CHL's top ten rankings, being called to place behind Tri City and Kelowna in their division.

They were 3-0 entering their home opener against Bob Brown's American's. Memorial Cup Banner raising night, Bob Brown leading the opposition, former Blazers in the stands. You could safely say it was an emotional night all round. It took an overtime goal by Brad Lukowich to give the home side the 5-4 victory.

They were 5-1 when they hosted the Chiefs at Riverside. The 4-3 score didn't favour the Blazers and it began a frustrating battle with Spokane who were the only major stumbling block to the blue, orange and white all season.

The roller coaster season saw them embarrassed 8-1 in

Calgary by Rod Branch, who was named first star after stopping 46 shots, and then turning around a few days later to flatten league leading Brandon 6-3 at the Key Arena.

With word Baumgartner was returning in November optimism blossomed. When they secured a 4-3 win over the Americans on Nov. 17/95 they were back on familiar ground; a first place tie for the league lead. Domenichelli was vying for the league scoring title and all looked good in Blazerville. Then came black December.

Blazer talent proved its downside. The squad lost Iginla, Domenichelli, Holland, Baumgartner and Lukowich to the junior nationals and began a slide which proved hard to brake. At the end of December they were toiling in third and anxiously awaiting the return of its stars.

They returned, gold medal in hand. Iginla scored the shorthanded winner in their 4-3 win over the Russians in the semi and two goals in the 4-1 championship win over Sweden. Domenichelli potted a goal and assist. Iginla was voted the best forward in the World.

Spike Wallace also returned home with a World class trophy. He was overseas as the equipment manager of the Canadian team that won the prestigious Spengler Cup in Switzerland. Now he proudly brought home the crystal trophy for all to see.

With all hands back on board they began their climb back to prominence. All save for Spokane were fodder for the mill. By late January they were fighting the Chiefs for first and riding a 15 game unbeaten streak. Despite losing all of their Spokane matches they were tied for first in mid February with both teams having 12 games remaining. It was neck and neck with the Blazers facing a tough eastern road swing.

A 7-1 loss in Brandon set them behind the Chiefs and they now faced a daunting task of playing in Prince Albert against a Raider team undefeated in 13. They came out ahead 4-1 to sit two points behind Spokane with each team having five games left.

The schedule was now kinder to them but when they lost to lowly Prince George and Portland the jig was up. Spokane took the division by six points. The second place Blazers managed only one tie all season against the front runners. Save for the Chiefs there would have been another banner hanging at Riverside Coliseum.

Domenichelli finished third in scoring followed closely

by Iginla in fourth.

Playoffs; round one, T-Birds, with news Winnipeg was returning star defenceman Darren Quint to Seattle but not Doan to Kamloops. The T-Birds finished well back in the standings but history showed it was dangerous to take any opponent lightly. In game one it took a late goal by Iginla to secure a 3-2 win. He starred again in a close game two match with two goals in a 4-2 victory. Seattle turned the tables with a 3-2 victory on home ice and gave every reason in game four to make their fans think an even series was a possibility. Their hopes were dashed when Brad Lukowich popped in 5-4 OT winner. Kamloops was up 3-1 in their series and were going home.

95/96 Kamloops Blazers **Top Left to Right** Peter Friedel (trainer), Blair Rota, Jordan Landry, Donnie Kinney, Konrad Brand, Don Larsen (marketing), Chris St. Croix, Steve Albrecht, Ajay Baines, Shawn McNeil, Greg "Spike" Wallace **Middle** Brian Henderson (asst. coach), Steve Gainey, Ryan Rishaug, Greg Hart, Jeff Oldenborger, Rob Skrlac, Jarome Iginla, Cadrin Smart, Jeff Ainsworth, Peter Bergman, Al Glendenning (asst. coach) **Front** Kevin Harris (stick boy), Scott Reid, Aaron Keller, Ed Dempsey (coach), Jason Holland, Stu MacGregor (GM), Hnat Domenichelli, Colin Day (President), Bob Maudie, Brad Lukowich, Randy Petruk, Trevor Kennedy (stick boy) (C. Brian's Photography) **Also suiting up** Nolan Baumgartner, Dean Kletzel, John Bradley, Jake Deadmarsh,

Spokane was in shock. They were down 3-0 with the next match in Portland. Iginla fired his third winning marker of the series as the T-Birds were eliminated at the Riverside Coliseum after a 7-5 loss.

Meanwhile the Chiefs staved off elimination and Kamloops waited. Not only did Spokane stave it off they came all the way back to take game seven 4-3 in overtime and advance. In doing so they got a bye and waited for the winner of Tri City/ Kamloops best of five. Bob Brown was back but a confident Daily News predicted Blazers in five.

Despite outshooting the Americans the home side went down 2-0 in game one and were down 2-0 in game two. It looked bad until Iginla scored the power play overtime winner to take the game 5-4 and knot the series. When the Blazers fell 5-2 in game three they faced elimination on Tri City ice. Finally they found their wheels and skated to a convincing 6-1 win to send the series back to Kamloops for the deciding match.

This time there was no question. Lesser lights on the team came to the fore and secured a series clinching win 5-1 in front of the home town fans. Outshooting the Americans 39-18 it was Ryan Rishaug's goal to make the score 3-1 with 48 seconds left in the second period that broke the Americans' back.

The Blazers were on their way to their 10th straight division final. Awaiting them; a team they had not defeated all season, going 0-7-1.

A less confident Daily News called for Spokane, who finished #1 in the nation, in seven.

Games one and two, both at Riverside Coliseum went as predicted in heart breaking fashion. In game one Iginla came back to tie it at 19:27 only to see the Chiefs secure a win 14 seconds later. Game two had Kamloops up 5-3 but the Chiefs poured it on to tie at 16:19 and win at 19:12. Demoralizing losses. When they went down 7-3 in game three in Spokane, despite outshooting the Chiefs, it looked to be all over.

Never say never. Iginla was the hero in game four in Spokane, with the winner, as the Blazers pulled out a 6-5 nail biter. They didn't stop there as they came back from a 5-4 deficit in the third to take game five 6-5. They were coming home down 3-2 and very much alive.

Spokane were not to be denied though. In front of the Kamloops faithful they pulled the plug on the Blazer season with a 6-2 series ending victory. They went on to face Brandon while Kamloops pondered what might have been had there been a Doan in the lineup.

Iginla didn't have time to ponder as he was whisked off to Calgary to help them with their playoff run. Impressing from the start his days with the Blazers came to an end.

Victorious Spokane coach Mike Babcock was gracious in acknowledging the Chief's victory.

"Its is an honour to win but its probably a bigger honour because we beat such a class organization."

Kamloops in turn credited Spokane depth, defence and goaltending as the difference.

Domenichelli, Iginla, Holland and Baumgartner all landed on the west division all stars.

Shawn McNeil was drafted by Washington and Petruk by Colorado. Peter Bergman went to Pittsburgh and Jake Deadmarsh to San Jose.

Iginla won league player of the year, Domenichelli grabbed the most sportsmanlike player and Baumgartner garnered the top defenceman award for the second straight year.

Iginla has gone on to stardom in Calgary where he was briefly joined by Domenichelli on a sojourn between Hartford and the new Atlanta Thrashers. Holland has bumped up and down between the minors and the NHL with the Islanders and Buffalo while Brad Lukowich found his way from the Islanders to Hitchcock's 1999 Stanley Cup winning Dallas Stars. Baumgartner has sprinkled a few games with Washington Capitals while biding his time in the AHL. Tucker skated away with the AHL rookie of the year.

Dempsey's Blazers had done well and the tradition had been maintained. Despite big personnel losses on and off the ice the team landed fourth overall and made the division final. They set a record for six consecutive 40 plus win seasons and a league benchmark of 14 straight plus .500 campaigns.

Next season the losses to graduation and the pros would go deeper than anyone anticipated. It would be gut check time for players and fans alike.

51

The Measure of Adversity_____1996/97

It has been said the measure of champions is how they handle adversity. The 1996/97 season offered the proud Blazer dynasty a yardstick.

The losses in personnel went deeper than ever before. The defence lost Keller, Holland, Baumgartner and Lukowich. The forwards lost Iginla, Domenichelli and Bob Maudie. No amount of promising rookies could make up the slack. Petruk returned along with enforcer Rob Skrlac but veteran guns were gone.

For Dempsey the challenge was formidable as he looked up at the fortunes of his predecessors. Both Don Hay with Phoenix and Tom Renney with Vancouver joined Ken Hitchcock coaching in the NHL. Craig Bonner rejoined the team; behind the bench.

Talking about coaching in Kamloops Don Hay remarked "Kamloops is a blue collar town. You had to answer when the team didn't do well - answer to fans, answer to media. That kind of pressure helped coaches develop."

"The work ethic the three coaches (Laforge, Hitchcock, Renney) demanded from the players, just the tradition, no one wants to let that tradition down. Its an important factor to have on your side."

There was promise in the rookies trying out such as Mickey Dupont, John Hobson, Allan Manness, Steve Shrum and, most impressive Robin Regehr, but they were still rookies. Portland and Spokane were picked #1 and #2 for the season and the young Blazers set their sights on the playoffs and a .500 campaign.

The pre season looked good at 5-1 but the guns fell 3-1 in their season opener in Portland. It had not happened for 14 seasons. Before the next game captain Dean Kletzel hung up his skates and the job fell to local Ajay Baines to take on the heavy mantle. He did it proud and became the longest serving team captain in Blazer history.

As the squad struggled player moves began. Bergman was sent to Calgary for 15 year old Blaine Depper. He would face his former mates in the WHL final two years later. Jordan Landry was shipped to Edmonton for 20 year old Darren Wright in an effort to shore up the defence.

Wright's feeling about coming to the Blazers were summed up

"I think its every kids dream in B.C. to play in Kamloops, just because of the tradition they have."

96/97 Kamloops Blazers **Top Left to Right** Wade Burt, Jonathan Hobson, Blair Rota, Alan Manness, Thomas Scantlebury, Micki Dupont, Steve Shrum, **Middle** Don Larsen (marketing), Peter Friedel (trainer), Brian Henderson (asst. coach), Steve Gainey, Gennady Razin, Drew Kehler, Konrad Brand, Jake Deadmarsh, Nils Anton, Robyn Regehr, Chris St. Croix, Steve Albrecht, Craig Bonner, Greg "Spike" Wallace **Front** Kevin Harris (stick boy), Clayton Pool, Darren Wright, Ed Dempsey (coach), Donnie Kinney, Stu MacGregor (GM), Rob Skrlac, Ajay Baines, Colin Day (president), Shawn McNeil, Darcy Smith, Al Glendenning (asst. coach), Jeff Ainsworth, Randy Petruk, Trevor Kennedy (stick boy) (C.Brian's Photography) **also suiting up** Dean Kletzel, Peter Bergman, Jordan Landry,

Despite the struggles the team had some nights to remember. Early in October Blazer fans roared with delight when tough guy Rob Skrlac scored two goals in 90 seconds, including the winner, in a 4-2 home ice victory over Prince George. Later the same month Baines notched 3 goals and 3 assists while Petruk stopped 44 shots to win in Prince George and end a 9 game losing streak. At the end of December they were in third with an unfamiliar sub. 500 record of 17-19-4. Despite the record Dempsey was pleased with how his rookie squad was holding up.

The new year started well enough and on a couple of occasions they got to within one game of reaching .500. Then came the dark cloud with a silver lining.

Front running Portland came to town and made a point. Before the Kamloops faithful they throttled the Blazers. Final score 12-1. Yet in the midst of this, one goal stood out as the team's measure against adversity. Heavily outshot and succumbing to the waves of Portland attackers Kamloops gave it everything they had and began storming the Portland net. The fans roared as the Blazers cycled the puck and fought for every inch. Gainey fired in their only goal of the game and the crowd responded. This was no team scoring a lone goal to make the score 10-1 and hanging their heads. This was a team that stood up and fought back when they could have folded their tent and gone home. The crowd reacted like they had scored the overtime winner in a playoff series. It was the stuff the Seventh Man savoured and noticed.

Late in the campaign, adversity came knocking again, Petruk was injured and put out for three to six weeks. Clayton Pool came in with 15 year old Bill Dick as backup.

The season ended with Kamloops experiencing its first sub .500 season since 81/82. Former GM Bob Brown called for Seattle to oust the Blazers in the first round on the basis of their star, Patrick Marleau, and Kamloops losing their star Petruk. The paper backed him by calling for Seattle in six. Facing his hometown in the T-Birds net was Jeff Blair.

Games one and two went to Seattle handily by scores of 5-2 and 7-3. When the Washingtonians took game three 4-1 at Riverside it looked like lights out. But the Blazers were not about to go down without a fight in front of their fans. Clayton Pool came forward in a gutsy game by the squad as they pulled off a 3-2 win to reward their faithful followers and stay alive for another day.

They took the same act into Seattle and held leads of 2-0 and 4-2 before eventually succumbing to Marleau's magic. He scored the ultimate winner at 2:52 of the third and Kamloops was eliminated in the first round for the first time in 13 years.

Darcy Smith, Darren Wright and, most emotionally, Rob Skrlac were graduating. For the rugged Skrlac he sat for some time hanging on to his Blazer sweater knowing he would not be back to play in the colours.

The draft saw Steve Gainey picked up, fittingly, by the

Dallas Stars, Chris St. Croix by Calgary and Gennady Razin by the Montreal Canadians. None were taken in the first two rounds.

There were no Blazers in the top scorers, on the all star squad or picking up hardware but the Seventh Man didn't care. They had kept it respectable, had some big nights and shown that the work ethic was still there.

Throughout the season they dressed four 16 year olds, seven 17 year olds and three of their rookies were 18. In a test against adversity they did not fold. They did not trade off their star players to accept losing today as a means of winning tomorrow. They did not accept the easy way out.

The boys were on their way back.

What's Old is New Again_____1997/98

Once again rumblings, rumours and differing perspectives clogged hockey talk along the Thompson. Local boy Ed Dempsey was gone as coach; replaced by a returning star. Everyone had an opinion. Ed would be back.

Former Junior Oiler, albeit briefly, Marc Habscheid came on board as the 8th coach in Oilers/Blazers history. During his stint with the junior Oilers he excited the fans before injury and eventual call up to Edmonton ended his tenure. His playing days over he went on to coach, ironically, in Melfort where the franchise had touched down for two seasons. After but one year there he moved up to major junior with Kamloops.

As for Dempsey he had an eye on the opening in Prince George left by departing Stan Butler. The Cougars were on a high after upsetting front runners Portland in the playoffs and Ed wanted to stay with coaching. On August 16/97 came the news he was the Cougars new bench boss. Henceforth games with Prince George took on new meaning.

Player changes continued. Promising Shawn McNeil was off to Red Deer for rugged Mike Brown, a Florida Panthers draft pick and rear guard Kevin Mackie was obtained from Medicine Hat. Overagers Jeff Ainsworth and Blair Rota were cut and 20 year old tough guy Mark Scott followed Habscheid from Melfort. St. Croix and Petruk returned from their pro camps and there was optimism about the play of rookies Gable Gross, Shaun Thompson and local Brett Draney.

The season started poorly.

For the second straight year they lost their league opener, this time to Seattle 5-3. It was followed by convincing losses in Kelowna and in Prince George. The bleeding ended when they stopped highly touted Portland 2-1 at Riverside on the strength of a goal and assist from recently acquired 20 year old Tyler Perry, picked up only hours before from Swift Current. Unfortunately for Perry and the team his tenure was short as a season ending ankle injury took him out less than a month later. In late October Thomas Scantlebury was sent packing to Lethbridge for overage defenceman Shane Belter who blossomed into a contributing point man and solid rearguard.

Two days later Dempsey brought his Cougars to town for the first time. Relieved Blazers fans saw the improving home side skate away with the 4-2 decision. The season long battle eventually favoured the Cougars by a narrow margin of 6-5-1.

The squad battled to stay at .500 as the year neared a close. Teams taking them for granted paid a price as they stopped league leading Swift Current and were more than holding their own against Prince George. On any given night they were in the games but consistency suffered. By December's end they were playing .500 hockey and holding down 4th place.

No Blazers made the Canadian junior squad but Chris St. Croix laced up for the USA and Nils Antons for Germany. Petruk landed on the west division all stars and promising Robin Regehr was selected to play in the CHL (draft) prospects match.

97/98 Kamloops Blazers **Top Left to Right** Micki Dupont, Brett Draney, Alan Manness, Steve Shrum, Shane Belter, Gable Gross, Kevin Mackie, Jonathan Hobson, Wade Burt **Middle** Pete Friedel, Gennady Razin, Mark Scott, Adam Dombrowski, Jason Norrie, Mike Brown, Nils Antons, Robyn Regehr, Ryan Thorpe, Shawn Thompson, Greg "Spike" Wallace **Front** Garnet Stephenson, Don Larsen, Donnie Kinney, Stu MacGregor, Ajay Baines, Colin Day, Chris St. Croix, Marc Habschied, Steve Gainey, Craig Bonner, Randy Petruk Sticks boys - Craig Karwander, Trevor Kennedy (C.Brian's Photography) **Also suiting up** Tyler Perry, Drew Kehler, Scott Farrell, David Klatt, Thomas Scantlebury, Brad Hickes, Ryan Epp, Jared Aulin, Ryan Rishaug

The New Year started with some promise as they shut out the visiting Swift Current Broncos 3-0 at Riverside to sweep their season series against the league leaders.

Former T-Bird Jason Norrie was picked up as another overager and contributed in an 8-4 victory over his old team in January. A big win as the birds were trying to catch the Blazers for 4th.

On March 6/98 they clinched 4th with a 4-3 win over visiting Spokane. They could not catch 3rd place Prince George. Mike Brown, with a few games still remaining in the season, set a new Blazer record for penalty minutes as he surpassed the record set by Paul Kruse in 89/90.

They closed out the season with a 4-2 win over Kelowna at Riverside and saw their record improve to 37-32-3. They were back over .500 with an improved second half.

Their first round opponents were the favoured but uneasy Prince George Cougars. Dempsey preferred to avoid the Blazers as the teams played evenly over the course of the season. The Cougars came with the asset of the intimidating Prince George crowd, home ice advantage and the presence of first round pick of the Islanders, Kamloops own Eric Brewer. Despite being a home boy Brewer wanted revenge on a Kamloops team that for so many years humbled the Cougars. The Daily News called for Prince George to take the series in six games.

Petruk silenced the Cougar faithful in game one. The winner of the Dean Evason Award for the player with the most inspirational leadership ability Randy went out and proved the point. Just after a Donnie Kinney goal had been waved off Prince George got a power play opportunity but Randy stoned the Cougars. The visitors escaped with a 2-1 win. The Cougars got untracked in game two and, despite giving up 13 power plays to Kamloops, secured a convincing 6-0 win to even the series.

In Kamloops it was the Blazers' turn to turn it on. They outshot the visitors 42-28 and skated away with a 5-3 victory. It got better yet. Petruk was at his best for game four as the Cougars poured it on. Outshooting Kamloops 41- 22 they ended up on the short end of the 2-1 score as Shrum put in the winner with only 37 seconds remaining. Surprisingly the Blazers had a 3-1 series lead.

A 4-1 loss in Prince George set up the pivotal series game in Kamloops. Win it and the Blazers advanced. Lose and the momentum swung back to Prince George. The bad news was key power play man Shane Belter was out along with Robin Regehr. The Cougars were ahead late in the third. With 1:47 remaining Habscheid pulled Petruk. Eight seconds later Mike Brown tied it to force overtime. The crowd was elated but the air went out of the balloon when Jarrett Smith extended the Cougars season with the winner at 8:56 of OT. They were off to Prince George for the seventh and deciding game, still without Belter or Regehr.

The Blazers refused to be intimidated by the crowd and took the lead on a goal by Ajay Bains at 3:01 of the second. The Cougars tied it up at 11:16 on the power play. The third period decided the game and the series. Despite outshooting the home side it was the Cougars who escaped with the winner, by Blair Betts, with 3:09 remaining.

For the second season in a row the Blazers went out in the first round but did not go quietly. They took a team finishing 14 points ahead of them to the wire and demonstrated marked improvement over the previous season. There was much to be optimistic about.

Robin Regehr was the only Blazer to get drafted the coming summer as he went in the first round to Colorado. Petruk was the only member of the squad to make the west division all stars.

Off in the NHL former Blazer Craig Berube got within sight of the Stanley Cup before his Washington Capitals lost out to Detroit.

Kamloops could look forward to many players returning for the coming campaign though Norrie, Belter and Scott would not be amongst them.

Outgoing GM Stu MacGregor, who had been picked up as a scout for the Dallas Stars, prophesied the team had to win next season or replace its past mystique for present day mediocrity.

The challenge would have to be met, in all likelihood, without the services of star netminder Randy Petruk. There was no clear replacement in the wings but Estevan was slated to once more play a role in the Seventh Man's story.

53

The X Man Cometh 1998/99

The season brought surprises; some immediately noticeable and others that evolved as the season progressed.

Last season the Blazers contended with a former coach heading up the Prince George Cougars who eventually ousted them from the playoffs. This campaign they faced Kamloops' Golden Boy himself. Don Hay joined Bob Brown in Tri Cities and went behind the bench along with former Blazers assistant coach Terry Bangen.

It began to look like the Kamloops Hockey League as former Kamloops Rockets goaltender Garth Malarchuk took over the bench in Kelowna and former Junior Oiler Dean Clark guided the Calgary Hitmen. Before the final whistle another familiar face entered in dramatic fashion. Former Calgary assistant GM Mike Moore came over to pick up the reins from Stu MacGregor. He was more than familiar with the Blazers having scouted for them for three years and tagged both Gable Gross and Mickey Dupont as prospects.

Optimism surrounding the host of returning players was buoyed by the addition of two talented Russian rookies in Konstantin Panov and Anton Borodkin. Sixteen year old Jared Aulin from Calgary was pegged as a can't miss prospect and carried his own cheering section with his grandmother and extended family being Kamloops and area residents.

During the campaign buildup the alumni gathered. First was the annual Don Hay Charity Classic Golf Tournament and then the annual Pro Am game. They came to play and socialize. Scott Ferguson, Jason Holland, Greg Hawgood, Brad Lukowich, Jason Strudwick, Jerome Iginla, David Chyzowski, Tyson Nash, Ed Patterson, Rod Stevens, Steve Passmore, Mark Ferner, Nolan Baumgartner, Tod Carnelly, Darryl Sydor, Ryan Huska, Shane Doan, Blair Rota and Mark Recchi all suited up for the event. Links in the chain from past to present.

All fronts looked good with the exception of goaltending.

Local Bill Dick and returnee David Klatt went head to head but both lacked experience. On the Prairies a compelling story began unfolding. Regina's nineteen year old Kenric Exner had been playing backup goal for the Estevan Bruins of the SJHL. Managing only 14 games he posted six wins and a 3.30 average. He was not optimistic about his chances of pursuing his hockey career any further.

He made a deal with his parents that if he was not getting more ice time by Christmas he would leave junior hockey to go to University in Regina and play for their team. Hockey was not his only concern at the time for father Jerry had been diagnosed with leukemia.

Kenric journeyed to Swift Current for the summer to work at a hockey school run by his old coach from Regina, Jim Dekowny. Once there he got the urge to tryout with the Broncos and asked Dekowny if he could set it up. On Aug. 18/98 Kenric got a call from Jim telling him he had been talking to an old friend who had just taken over the coaching reins of a WHL team and was in need of an experienced goalie. The coach's name was Marc Habscheid. Jim told Kenric to wait by the phone and shortly afterwards he got a call from GM Mike Moore. Even after Kenric told him he hadn't been a particularly good goalie the offer was made for a tryout. Seems somebody highly recommended the young man. Kenric took the offer and came out. His story unfolded like a made for TV movie. On arrival in Kamloops who should be there to drive him down to the rink but Randy Petruk who had stood on his head as a rookie himself.

The sports columnists were mixed in their projections calling on the Blazers to land anywhere from first to third.

An additional incentive for the matches against division rivals Kelowna and Prince George was the battle for the inaugural Denny's Cup, for B.C. bragging rights. What with the strong connections all three coaches had with Kamloops, the Cup took on extra meaning.

The campaign opened on an uncertain note. Dempsey's Cougars came calling and were down 3-0 in the third. They roared back and Kamloops escaped with a 4-4 tie despite outshooting the Cougars 44-22. Doubts about Exner's ability to fill the shoes of Petruk weren't removed. Fans remained hopeful the "Wild Thing" might return. Klatt didn't seem ready for prime time either when the Blazers lost the next match 5-4 in Seattle, despite barraging them 52-25 in shots.

Game three was better as they got some revenge over Portland for the 12-1 drubbing a couple years before. Their first win was a 9-1 shellacking in front of the home crowd. Game four saw Exner get his first shutout of the season 8-0 over Seattle. On top of Exner's play the Manness, Shrum Burt line garnered four goals. Only one of the threesome would still be there at seasons end. Wade Burt was off to the Kootenay Ice just as word came Robin Regehr was returning from Colorado.

Good news for Exner came with the goalie of the week award but was off set by an injury forcing him out and bringing in Chris Thompson from Ontario. Thompson had played for the Guelph Storm in their Memorial Cup appearance. The experiment was short-lived. Don Hay's homecoming game with Tri City was a humbling 7-2 setback by their old coach. Goaltending anxiety was high amongst the fans.

Exner returned and began where he left off, winning. The backup from Estevan was destined to go undefeated in his first 24 games as a Blazer.

As the season progressed it became increasingly clear the battle was between the two ex Junior Oiler teammates Habscheid and Dean Clark of Calgary. Their first encounter, at Riverside, saw the Hitmen undefeated and holding on to first overall. Exner backstopped the Blazers to a 4-3 win ending Calgary's streak and pulling Kamloops to within one point. The Blazers were on an undefeated streak of their own.

Within three days they were running ahead of Calgary but heading out on a gruelling eastern road swing. It didn't stop them and their 4-2 win in Medicine Hat set a new franchise record of 6-0 on an eastern road trip. Again Exner was voted player of the week and the Blazers found themselves ranked #4 in the country, ahead of Calgary at #6. The team continued to pursue franchise records.

In November their 3-1 win over Kootenay at Riverside set a new franchise record for an unbeaten streak, at 17. The new benchmark reached 26 with a 10-2 sweet revenge win over Tri City at Riverside. They came within three of matching the CHL record set by the awesome 1979 Brandon Wheat Kings. By December 14 Kamloops was number one in the nation.

Exner, Brown and Regehr were all called up to the Canadian National Junior tryouts while St. Croix laced up for the Americans. Only Regehr stuck. Brown, Kinney, Baines, Exner, St. Croix and Regehr all made the west division all stars with

Baines being voted team captain by the players. This was more like what Kamloops fans were used to.

Perhaps due to all the player moves the team began to struggle as did Exner. Behind the scenes he was contending with news his father required more surgery along with the doubts coming from his unsuccessful bid for the national squad. Calgary closed in for first overall and the team slipped in CHL rankings. Still, when 1998 ended Exner's conditional promise to his parents didn't have to be met. He was more than getting enough ice time. The team was first overall with a 26-6-8 record.

98/99 Kamloops Blazers **Top Left to Right** Steve Shrum, Jonathan Hobson, Brett Draney, Kyle Calder, Konstantin Panov, Micki Dupont, Gable Gross, Anton Borodkin, Paul Deniset **Middle** Kent Wagner (trainer), Don Larsen (marketing), Kevin Mackie, Jared Aulin, Aaron Gionet, Mike Brown, Chad Starling, Robyn Regehr, Ty Jones, Kyle Kos, Jordan Flodell, Peter Friedel (trainer), Greg "Spike" Wallace **Front** Trevor Kennedy (stick boy), David Haun, David Klatt, Brian Henderson (asst. coach), Chris St. Croix, Mike Moore, Ajay Baines, Colin Day (President), Donnie Kinney, Marc Habscheid (coach), Steve Gainey, Craig Bonner, Kenric Exner, Craig Karwandy (stick boy) (C. Brian's Photography) **Also suiting up** Wade Burt, Chris Thompson (goal), Adam Dombrowski, Alan Manness, Ryan Thorpe, Shaun Thompson

The squad's performance gave every reason to believe they had a chance at the Memorial Cup. Tinkering began. Jordan Flodell had already come over from Moose Jaw. Now they nabbed Kyle Kos from Red Deer. Then came National Junior Team star Kyle Calder from Regina for Allan Manness; a heartbreaker for the popular forward. Ty Jones and goalie David Haun arrived from Spokane as the Chiefs went in the tank for better prospects next season. Haun, who had Memorial Cup experience with both Brandon and Spokane, was seen as netminding insurance.

Calgary loaded up as well and was vying for first overall. By the beginning of February Kamloops was one point up on the Hitmen but the Albertans had five games in hand. When they beat Swift Current 4-0 on March 10th they secured their 11th divisional regular season title. Exner's 5th shutout tied him for the team record with Rod Branch and Corey Hirsch. First overall still wasn't out of the question either.

When the final weekend of the regular season arrived they were three points behind the Hitmen. They took both their final games but a lone Hitmen win in Cranbrook secured them the Munro Cup. The Blazers finished one point back and ranked #6 in the CHL behind #3 Calgary.

The post Bob Brown Blazers amassed an incredible record considering the achievements of the Blazer squads preceding them. Franchise records were set for the fewest losses (at 11), fewest goals against and longest undefeated streak. To this Kenric Exner added his own record as the league's top goaltender. His 2:31 goals against average erased a 2:37 record set by John Davidson of the Calgary Centennials back in 1972. The former Estevan backup ended with a season record of 34-6-8, a saves percentage of 91.2, a playoff record of 7-4 and 91.9% saves average. That he should be a WHL all star was no surprise.

The Kelowna Rockets, big underdogs and after going down two games to none to start the series, one of which was another shutout for Exner, looked to be gone in a hurry. Facing elimination on Kamloops ice they hung on for a 4-3 win to send the game back to Kelowna for a 6th game. In taking the win they stopped a record 32 game home undefeated streak by the Blazers. There was no game seven and Kamloops enjoyed a bye, awaiting Tri City or Seattle.

Meanwhile Calgary was taken to seven games by upstart Kootenay. No sooner had they taken the series than they announced the addition of a hero from Kamloops' hockey past. Dean Evason came on board to assist his former team mate in Calgary's battle for the Memorial Cup.

Bad enough the Blazers contended with Dempsey in Prince George and were looking at going against local hero Don Hay in the division final; they may now have to contend with Dean Evason in future rounds. It somehow just didn't seem right these guys were on the other side.

Indeed the Blazers road to the Memorial Cup did face the dominant presence of Don Hay in the divisional final; the team's 11th appearance. Facing them in net in his final season was local product Jeff Blair. He enjoyed ousting his hometown two years earlier with Seattle and he and fellow local Darrell Hay wanted to do so again.

In game one the Americans were in it to the last before Calder got the 4-3 winner at 18:02. Exner did his part stopping McKay on a penalty shot when the score was 3-2 Blazers. Game two was no contest as Kamloops shutout Tri City 6-0. On home ice the Americans, minus star Gomez, played it close and tied it up on a penalty shot by Gyori on Exner. It wasn't enough as the Blazers' Panov ended it 3-2 in overtime. Down to their last gasp the Americans showed the character of a Don Hay team. Despite missing their number one player they bounced back from 3-0 to make it close before bowing out 4-3.

Kamloops was back in the western final for the first time in four years and the 9th time since the franchise came to Kamloops 17 seasons before.

Don Hay did not end the season without accolades. When the WHL named its all time all star team franchise alumni Barry Beck of the New Westminster Bruins and Don Hay as coach of the Kamloops Blazers were named. Considering all the players and coaches to have graced the WHL it has to be one of the greatest achievements any coach or player could attain.

Right now another former coach was smiling. Three of his former players were behind the bench in the western final and giving him considerable credit for their successes on and off the ice. The two Deans, Clark and Evason, referred to their competitive spirits being forged in Kamloops under fiery Bill Laforge. Clark had repeatedly spoken about using the Kamloops blueprint to build a team.

Recalling his days with Laforge he commented "We never had the most talent in the league. But teams knew it was not going to be an easy game....teams absolutely hated to play us. Effort wise nobody beat us, win or lose, we were going to be in every game."

Game one went in Calgary and it was once again time for the story of Kenric Exner to take centre stage. The goalie who had just about packed it in realized a dream and there in the stands with over 13000 others were his parents, Denise and Jerry, to watch. Jerry had won his battle with leukemia and was on his way back. The script writer couldn't have done it better.

Taking a 3-1 lead into the third the Blazers were met with an onslaught. Outshooting Kamloops 19-7 the Hitmen were getting nowhere until they pulled their goalie with over two minutes remaining. They notched a goal at 18:01 to draw within one but Steve Gainey salted the match away with an empty net marker. With his parents looking on Kenric skated out on to the ice as the games first star.

The Hitmen were not to be denied in game two as they pulled off a 4-0 win despite being outshot 29-21. Still, Kamloops was coming home having garnered home ice and knowing Calgary had never won at Riverside. The jinx did not hold as Calgary scored two late goals to take game three 4-2 and regain home ice. Game four was pivotal.

Haun was in net. Calgary took a 2-0 lead but within 13 seconds of getting it Ty Jones got the Blazers on the board. Calder tied it and part way through the third the fans had something big to cheer about as Kamloops went ahead 3-2. The lead did not hold as Brad Moran tied it up on a breakaway slapshot to send the game into OT. It took triple overtime before the red light went on and the hopes of the faithful were dashed. Despite outshooting the visitors 57-43 the Blazers lost and were down 3-1 heading back to Calgary. A telling point; Kamloops was 0-22 in series power plays.

Game five in Calgary was the last gasp and despite outshooting the Hitmen 26-20 it was Calgary who skated off with the 5-2 win and a trip to the Memorial Cup. The Blazers finally got a power play marker, by Ajay Baines, but still went only 1-29 all series long.

They had nothing to hang their heads for. The series could have gone either way and they kept the work ethic going. They more than met the challenge left by departing Stu MacGregor. The Seventh Man was not displeased. They met adversity two years earlier and did not lose the tradition.

Baines, Kinney and Haun were lost to graduation. Baines in particular had left his mark as the local hero who became the longest serving team captain in Blazer history and epitomized the work ethic. It was unlikely Calder, Kos or Jones would return from the pros. Hopes were some of the stalwarts would be back but there were real concerns the squad would lose Gainey, Brown, St. Croix and possibly even Regehr. At least they were set in goal, or so it seemed.

Panov (Nashville), Borodkin (Detroit) Starling (St. Louis) and Draney (Dallas) all got picked up in the draft but management felt confident all four would return.

The inaugural Denny's Cup had gone to Kamloops.

Off in the NHL the Blazer alumni did more than passably well. Paul Kruse was on the runner up Buffalo Sabres squad in the Stanley Cup. Ken Hitchcock, twice denied the Memorial Cup with Kamloops, took home the grand daddy of them all as he joined Darryl Sydor and Brad Lukowich in hoisting the 1999 Stanley Cup with the Dallas Stars. Adding to the moment for Kamloops fans was local player Doug Lidster carving his name on his second Stanley Cup. Sydor and Lidster brought the cherished mug to the Riverside Coliseum for all to see.

The mystique was alive with more surprises in the offing.

54

Son of the Seventh Man____1999/2000

A moment frozen in time. Locked away in the recesses of the mind like some personal photo of Paul Henderson scoring the winning Canada Cup goal in 1972.

Such a moment had begun the return of the franchise to prominence after its arrival in Kamloops. Dean Evason's game tying goal against Regina in 1984 rekindled the spirit of the Seventh Man. And now he was back.

His NHL career had run its course and a new chapter was beginning for the franchise hero. It began where it should; in Kamloops.

Despite team success on the ice Habscheid and the Blazers did not agree to his return to the organization for a third term. As before with Brown and Dempsey the debates filled conversation at coffee shops and pubs; hockey being played as much in conversation as on the ice. Yet with word Evason was the new coach a sense of excitement and optimism bubbled over from those who remembered him. He symbolized the marriage of ability and determination that came to characterize the organization and the team. Who says you can't go home.

He had a daunting task. Like Dempsey in 1996 most of his veterans departed and he took on the task of moulding a young, rookie ladened team into a force commanding respect. It soon became apparent Mike Brown, Steve Gainey and Chris St. Croix were not coming back. There had been little hope that Calder, Kos or Jones would suit up. It recalled the rookie squad of 88/89.

Robin Regehr's situation was even more uncertain. He had been seriously injured in a car accident back home in Saskatchewan; leaving two people dead and questions as to whether his ravaged legs would ever allow him to walk normally again much less return to hockey. Almost twenty years before a car accident took the life of promising New Westminster Bruin Barry Smith. Once again hockey became secondary to the realities of life and the concerns were for his well being and compassion for his family. What transpired was a credit to the strength of human will.

When the home opening ceremonies commenced the evening was as emotional as the raising of Memorial Cup Banners.

The roving lights swung about the packed coliseum and centred upon a banner high in the rafters. The announcer recalled the glory of a past hero as the retired number of Dean Evason caught every eye in the building. Thunder rocked the house when Evason walked out before the admiring fans. He was back.

99/2000 Kamloops Blazers - **Front Left to Right** Richard Minaker (stickboy), Davis Parley, Craig Bonner (asst. coach), Steve Shrum, Mike Moore (GM), Micki Dupont, Colin Day (President), Jared Aulin, Dean Evason (coach), Kevin Mackie, Matt Recchi (asst. coach), Grant McCune, Jackson Morrell (stick boy) **Middle** Don Larsen (marketing), Kent Wagner (trainer), Brett Draney, Shaone Morrison, Jason Bone, Aaron Gionet, Chad Starling, Blaine Depper, Mike Munro, Mark Roonem, Konstantin Panov, Greg "Spike" Wallace (equipment manager), Peter Friedel (asst. trainer) **Top** Gable Gross, Chad Schockenmaier, Kyle Ladobrouk, Eric Christensen, Jordan Walker, Anton Borodkin, Jonathan Hobson, Paul Deniset (C. Brian's Photography) **Also suiting up** Trent Klatt (goal), Curtis Austring, Kyle Bruce, Jeremy Cominotto, Conan Sedler, Tyler Boldt, Derek Krestanovich

It did not end there. The announcer recalled the accident of the past summer that had so nearly cost the life of Robin Regehr. Thunder rolled again as the Blazer star strode out to the lights and heart felt applause.

Then came the hoisting of the banners for finishing first in the regular season and winning the divisional title in 1999.

More beacons of success amid rafters heavy with emblems of previous accomplishments. Former coach Marc Habscheid was amongst those sharing in the moment; for him a bitter sweet evening. He would be back.

The only thing missing was the X man. The remarkable young man who had captured the hearts of Kamloops continued his storybook rise. His free agent tryout with St. Louis went so well he was signed to a minor pro contract. His star rose and Kamloops became part of the history.

The Regehr story continued as well with his amazing recovery. By December he had worked himself into the Calgary Flames lineup. Hopes for his return faded with every game he played but were mixed with best wishes for his success.

On the ice the task facing Moore and Evason grew even tougher with the unexpected loss of the two key players. With a team ravaged by the pros and graduation the rookie coach took on the Seventh Man's mantle with adversity hogging the bench.

It started as it should. Visiting Portland went down 7-2 as Aulin, Panov and Dupont exploded out of the gate. Early going reviews were mixed as Davis Parley notched a couple shutouts but the team tumbled to fifth place with inconsistent goaltending. The tinkering began with 16 year old Kyle Bruce going to Prince Albert for 19 year old backup goalie Grant McCune.

McCune's first test was in Seattle where his 6-3 win started a streak that went 10-0-3 before he tasted defeat. Included in the run was a 1-1 tie against visiting Prince Albert where Kyle Bruce popped the Raiders goal. The team was flourishing as well and took their own streak to 12 games undefeated.

In November came word Garth Malarchuk was released by struggling Kelowna who reached into the franchise legend to nab Marc Habscheid as their new bench boss.

In December the Seventh Man's shadow grew larger yet as the Kamloops Blazers were selected 16th on the list of the best sports teams of the century. A list headed by the 1972 Canada Cup winning national team.

Later the same month Mark Recchi was voted Kamloops athlete of the 20th Century and had a portion of Lorne Street, near the Coliseum, renamed Mark Recchi Way.

On the ice the season proved a roller coaster of feast and famine with alternating winning and losing streaks. McCune remained the backbone as the squad climbed to third and battled to the end to hold it against a late charging Seattle.

In February the CHL #1 ranked Calgary Hitmen came to town for a return match. They had handled the Blazers in Calgary and were running away with the WHL. Evason took it to his old buddy Clark as his charges won the day 6-3 for their biggest win of the campaign. Before the month was out they secured a playoff spot for the 19th straight season.

With Seattle mounting a late season charge the weekend of March 17 proved dark. Not only did the T-Birds win their game the Blazers were upset 2-1 by cellar dwelling Portland and lost the services of top scorer Konstantin Panov. Seattle moved to within one point. Assured of playing each other in the first round the question was one of third place and home ice.

It came down to the last game. Seattle hosting Hay's Americans and Kamloops hosting Prince George. The Blazers needed a win and a Seattle loss. Down 3-1 to the second place Cougars in the third it appeared to be over; but it wasn't. Rookie Kyle Ladobruk tied it up, Hobson gave them the lead and Shrum sealed a 5-3 win with an empty net marker. Unfortunately Tri Cities dropped their game and Seattle garnered home ice.

At the end the rebuilding squad secured fourth and another plus .500 season. Adversity was kicked off the bench.

Micki Dupont, the team's leading scorer, led the Panovless Blazers in to the opening round series against a T-Bird team that took the last three encounters and had home ice. Former Blazer Allan Manness led the Seattle charge as the Birds took the first two games convincingly, despite being outshot. Proving a point in game two Manness notched a hat trick.

Game three in Kamloops had the local heroes up 2-0 at the end of the first but heartbreak struck in the second frame. First Seattle tied it and then potted a shorthanded marker at 19:52 to take a 3-2 lead. It stood up as the winner and the Blazers were on the edge of elimination. The player woes got worse as Steve Shrum was lost to injury and Gable Gross to a one game suspension.

Game four told all. Seattle jumped out to a 2-0 lead but at 18:46 the Blazers tied the contest. The T-Birds took a 3-2 lead on a power play in the second but the Blazers roared back to tie it. Or so they and their fans thought. Instead the goal was called back because the Blazers were being called on a penalty. Seattle made the power play count. At 4-2 the wind was out of the sails. In Blazer tradition the boys kept fighting and for the fourth straight time outshot the T-Birds. The last goal was into an empty net and the Blazers' season was over.

Yet with time winding down a thunder began to rise from the stands. The fans rose to their feet. Applause and cheers filled the coliseum. If a visitor had walked in they would have thought it was the Blazers who had won. They had won the hearts of their fans for a great season and for keeping the tradition alive. They went down fighting and with class.

Dean Evason, the Blazer organization and the players faced adversity and emerged the victors. Rookie ladened they had few player losses to face next season; the first full season of the new Millennium. The promise was reborn.

Micki Dupont's stellar season earned him accolades as the WHL and Canadian Hockey League (CHL) defenceman of the year along with a starting position on the CHL all star team. He joined Jared Aulin (Colorado), Davis Parley (Florida) and Aaron Gionet (Tampa Bay) as drafted Blazers when his hometown Calgary Flames picked him up.

The alumni saw Ken Daneyko and Scott Niedermayer's New Jersey Devils wrest the Stanley Cup from Hitchcock and Sydor's Dallas Stars in the Cup Final.

The Seventh Man had come a long way from his tenuous beginnings in Humboldt.

55

The Seventh Man's Shadow

Most stories that have a beginning have an ending but this is not one of them.

The Seventh Man continues to weave his magic with the franchise as he has since the formative years in Humboldt. The players come and go; each taking a bit with them and leaving a bit of themselves. There are the memories that remain with the many fans in all of its stops and the recollections of all those who have played parts, big and small, in the never ending story.

The achievements, the adversity, the tragedies and the humour are all a part of the legacy old team mates share when fortune sees their paths cross. Yet it is not just what transpired on the ice that makes the Seventh Man what he is. There are the people behind the scenes; the scouts, managers, coaches, volunteers, booster clubs, society members. media and fans. Some stand out amid the throngs but all are a part of what has come to be and what was.

Leo Parker, Scotty Munro, Ernie McLean and Bill Shinske were the emissaries for so many years until the link was broken and the franchise came to its present home. New emissaries arose in the persons of Bill Laforge, Ken Hitchcock, Tom Renney, Don Hay, Ed Dempsey, Marc Habscheid, Bob Brown, Stu MacGregor and now Dean Evason and Mike Moore. In the background emerged the collection of dedicated believers who captured the franchise in the first place, gave it a permanent home and have been the rock foundation on which it now stands. Andy Clovechok, Colin Day, Harvey Roy, Loy Hoffbeck, Ken Almond, Dennis Coates and Gary Cooper were the spearhead for a community that rallied to give the Seventh Man a home and continue his ongoing quest.

For them all the past, present and future are alive as the tale continues to unfold.

For the players their time in the Sun passes and the future takes them on differing roads. But they have something special. For a moment in their lives, when they were in the Spring of youth, when life was at its most intense, they were a part of an incredible story. The influences of that oh so brief time are forever impressed upon them. For in their time they skated with the Seventh Man and donned his jersey. The jersey which carries with it the pride of the past and expectation for the future.

As the years pass they all remember.

They leave but the Seventh Man remains. Forever young and forever a part of them.

The Team Behind the Team

To list all those people over the years who have contributed to the success of the franchise would be immense and virtually impossible. There is however a need to acknowledge a special group, without whom the Seventh Man would not be skating in Kamloops. Behind the rescue team was an array of people, organizations and businesses who put money and time in to the community effort to keep the team. Their efforts remain acknowledged in the list of members of Kamloops Blazers Holdings Ltd.

They are Cooper Market Ltd., Colin Day, Ken Almond. Loy Hoffbeck Andy Clovechok, Frank Rossi, J. Alan Miller, Jim Walsh, Capital Tire Inc.,Murray Pratt, Dale Scherer & Terry Turnbull, Wilf Tantrum, Barney Lukas, Jack Rea, Peter Doyle, Paul & Glenda Bourque, Nathan Saunders, Dave Blackwell, Keith Tordoff, Craig Sturgeon, Maurice & Isabelle Owen, Ken Ezzard, Ray Christensen, James Booth, John Payne, Louis Holowaychuk, Waverley Conan, Oscar Bepple, Norio Sakaki, Eldon Dever, John Nelson, Jackie Roy, Bob Winters, Babs Nicholson, Roan Holdings Ltd., Dave Kerr, Randy Maduik, Francois Lambert, Bill Anger, Dr. Bob Smillie, Lorraine Ritchie, Ken Moffat, Rick Harris, Harry Thomas, Robert McConnel, Grant Roberston, Enzo Lizzi, Jack Hollstedt, Richard Strutz, Tom Wallace, Mike Bruno,Roy Baron, J.M. Crawford, B. Crawford, Bill Swain, Jack Farley, Lara Management Corporation, Craig Harrold, Dr. George Monkman, Garden Court Investments, Chuck Rachar, Doug Prefontaine, Kamloops Sports Racers Ltd., World of Wicker, James International, Derek Johnston, Ernie Funk's Electric Ltd., Ian Middlemass, Roger Schreiner, Yellow Quip Rentals Ltd., Mas Tahara/ A. Banman, Victor Mahm, George Tetrau, Reg Fuoco, Peter Espig, Kamloops Branch Restaurant & Food Services of B.C., Jensen, Mitchel & Co., Canada West Coastlines, Local 900 Canadian Union of Public Employees, Ray Fuoco, John Van Horlick, Joe Leong, Necmart Enterprises, Rick Thompson, K.G. Scholefield, Lotus Enterprises, Noel Hunt, Mel Recchi, Dr. Gordon Olsen, Randy Madiuk,Victor & Brandan Martin, Booster Club, Abe Riesbrecht, Murray Owen, George & Manny Mattis, Francis Ferguson, Bill Sankey, Gary & Janet Westphal, Paul Piwek, Bill Van Zandt, Harry Nishimura, Peter F. Van Hoof, Big Brothers of Kamloops Inc., Kevin Jardine, Stu Beatty, Headhunters Enterprises Ltd., Bert Day, George Gatehouse, Syd Smith Employess, Fred Leake, Floritto Egg Sales, Bruce Kulla (Harold Dreyer), Gerald Shandro, Dr. Gur S. Singh, Bernie Deys, Central Print & Screen Co.,

Keith Boychuk, Ted & Brenda Fisher, I.J. Building Industry Services Ltd., Ladies Auxilary to Minor Hockey, Robbie Dunn, Irvin & Jan Weiss, Don-Bar Holdings Ltd., Ray McInnes, Western Industrial Relations Ltd., Case Van Diemen, M.J. Day, Walter A. Wende, Larry Coupal, Robert & William Kershaw, Mike Graas, Mort Nielsen, Don Stewart, J. Obana, Edwin Ferner, 523 Group, Kamloops Minor Hockey Association, Central Sten Ad Ltd., Ken, Almond & Co., Radio NL, Ken Hitchcock, Kamloops Minor Hockey, Vern Smith, Ted Smigielski, Jim Stuart, Gerald Sauve, Paul Adams, Frank McRae, Arne Saastad, Ted Alexandre, Gordon Harris, Jim Stephens, Bob Becker, Bill MacGillvray, Don Hoover, Dean Lagrandeur, Mike Russell, Fred Gilliland, Ed Begg, Earle V. Morice, Dave Agar, Wayne Qualtiere, Aqua Chem Enterprises Ltd., R & M Emery Enterprises, Gerry Hartley, Recchi Holdings Ltd., Artnor Holdings Ltd., Piwek Reefer Express Ltd., Clifford Roy Youwe, Price Waterhouse, Don & Sandra Stuart, Robert A. Wills, Case Van Diemen, Westwin Realty Ltd.,Archie Green Kamloops Ltd., Kamloops Blazers Hockey Society, Jack Jusola Enterprises Ltd., Craig Michael Day and Weyerhauser Canada Ltd.

Players who suited up for the franchise but whose actual seasons are unknown include Rich Brost, Murray Worley and Cam Stratichuk with New Westminster and Bob Foglietta, Troy Bakogeorge, Craig Kalawsky, Darren Kwiatkowski, Dave MacKenzie, Darren Sivertson and Darren Stolk with Kamloops.

About the Author:

Glen Cowley is a local Kamloops writer whose interest in hockey, history, travel and things Canadian have found expression in local newspapers, magazines and in his first book, *Wind & Ice (100 Years, almost, of Kamloops Hockey).* A long time hockey fan he found Heaven in Kamloops when he, his wife Karen, and two children landed in the home of the Kamloops Blazers in 1985. A graduate of Simon Fraser University, in the relatively unknown field of historical geography, writing took a back seat to forging a career in corrections as a probation officer until the start of the 1990's.

The Big Picture

Humboldt

46/47	Finished 5th	Missed Playoffs
47/48	Finished 4th	Lost **first round** to MooseJaw 0-3
48/49	Finished 2nd	Lost **League final** to Prince Albert 1-3
49/50	Finished 3rd	Lost in **first round** to Flin Flon 0-3
50/51	Finished last	Lost in **first round** to Flin Flon 0-3
51/52	**Regular Season**	**Champs**
		Lost **League final** to Flin Flon 2-3
52/53	Finished 2nd	Lost **League final** to Flin Flon 1-4
53/54	Finished 3rd	Lost in **first round** to Prince Albert 1-4
54/55	**Regular Season**	**Champs**
		Won League, lost **Provincial final** to Regina 1-4
55/56	Finished 4th	Lost in **first round** to Flin Flon 1-4
56/57	Finished 4th	Lost in **first round** to Flin Flon 1-4

Humboldt Indians - Regular Season League Champs twice, reached League final four times, won the League once and made the playoffs ten out of eleven years.

Estevan

57/58	Finished 4th	Lost in **first round** to Regina 1-4
58/59	Finished 2nd	Lost **League final** to Flin Flon 2-3
59/60	Finished 6th (last place)	Missed Playoffs
60/61	Finished 2nd	Lost **League final** to Regina 0-4
61/62	**Regular Season**	**Champs**
		Eliminated in Round Robin by Moose Jaw & Regina
62/63	**Regular Season**	**Champs**
		League & Provincial Champs over Melville 4-1
		Lost **Western final** to Edmonton 2-4
63/64	**Regular Season**	**Champs**
		League & Provincial Champs over Regina 4-2
		Lost **Western final** to Edmonton 1-4
64/65	Finished 4th	Lost **first round** to Regina 2-4
65/66	**Regular Season**	**Champs**
		League & Provincial Champs over Weyburn 4-3

Regional Champs over Ft. William (Ont.) 4-3
Lost **Western final** to Edmonton 2-4

Start of WHL

66/67	Finished 2nd	Lost **second round** to Regina 1-4-1
67/68	Finished 2nd	**League Champs** Lost **Memorial Cup** to Niagara Falls 1-4
68/69	2nd in division 2nd overall	Lost **second round** to Flin Flon 0-4-1
69/70	2nd in division 4th overall	Lost **first round** to Winnipeg 2-4-1
70/71	**1st in division** 2nd overall	Lost **first round** to Winnipeg 2-4-1

Estevan Bruins - Regular Season Champs four times and regular season division Champs once. Reached League finals six times, league champs four times, Saskatchewan Provincial Champs three times and reached the Memorial Cup once. Missed the playoffs once in fourteen years.

New Westminster

71/72	3rd in division 4th overall	Lost **first round** to Edmonton 1-4
72/73	4th in division 6th overall	Lost **first round** to Edmonton 1-4
73/74	2nd in division 3rd overall	Lost **second round** to Calgary 2-4
74/75	3rd in division 4th overall	**League Champs** over Saskatoon 4-3 Lost **Memorial Cup final game** 7-3 to Toronto
75/76	**Regular Season League Champs**	**League Champs** over Saskatoon 4-2-1 Lost **Memorial Cup final game** 5-2 to Hamilton
76/77	**1st in division** 2nd overall	**League Champs** over Brandon 4-1 **Won Memorial Cup final game** 6-5 over Ottawa
77/78	2nd in division 4th overall	**League Champs** over Billings 4-0 **Won Memorial Cup final game** 7-4 over Peterboro
78/79	3rd in division 6th overall	Eliminated in **first round robin** by Portland & Victoria

79/80	Last in division, 2nd last overall	Missed playoffs
80/81	4th in division 12th overall	Missed playoffs

New Westminster Bruins - Regular Season League Champs once and division Champs twice. League Champs four times and Memorial Cup winners twice. Missed the playoffs twice in ten years.

<u>Kamloops</u>

81/82	4th in division, 12th overall	Lost **first round** to Portland 0-4
82/83	3rd in division 5 overall	Lost **first round** to Victoria 3-4
83/84	**Regular Season League Champs**	**League Champs** over Regina 4-3 Went 1-4 in **Memorial Cup**
84/85	**1st in division** 2nd overall	Lost **League final** to Prince Albert 0-4
85/86	**1st in division** 3rd overall	**League Champs** over Medicine Hat 4-1 Went 2-3 in **Memorial Cup**
86/87	**Regular Season League Champs**	Lost **division final** to Portland 3-5
87/88	**1st in division**, 3rd overall	Lost **League final** to Medicine Hat 2-4
88/89	3rd in division, 7th overall	Lost **division final** to Portland 3-5
89/90	**Regular Season League Champs**	**League Champs** over Lethbridge 4-0 Went 0-3 in **Memorial Cup**
90/91	**Regular Season League Champs**	Lost **division final** to Spokane 0-5
91/92	**Regular Season League Champs**	**League Champs** over Saskatoon 4-3
	Won Memorial Cup final game 5-4 over Sault Ste.Marie	
92/93	3rd in division, 6th overall	Lost **division final** to Portland 1-4
93/94	**Regular Season League Champs**	**League Champs** over Saskatoon 4-3
	Won Memorial Cup final game 5-3 over Laval	
94/95	**Regular Season League Champs**	**League Champs** over Brandon 4-2
	Won Memorial Cup final game 8-2 over Detroit	
95/96	2nd in division, 4th overall	Lost **division final** to Spokane 2-4
96/97	5th in division, 13th overall	Lost **first round** to Seattle 1-4
97/98	4th in division, 8th overall	Lost **first round** to Prince George 4-3

98/99 **1st in division**, 2nd overall Lost **League final** to Calgary 1-4
99/2000 4th in division Lost **first round** to Seattle 0-4

Kamloops Junior Oilers/Blazers - Regular Season Division Champs twelve times and League Champs eight. Reached division finals fourteen times, League finals nine and won the League six times. Won the Memorial Cup three times. Have never missed the playoffs in nineteen seasons.

Overall

Regular Season League Champs 14 times League Champs 15 times
Regular Season Division Champs 20 timesLeague finals 23 times (since 68/69)

Division finals 17 times (since 68/69)
Memorial Cup appearances 11 times
Memorial Cup wins 5
Missed the playoffs 4 times in 54 seasons

Sources

Newspapers - The Humboldt Journal, The Estevan Mercury, The Columbian (New Westminster) The Kamloops Daily News Special credit to an article on Kenric Exner written by the Daily News' Tracy Elsaesser

Organizations - The Estevan Bruins (Saskatchewan Junior Hockey League), The Kamloops Blazers

Museums/Libraries - The Humboldt & District Museum & Gallery, The Kamloops Museum & Archives, The New Westminster Public Library,

Reference Books -1999/2000 Western Hockey League Guide - Western Hockey League; Total Hockey (Official Encyclopedia of the NHL) by Total Sports; The Memorial Cup by Richard Lapp and Alec Macaulay (Harbour Publishing); The Western Hockey League Yearbook

The People - Sharon Domotor, Jennifer Hoesgen, David Stewart, Jim Stewart, Reg Beliveau, Ernie "Punch" McLean, Dick Meissner, Harold Hall, Glenn Hall, Dick Warwick, Norm Park, Ken MacDonald, Jamie Durr, Nick Serregela, Glen Watson, Jim Harrison, Bernie Lukowich, Earl Seitz, Rick "The Bear"Wile, Colin Day, Andy Clovechok, Dennis Coates, Loy Hoffbeck, Ken Almond, Gary Cooper, Dean Evason, Ed Dempsey, Don Hay, Gerry Poeschek, Vern Smith, Doris Rubel, Kerry Rubel, Randy Rota, Dave Simpson, "Spike" Wallace, Doug MacLeod and Doug Kostynski